Meetings at the Edge

D1637780

Also by Stephen Levine

GRIST FOR THE MILL (with Ram Dass)

A GRADUAL AWAKENING

WHO DIES?

HEALING INTO LIFE AND DEATH

GUIDED MEDITATIONS, EXPLORATIONS AND HEALINGS

EMBRACING THE BELOVED

*Cassette recordings of
Stephen Levine's guided meditations
and talks are available:
write to Gateway Books for catalogue*

Meetings at the Edge

DIALOGUES WITH THE
GRIEVING AND THE DYING,
THE HEALING AND THE HEALED

Stephen Levine

GATEWAY BOOKS, BATH

Published by
GATEWAY BOOKS
The Hollies, Wellow
Bath, BA2 8QJ

Copyright © 1984 by Stephen Levine

This Edition 1993
Reprinted 1996

Cover design by Studio B, Bristol
Cover photo by Mark Ranshaw

British Library Cataloguing-in Publication Data:
A catalogue record for this book is
available from the British Library.

ISBN 0 946551-88-X

Printed and bound in Great Britain by
Redwood Books, Trowbridge, Wiltshire

In the Buddhist tradition, at the end of a period of meditation there is a practice called "sharing the merit." One might silently in their heart say something to the effect of "I share the merit of this meditation that it might aid all sentient beings on their path to perfect liberation." So rather than "dedicate" this book in the traditional sense, I would prefer to share whatever merit there may be with all sentient beings in general, and, in particular, with my wife and spiritual partner, Ondrea. While she never grew accustomed to recording her calls, she worked on the "dying phone" more than I, and her presence can be felt throughout this book. The "we" of these writings is not the royal "we" but the collaborative "we."

We would also like to thank Jakki Walters, who transcribed the "dying phone" tapes and helped produce this manuscript.

Contents

Introduction

Section I

Most live as though life was something yet to come. But as John Lennon pointed out, "Life is what happens while we are busy making other plans."

For some this may not be an easy book to read. It explores the fear and doubt, the courage and determination which arise in turn to confront the uncontrollable—the unpleasant, the long-feared, the newly discovered.

This is a book of the unexpected and often unprepared for. This is a book of the growth that occurs as we come to the mind's edge, past seemingly solid fears and long-conditioned doubt, and enter the heart of the mystery. Love is the bridge.

This is a high-wire act. To keep the heart open in hell, to maintain some loving balance in the face of all our pain and confusion. To allow life in. To heal past our fear of the unknown.

Some may feel unprepared to face this much suffering. We have so much doubt and so little confidence in our own natural greatness, in our original nature. But the suffering we experience while reading these stories is our own suffering. When reading these stories note the furrowed brow, the wincing about the eyes, the clenched jaw. This is our scramble for safe territory, this is our difficulty in dying, in living.

This is the suffering that connects us with all suffering. These are not isolated stories. This is the "cosmic suffering" that opens us into the universal and allows us to go beyond "the separate self," to touch the deathless within us all.

Let this book tear your heart open. But see beyond the individual suffering to the holding that creates our pain. This is a book of shared learning, of letting go, of entering into the edgelessness of being that lies just beyond the edge of our old concepts and shopworn ideas, of our deeply imprinted fears and self-doubt.

These are stories of those who have been brought to their edge. Each has taken a step into unexplored territory, and entered the no-man's-land of uninvestigated life. These are our meetings at the edge, at the point from which all growth originates—these are stories of the first faltering steps beyond our fears, beyond our image of who we are, into the direct experience of life.

There is no need to tighten the brow or tense the jaws. We have within us all that it takes to face the immensity of this pain, to let it soak in, to learn to breathe it into the heart, to let it burn its way to completion.

Section II

Ondrea and I have been working with the terminally ill and those investigating the process of grieving and healing for many years. Having directed the Hanuman Foundation Dying Project at the invitation of Ram Dass, who began the foundation as a means of spiritual friendship and social action, we have for the past seven years predominantly focused our "practice in the world" (what is called "service" by some and "meditation in action" by others) on the dying and the grieving.

For the last three years (1979–82), we have offered through the Dying Project, a free consultation phone for the "terminally ill and those working closely with a death." Most of the material in this book comes out of the recorded sharings on the "dying phone." Most callers were responding to various announcements that our counseling had to do with "using the exploration of death as a means of spiritual awakening." A number of the people who called were referred by physicians or other counselors who knew of our work and the existence of the phone. Many, however, called because of articles on our work in various national magazines. I think it would be fair to say that we did not receive the same kind of "clientele" that perhaps the majority of "help phones" are accustomed to. Even those who called because they were contemplating suicide often had something of a spiritual context, at least philosophically if not perceptually, which allowed a certain shared communication that may not often arise in more standard exchanges. Several called not because they were dying or had lost a loved one, but because of a loss of great expectations in the birth of a Down's syndrome child or the amputation of an arm or the loss of faith. In many could be heard the world-weariness that so often is experienced in moments of disappointment and unfulfilled dreams.

If any were to ask us what our "technique" is for working with those in crisis, I would have to say that it is the "braille method" —feeling our way along from moment to moment in uncharted territory, meeting the next unknown moment with a sense of wonder and trust in the shared exploration. It is a very intuitive process. And even as I read some of these pages, the mind that responds in this moment says it might have said it differently at that moment. Or in more detail. Or in less. But then I recall the energy of those sharings and recognize how each communication was so much a response to something felt though unspoken in the instant of contact.

Our training over the last twenty years has been predominantly in Buddhist psychology and meditation, particularly in the Theravadan and Zen lineage. We have, however, investigated many other forms, including the use of mantras, visualizations, and devotional practices of the Christian, Sufi, and Hindu traditions, which we have found applicable to various temperaments at different times.

These are not therapy sessions in the usual sense. This is essentially a spiritual counseling. If psychology, in a very oversimplified way, can be said to deal with the mindstuff, the content of the mind, the perishable, the incessantly changing, then perhaps the spiritual can be said to be the investigation of the heart space, the vastness in which it is all happening, the infinite spaciousness out of which each thought and feeling arises and into which each moment disappears, the deathless, that which has no beginning and no end.

It might here be appropriate to clarify that when I say "being" I do not mean "being" as opposed to "nonbeing." I mean being itself, *isness*, the eternal in which all floats, including being and nonbeing. This is not being as concept, but being as experience, as the underlying reality, as the vast screen of

xii   INTRODUCTION

awareness on which all experiences change and mutate, arising
and passing away within a sense of edgeless presence.

Because our work with others, our "service," is simply work
on ourselves (and sometimes, as when a raw nerve is touched at
the bedside of a dying child or in the arms of a grieving husband, not so simply), many different techniques are employed.

Different temperaments draw from us different intuitive responses. With some we are quite devotional—we use the word
"God," for instance, out of exasperation for lack of a better term
to describe the indescribable, the unity out of which all forms
and definitions arise, the infinite spaciousness of being. In the
same way we use "Jesus" or "Buddha" with many whose most
familiar metaphor for their essence is a historical figure who
embodies the qualities of pure being: wisdom and love. With
many, we use techniques for deep meditative discovery. With
most we explore the fear or anger, which results in suffering.
For a few we might suggest the "Who am I?" investigation, the
Vichara Atman teaching of Ramana Maharshi, which some call
"the high path with no railing" and which is certainly not for
everyone; a powerful confrontation with the very nature of
experience and existence itself. With many we shared the writings of such great teachers as Neem Karoli Baba; St. John of the
Cross; Sengstan, the Third Zen Patriarch; and Kabir, the god-
drunken poet of the fifteenth century. But with all the investi-
gations of the mind, the encouragement of the heart was the
medium of communication, and we often used guided meditations to touch the cause of suffering, to accept it in compassion
and self-mercy, to open to it and let it float free in the heart.

Section III

Of the perhaps three thousand or more phone calls on the
free consultation phone over the past three years, only a small
percentage were recorded, so what follows are not really "the
best cases" but rather those that we had permission for and
access to on tape which seemed representative of so many other
communications we experienced.

In editing these tapes for publication, in order to tighten the
communication, removing the natural pauses and half sentences which are so much a part of spontaneous speech, I have

at times condensed sentences and ideas in such a way that as I
now reread some of these dialogues, I hear a certain echo of my
voice within theirs. This is the hazard and difficulty of formaliz-
ing the intuitive hum and flow of conversation into "the written
word." Though their natural speech may be somewhat neutral-
ized through editing, I trust the heart of these sharings will not
be lost.

Each chapter is a single aspect of a much longer and more
complex process, often shared over a considerable length of
time. Indeed, these stories have been edited so that each de-
fines a particular predicament that we found recurring in dozens of different circumstances. In a way each of these stories is
an archetype of the multiple directions from which we approach crisis and the unknown. In some stories more than one
patient's process has been included to form something of a
composite which more clearly displays the particular arche-
typal situation to which the story refers.

I have attempted not to "put words in others' mouths," to
make them clearer or holier or any more or less confused than
they may have been. On a few occasions, however, I have dis-
tilled months of hard introspective work into a few sentences or
paragraphs of deep recognition.

Indeed, this was an odd work to approach, as I had some
concerns about honoring the privacy of various individuals. Because all who called knew their calls were being recorded, in
recognition of their candor and trust each has been disguised by
the changing of various particulars that might identify them.
Names and places have been changed, as have circumstances,
but the heart of the individual and its voice have not been
altered.

These are not the "highest" or clearest people we have
worked with but only those from whom we had letters or tapes
—which feels just right, so this book will not appear to make
death any more special than it is or to make the process of dying
seem any easier or more difficult than is experienced by many.
These are only a few beings in the process of discovery and loss,
fear and courage, doubt and confidence in the value of life/
death. Some think of this process as a wonder. Some are healing.
Some are not. What was for some an exploration of the deathless
was of necessity for others a nitty-gritty finishing of incomplete

relationships. But for each, love seemed the ultimate teaching, and priorities changed for all.

These are, in certain ways, "incidental stories," which may be of use to those who have spent some time with *Who Dies?*

Section IV

When recently asked, "Is death real or an illusion?" one of the remarkable, nearly translucent, teachers of the Tibetan Buddhist tradition answered, "Death is a real illusion." In a sense these stories too are "real illusion." They can be very misleading if one takes these words and swallows them whole, feeding the mind with more information and another menu for controlling the universe. But if one sees these stories rather as "skillful means," as ways through the holding of the mind and the armoring of the heart, then the "truth" in them will surface as one's own. These stories are real insofar as they are the direct experience of various beings in their confrontations with life and death, with pain and grief, with healing and letting go, but they are illusions to the degree one may feel these predicaments to be "any realer than they are." It would be shortsighted to see these patients simply as their personalities rather than recognizing them as process-in-motion, ever changing, never as neatly described as words would have it. Indeed, these words are not the truth, but only indications and directions of paths we may travel for ourselves in this search of self-discovery.

These stories are not of others but of us all in the process of purification and growth, coming into some deeper sense of being. The process of growth is, it seems, the art of falling down. Growth is measured by the gentleness and awareness with which we once again pick ourselves up, the lightness with which we dust ourselves off, the openness with which we continue and take the next unknown step, beyond our edge, beyond our holding, into the remarkable mystery of being. Going beyond the mind, we go beyond death. In the heart lies the deathless.

Meetings at the Edge

Opening to Grief

DOROTHY

Dorothy called one morning to say that her nine-year-old daughter was dying of lymphoma. After an unexpected, six-week illness the lymph nodes had begun "popping up like popcorn," to which she added, "It feels to me and to the doctors as if it is already a bit too late for any sort of intervention."

S: "Does your daughter understand what is happening to her?"
D: "No, not entirely. She asked me the other day, 'Mom, I am really pretty sick, aren't I?' and I said, 'Little girls nine years old don't usually get so lumpy.' "

Her mother added, "We will take it quiet now and do the things we are able to do. She has been out of school but I have not pressed it. She asked me what they were running the test for and I said cancer. And she said, 'People die with that, don't they?' And I said, 'Certainly they die with that and they also die crossing the streets.' I tried to be very casual with her."

I asked Dorothy if she thought her fear at that moment may have caused her to miss a moment of truth. If indeed her daughter wasn't trying to see past the barrier of Dorothy's motherhood and protection to some place essential where she could share her fears and her confusion of what she was moving toward.

D: "At this point, as long as she is active, I am not going to say much of what is happening. The night before last two lymph nodes in her groin began swelling and one on her neck about three days before that. And she said, 'Why am I getting these, Mom?' "

I mentioned to Dorothy that she sounded very matter-of-fact. That rather than holding back, as painful as it might be, perhaps she might investigate more deeply what she felt, and I asked her, "What if your daughter died tonight? What would remain unsaid? What have you not shared with her that you might wish to?" To which she replied, "At first I cried at night, but in the days I try to deal with it objectively." I pointed out that her daughter only saw her during the day, however; that her daughter might benefit from sharing in some of those tears so she might see some of the softness that her mother felt at night when they were both apart. Dorothy said, "I decided not to go through all that."

S: "Do you think emotions are something you can just decide about?"

D: "To a large extent, yes, at least the display of them."

S: "What seems inappropriate about sharing your concern?"

D: "At this point I would just like to try and remain as normal as humanly possible."

S: "What do you mean by normal? Isn't the sharing of this grief normal under the circumstances? Mightn't it open a deeper contact between you two, a healing of the confusion and isolation which is so frightening for you both? Truly, you can't go through the door with her, but you can accompany her more fully to the threshold."

D: "I have felt so alone for the past weeks and I guess she must too. I have lost so much in my life. My husband died of cancer three years ago. I have lost two other children to cancer as well. There is so much grief, I don't know where to start. I think basically we are always alone. I don't like it but I don't know what to do about it."

S: "You have pushed so much away that now it seems impossible to make room for it all, but that is your daughter's legacy to you. Each grief demands to be recognized—the pain around your heart is its voice. Can you feel that sensation in the middle of your chest over your heart?"

D: "No."

S: "No soreness?"

D: "Well, yes."

I explored with Dorothy that she might find a quiet place in the house some evening and start to focus on that sensation in the center of her chest. To start to open to whatever pain arose there because the heart armors itself, and her work now is to allow her heart to be torn open to the truths of the present moment. Focusing on the sensation, she might find that it would become very distinct and that she could start breathing directly into it as though it were a vent opening into her heart. That the soreness was the touch point of her heart, and as she entered this great soreness of heart all sorts of associated images might arise in the mind, glimpses of the deaths of others and the hard swallowing of long-held tears. To open to this fear and notice how it forms a shell around each stiff breath. To meet this fear with a willingness to be in this pain as a means of going beyond it into the vast love just beneath. If she wished her heart to touch her daughter's heart, she must focus on whatever old grief and broken longings blocked that touch point. I shared with her that this was not a time to seek safe territory as obviously there was no way she could protect her daughter from the experience of this time. All she could do was open in love to these precious moments that remained.

S: "How merciless we are with ourselves. How little we are available to ourselves and to others when we are maintaining this sort of self-protection which we have been told to cultivate our whole life through. Indeed, your daughter's teaching for you may be to start to tune in to the suffering which has so long been present in your heart. But by pulling back, as you have so many times in the past, you may find just another dark veil drawn across the heart, another moment missed that you wish to share with your daughter. I know it is a tough one."

Dorothy shared with me her fear of opening to those feelings. "When I was just a child, I was given a puppy for Christmas, a little cocker spaniel. He was like one of my dolls but better—he was alive—but he got run over two months later and that same week my grandmother died—no one wanted to hear about my puppy and we weren't allowed to talk about Grandma. I guess I just didn't know what to do with it all—something in me shut down, I guess. I've put each death in my life behind me as quickly as possible. I almost never cry. I would like to get out all this grief but it sounds like such a bummer."

S: "How much more of a bummer is it to feel cut off from the world? From your daughter at a time of such need? We keep guarding our heart—we want to be so together, and in being so together we retract from the world into a kind of drowsy blindness that lets life slip by unshared."

D: "But it has always seemed so much safer to hold back from all this pain."

S: "That is what we have so often been encouraged to do. But you know, it is pretty hard to kiss someone who is keeping a stiff upper lip. How does this stiffness feel? Does it leave you sore all over? Where is the safety? You can't keep from dying, you can't keep your heart from aching—the pain just becomes more unbearable, seemingly unworkable. You have to do exactly what you wish your daughter to do right now—to open, to soften around the pain, to make contact with something essential. All the holding back of a lifetime has become focused now in this predicament. It is time to be kind to yourself, to use these days or weeks as a deepening of your opening to life—by just loving her and being with her as your heart allows.

"As we speak now, just close your eyes and gently move into the pain. Allow the heart's armoring to melt. There is a vastness you share with your daughter. An edgeless unity with her, and all that is, which can be discovered when the heart allows itself to be torn open. Allow the pain to penetrate into the very center of your heart. Let go of any resistance that falsely assures you it is your only defense. Share in the deathlessness of just being in the moment, with whatever it offers. Allowing yourself to go beyond the defenses of the mind. Move into the very heart of the moment. It can allow an experience of much greater context than the fearful attachment to the body. This is the unfinished work we are so frightened to move into. Clearly death is not the enemy. It is our lack of self-trust. Our forgetfulness of the extraordinary nature which inhabits this tiny body for a moment. I don't mean just your daughter's tiny body. I mean your tiny body as well. Go gently through without force. Just opening a moment at a time to the feelings and pain that arise there in the middle of your chest. With great kindness to yourself, remember how force, again and again, closes the heart."

D: "You know, even though my mind is fighting against what you are saying, the sensation in my heart is beginning to make me feel like my heart will burst. I just want to cry."

S: "Good. Let your heart break. Let go of the suffering that keeps you back from life. Do you hear yourself now? Your heart is so open and the pain is right there. You are doing now just what you need to do—to just feel with so much compassion for yourself what you are going through.

"There is no rush to this process of opening, there is no emergency. Just slowly begin to make room in your heart for yourself. Perhaps tonight you will sit down with your daughter and feel that pain and just share it with her."

We spoke of the resistance to life which filters every perception, which pushes away our connectedness with all that we love and leaves us feeling so isolated. And I encouraged her to just start to breathe in to her heart with whatever love might mean to her at that moment and to breathe it back out, to send it to her daughter. To allow herself to move into her experience and not hold back. That her essential connectedness with her daughter would become apparent beyond the ancient barricades which had so often kept her separate from the moment. "Let your pain be there and open around it. Open so that you can feel her pain and your pain together. You know, if pain made a sound, the atmosphere would be humming all the time. What you are sharing with your daughter now is being shared by tens of thousands of other beings at this very moment. Let it be in love instead of fear. Let her death be surrounded by your care for her and a willingness to go beyond your fear. To open to her death in a kind of new birth shared now for you both."

D: "I can't talk much now, my chest hurts so, but in my heart I hear my daughter saying 'thank you.' "

Before Dorothy's daughter died, they had many long "midnight talks" about her father's and brother's deaths. Dorothy said at first she was "terribly uncomfortable bringing this all up" but that it seemed to put her daughter more at ease. "We talked at length about cancer and God. And I told her I loved her in a way that even losing her could not diminish. I don't think I have ever acknowledged my feelings to anyone so directly. It felt terrible. It felt wonderful."

In the years since Dorothy's daughter's death, she has been "working hard on this grief, or should I say it has been working hard on me. My youngest son says 'I love you, Mom' all the time. I don't think we were ever so demonstrative. I am less afraid but more often in pain than I ever have been." She has since adopted two severely disabled infants and accompanied them to "the threshold." The last time we spoke Dorothy said, "You are right, death is not the enemy, fear is. You know, I have never felt so bad or so good, in my whole life."

Allowing Death

DORIS

Doris, a thirty-eight-year-old attorney from Pittsburgh, called
one morning to ask us to "therapize" her mother. "I am calling
because I would like you to speak to my mother. She is very sick
from cancer, almost dying, and I want her to continue her
treatment. She says she has had enough, the treatments make
her sick, and she refuses to go to the hospital or continue the
therapy that the doctors say might help." Doris, who had two
children, was angry and saddened by her grief at her sixty-five-
year-old mother's "lack of care for herself after suffering from
cancer for nearly three years." Barbara, her mother, had gone
the full route of the medical model for treating her cancer. She
had surgery followed by chemotherapy and a full schedule of
radiation, and now the doctors once again were saying that
chemotherapy "might be of some help." But the treatment
made her ill, and Barbara wanted only to stay in her own home,
in her own bed, to "meet the end with some quiet, and not so
damned nauseous."

Speaking with Doris, I told her it was not our custom or
intention to talk to someone who did not wish to speak to us.
That if her mother's desires were such, that it was our sense that
it was most appropriate to treat her with the dignity of her own
wishes in these last days or weeks or months of her life.

D: "But if you don't talk to her, she is just going to let herself die.
She is so bullheaded. She just won't do what I am asking her to
do. If she won't do it for herself, she can at least do it for me."
S: "You know, Doris, the more you want her to do something,
the more you put her out of your heart. As long as you want
anything from her, then she becomes just another object in

your mind from which you wish to wring satisfaction. Instead of a living human being going through a very difficult time. This is her time of completion. And it is your time of completion with her as well. Why don't you trust her sense of what is right for her?"

D: "I don't want her to die."

S: "But she is dying. How are you going to stop that? How is your differing with her now going to make this situation any better for either of you?"

D: "But I think emotional growth is occurring even now and that is why I encourage her to continue. Because I need her and I love her and I don't want to lose her."

S: "But the more you want her to do what you think is right, the further away you push her. In a sense, you are losing her before she even dies. Imagine what it might feel like to be someone just about to jump off a diving board and as your toes leave the edge, all around you yell, 'Don't dive! Don't dive!' What can you do? It is impossible to get back on the board and gravity is pulling you toward the pool. The dive is going to be very awkward and self-conscious. If someone is dying and those around them insist that they do not die, the person dies in isolation, alone and without the love that can offer such support and such a sense of completion at the end of sixty-five years. You say you don't want her to die, but she *is* dying. You can't stop that process. All you can really do is be an open-hearted space into which that person can let go of whatever holds them back from their next perfect evolution."

D: "Well, it is OK with me that she is dying. I just don't want her to die right now."

S: "I understand how you may wish to be with her as long as possible. But in a real sense you have stopped being with her when you deny what her heart tells her is appropriate. You say it is all right with you she is dying, but I sense that is not altogether so, and this confusion may be transmitted to her and put her in yet another quandary. Dying is difficult enough without having to protect those around you who are confused by their own feelings and fear of abandonment.

"It is natural that you have these feelings, but perhaps there is some place within you where you can come to some resolution. It is all right that the mind is irrational right now. Emotions are not rational and of course needn't be. They are a whole other level of the mind. And we don't have to try to make them rational. In fact, those who try to make their emotions rational make themselves crazy. Emotions have their own nature and they are often in conflict with one another. I am suggesting that you examine this tension so it is not transmitted to your mother at a time when she needs peace, not conflict. When she needs trust in the next unknown moment, not someone scrambling to drag her back from the pull of gravity."

D: "I want her to go to the hospital, but she says she wants to stay home. I tell her that every week more is so precious, but she says that she is done and why bother. I need her love for me. It is something I have known all my life."

S: "Can you see how her dying is causing you to confront this world of impermanence, and even your own mortality?"

D: "Yes, but I still need her."

S: "Do you think that you are in some way trying to keep her alive as a means of keeping yourself alive? It is very difficult what you are going through, and I know there is no easy way to lose a parent. To lose a parent is to feel sort of like you have been cut loose. Like a boat that has lost its mooring. There is a sense of insecurity and instability in it which activates all our feelings of unworthiness and fearsomeness. It is frightening, but it is also, just as you said of her, part of your own emotional growth as well. You are probably going through great feelings of aloneness and abandonment, but so is she. Allow her her death as she wishes."

D: "Maybe that is true, but I just don't want her to give up the ship too soon."

S: "What do you mean by the ship? Her body?"

D: "Yes. I just don't want her to die any sooner than she has to."

S: "Are you asking her to die your death for you? Because really she only needs to do what she senses is right. No matter how long she lives, it will never be long enough if you continue to fear her death instead of support it."

D: "I understand, but it hurts so much to lose her."

S: "Well, you do understand and you don't understand. And that is natural too. But just as you did not appreciate her telling you how to live your life when you were a child, do you think she appreciates your telling her how to die her death as an adult?

"She is going to die. And it could be a month, or it could be a week, or it could be a day. And if you have fought with her about how it is to be, what do you think the aftertaste of that experience is going to be. How is your heart going to feel after pulling her back from what she thought was right for her? How will you feel any sense of completion if you have not honored her wishes, if you have fought death instead of honoring her life as she chooses to live it to the very end?"

D: "I just don't know what to do. I am so confused."

S: "Of course you are confused. This is one of the great confusions of a lifetime—to lose a child, to lose a parent, to break that mirror which has so often reflected your beauty and made you feel so safe. But you can't protect her from death any more than you can protect her from life. Any more than you can protect your own children. All you do is create more separation. Your mind is creating an abyss that your heart must eventually cross. Her dying holds perhaps the greatest potential for intimacy of a lifetime together. To be with one as they die and offer them love and compassion will allow your hearts to touch perhaps as never before. But if you push her decision away, you push her away, and she dies alone. And you die more orphaned than you suspect."

D: "Is there nothing I should do to keep her alive?"

S: "Give her what she asks for, but don't force her to stay alive. Just love her and share these last days in companionship and trust rather than fear and doubt. You too have an opportunity for a profound healing of all that has gone before—all the resentments, all the unsureties, all the unfinished business, can be finished in just a deep allowing of each other. A trust in the process."

D: "But perhaps if you could speak to her about the preciousness of what we are sharing now, she would wish to stay on a bit longer."

S: "Does she want to speak to me?"

D: "No. As a matter of fact, when I told her I was going to call you, she said, 'Have a nice conversation. Oh, and by the way, tell him I saw his picture on the back of the book and he has nice eyes.'"

S: "And tell her she has a beautiful heart and a very loving daughter. But do you understand the more you encourage her to 'not give up the ship,' the more you are encouraging her to hold on. The more tightly she grasps that ship, the more painful dying is going to be for her. In fact, in an odd way you are encouraging her to go down with the ship instead of letting go and floating free in the ocean of being. In a manner of speaking, as her ship slips its moorings and begins to depart, you are calling her back, but she is signaling to you that now is the time for her 'to catch the tide,' to proceed with her clear passage out to sea.

"What you are feeling is completely natural—it is the primal grasping of grief. I have been with many people who were dying surrounded by loved ones who encouraged them to 'hold on.' Often I find I am the only one in the room for whom it is really OK that the person is dying. Therefore the love between that person and me is so incredibly deep, because I am the only one saying to that person it is OK to be whoever you are, however you are right now, which is just what they need facing this great unknown of death. She has so much love to share if only you will allow her her way."

D: "I know I am holding to her. But I never really saw it in terms of holding her back, but I guess you're right. It's just that I am so afraid to let go."

S: "I understand. It is so complex, the loss of any loved one. Much less the loss of a parent or child. But in a sense, that is the contract we all have with our loved ones. It is the same as that which I share with my three children. I know I am either going to witness their death at some time or they are going to witness mine."

We shared for some time the reality that to be born is to sign the contract. Each is going to witness the other's exit from their body. And how for many people it is the most intense growth they go through together. Painful as hell. Incredibly painful. But it is the pain that tears open the heart to life; allowing life to unfold, not in fear, but in a new kindness, a deeper sense of being that does not pull back from impermanence but opens to it as a way of tasting each moment in its precious essence. "When you experience the loss of your mother, you are also experiencing the reservoir of loss within you. That place in which resides all the losses of a lifetime. The confusion of your-

self as the little five-year-old girl standing in the backyard, looking up at the sky, wondering, 'What is this all about?' All the
confusion, all the loves lost, all the pets that have died, all the
friends who have died or moved away, all the lovers who have
left—all the feelings of loss. It is not just the grief you feel for
your mother, it is the grief at life which you are feeling right
now. And to the degree you attempt to protect yourself from
that grief, you push away life, just as you may be pushing away
her death."

   We spoke of how grief has an incredible potential for deep
healing. How it is a process that drops the awareness into the
ancient reservoir of fear and holding. A place usually far below
the conscious level, but a place from which many of our most
confusing feelings of distrust and separation arise. Imagine, now
that you have access to these deep feelings, which have always
motivated us yet have been so seldom uncovered, how much an
allowing compassion for yourself might heal this area of confusion and pain. To meet these feelings, if only for a millisecond,
with understanding and forgiveness, with kindness, has the capacity to heal us and to offer so much more room for life, for
love. "And remember too that you are not the only one in grief.
So is your mother. You are losing one person, but she is losing
the whole world."

D: "You mean I should just let my mother die?"
S: "I mean you should let her live. Allow her to enter the next
moment as she wishes. Indeed, if she lived even a year more, if
that year is lived in tension and force, what have you really
shared? If you have put her out of your heart, in a sense she is
already dead to you. And you abandon her before she leaves the
world."
D: "How can I let her die when I love her so much?"
S: "How can you not let her die if you love her? See how it is not
her death which is separating you, because in a real sense she is
just as alive at the moment of death as she was at the moment of
birth. What separates you is fear—holding. Just allow that great
love you feel for her to be felt *by* her, to flow *to* her so that she
can take her next appropriate step."

As we spoke more, it seemed as if Doris was struggling to the surface to hear the words that were being said. "I ache so when I think of her dying, but it aches too when I think that maybe what you say is so and somehow I could be abandoning her, just as I fear abandonment, that I am doubling her difficulties by trying to stop her from setting sail when she needs my loving navigation so much. I will try."

A few weeks later Doris called to say her mother had died and that "when I let her go, when I just let her be, something happened that was so remarkable. We just loved each other. I am so glad that she died at home. That she didn't go to the hospital as she wished not to. Her sense of humor was incredible. One day not long before she died she thanked me for not 'pushing any longer.' She said, 'Dying is bizarre enough. I don't need to be sick from chemo and have my head in a wastepaper basket too. I've had enough nausea to last me a lifetime.' We laughed so much in those last two weeks. I never would have thought there could be so many moments of happiness when someone was dying. So much love. And you know, the day before she died she kept giggling. And when I asked her why, she said, 'Nothing is too good to be true.' And when I asked her what she meant, she just said she was happy and that 'everything is OK.' And she suggested we 'get on with the work at hand, get on with life.' I was so glad to be with her when she died. It was midafternoon, and right before she died she sat up in bed and had a big smile on her face and said, 'Your father has come for me.' But my father has been dead for fifteen years and all we could do was laugh and cry together. It was beautiful."

We spoke for some time more about her willingness to just allow her grief and love to be as it was.

She calls occasionally now to say how things are going for her and her children and how much closer she feels to them. "And I think I am not protecting them from living so much as I used to. And if it's possible, somehow I even love them more than ever."

Forgiveness as Healing

CASSIE

Cassie first called two days before Christmas 1979 to speak to us about the difficulties she was encountering opening to her cancer. "There is a distinct possibility I won't be around to see Christmas 1980. But that's not all of it. It turns out I have a very rare form of cancer that of all things my husband Mark is the world expert on. Of all the cancers I could have gotten, and there are more than a hundred, I had to get this one. And my husband is the leading researcher on this one. In fact he recently received a grant to do further studies on his findings. When the doctor finally diagnosed the type of disease and told me about it, he had a very strange expression on his face when he said, 'You know, your only hope is your husband. There are only about twenty cases of this potentially fatal form of cancer being treated in this country, and all of them look to your husband's research for a possible cure.' " The silence that followed was palpable. "And my husband and I have been having big problems for the last year or so since I found out the bastard had been womanizing for years on his many trips away from home. Do you think I am just trying to get his attention? This is a hell of a way of doing it. In a sense, I feel as though our relationship is killing me. And maybe will."

We spoke for a while about the blockages to communicating with Mark at any deeper level to share her feelings of abandonment and confusion. The conversation went on for some time and she admitted, "I don't even know if I want to take the treatment. When I told him what I have, he went pale as a ghost. I think that even if he does come up with something, I will try everything else first."

Investigating together her anger, we spoke of the quality of forgiveness. Of the power of that state of mind, when cultivated, to meet the fear and anger with a greater softness and an openness to what comes next. It was one of those conversations where one is in no way certain whether the other person can hear what is being said. But nonetheless the words speak themselves out of a sense of an appropriateness of their possibility of healing.

After about twenty minutes, as she continued to soften, she said, "And my husband has had two heart attacks in the last eighteen months but refuses to talk about the possibility of his dying. He might die and leave me with no cure. There is so much stuff between us, I don't know if we can ever get it all worked out in whatever time is allotted either of us. It may be that we are both dying, and now neither of us knows which will go first. It's a hell of a time."

She went on to say that her husband was about to go on another "business trip" and that it felt each time he left as though they may never see each other again but that it was never acknowledged because the anger and confusion accumulated over twenty years of marriage had resulted in "a huge wall between us." As we spoke, the underlying love, the years of connection and sharing, began to show through. Though the dishonesty of these years was causing great pain, still there was a foundation of many shared experiences, the raising of two children, the mutual growth, as she put it, "from a late adolescence into an early maturity."

It was suggested that she work with the forgiveness meditation as offered in *Who Dies?* and that she get in touch as it seemed appropriate.

Three weeks later she called. "I taped the forgiveness meditation like you said and I have used it daily and it's working. I am trying to open that part of my heart back up again. I had walled off my heart in that area into a tight little fist, and I started to go 'lightly' with it and allowed it to begin to open. I had a few cramps in that muscle, I have to admit.

"The neat part of all this is that I was able to be so gentle and loving with Mark before he left on this recent business trip. And he seemed able to talk a bit more about dying. I think the heart palpitations two weeks ago opened something up in him. The undeniable is becoming more obvious to both of us. And maybe the forgiveness is shining through all this resentment a bit. He may even be willing to talk now about his dying, which he hasn't said ten words about in the last year. He and I talked about how he believed that his womanizing so much of the time in the past twelve years was coming from a fear of death. As he spoke about this as all in the past, I felt we really began to deal with it, though I sure could feel the fist in my heart as he was talking—the distrust and fear. This time, thanks to whatever is happening in me, we spoke very graphically about dying instead of intellectualizing, about it, and I was able to be open and loving and allow the tears to come, both his and mine. It is one of the purest moments of the last years. My heart hurts."

S: "As the heart opens, sometimes the armoring and pain that has held life away become so distinct, we think we may die from it, that our heart will burst; but it is, in a manner of speaking, just contact with that place where you have been 'broken-hearted.' It is the healing pain. If it frightens you though, have it checked out. This is all such new territory you are exploring. Take it slowly and easily. This healing of the heart can be so painful yet so joyous."

She called two days later to say: "After we spoke, a warmth came from my heart up to the left side of my head, a kind of easing of tension. The heart pains continue but an EKG showed that my heart is just fine, so I am going ahead with the treatments that I had originally intended to undergo. Usually, when I get frightened about things going a certain way, I remember to remind myself that I could get well without any treatment or I could die in an instant from being hit by a truck or earthquake, or lightning or another disease! It's also true that living could be horrible and dying beautiful, but I don't so often remember that. The forgiveness meditation is opening me in a way I thought would have taken years. But it seems I am just letting go of my resentment. Living with it instead of dying from it.

"I guess the scenario I have in mind is that this treatment will bring about a remission. I will then have the energy to change my life. Meaning I might move away from Mark or maybe we will work out some arrangement. But things are changing so quickly now. Neither of us have a moment to lose, though there have been so many years of 'the wall' that I am not sure that a moment of openness will heal the abyss between us."

Encouraging her to "open to her anger so that she might have access to her love," we discussed what the qualities of anger in the mind are and how it closes the heart, how isolated we feel when anger is a predominant experience and how frightening that experience can be. What self-judgment it generates and what a feeling of aloneness it leaves us with. As we spoke of anger and its investigation, tears mixed with vituperative resentment poured from her. But amidst her agitation there was a spark, the light of an opening heart shining through, of a sense of love that had probably accompanied her during much of her earlier life. Also, as she spoke, she could hear in her own words the power of anger to close the heart, to make everyone else "an other," to close her off from life.

S: "And you know, Cassie, even when we speak about 'opening the heart,' that doesn't quite get at it—the truth is that the heart is always there shining and we must just learn to 'open to it.' "

A week after the conversation I received a letter. "I calmed down considerably since I called you. Mark returned from his trip and he and I have had several honest, open talks. It doesn't mean that all is open between us, but each talk, as far as it went, was honest, with little game playing, and each one listened carefully to the other.

"My interferon treatment is not going well. We will give it another week to be absolutely sure, but it looks like it is not going to work. It is a failure. I am terribly disappointed. I counted heavily on it. The doctor is again talking about chemotherapy, a new one, and I am feeling more and more backed against the wall. A woman from the hospital asked me, 'What are you going to do now?' And my mind didn't come up with any answer. How ironic that Mark's research should be perhaps my only hope. And that maybe we are both dying. And may never have the opportunity to heal each other in the way that I now sense is possible, as the honesty between us opens more.

"I know I talk like a dying person, so I want to add how everybody is telling me how well I look. Mark has received his grant and is working on the method he believes will be the best for treating me. With the situation being somewhat more peaceable between us, my resistance to his treatment has definitely decreased. It seems to move inescapably closer. I believe it was you who mentioned 'the divine choreographer,' that one sure knows how to dance the dance."

As the months went by and our communication continued, the power of the forgiveness meditation and the depth of her investigation of anger and the underlying love and sadness was allowing her what she called "a new life even though it appears I am dying."

In May, one day as we were speaking, she said, "You know, Mark and I had thought some years ago of writing a book about relationship and marriage together and had even started about two years ago to make some notes. This was before I found out about his philandering, but even before then something in me knew I wasn't getting all his love. And now I see how much denial was present for us to even imagine that we had worked through enough to try and help others. It is so easy to get stuck in thinking that fear and distancing is the only way to live, the only thing that life has to offer. It is strange how the possibility of my death has made me more open to life. Imagine if we had ever really published that book! How the underlying subtext of what we were saying would only have caused more confusion for people. Somehow I must have thought that because we could live together with so much anger that we had something to share about relationships. But my cancer and Mark's heart failures have forced me to see how we were both backing away from life. Indeed, the book about relationships was just another way we were conning ourselves. It was like sending a get-well card to someone in the morgue.

"And you know," she went on. "For some reason a lot of dying people have come into my life in the past few months. I had a dear close friend die in my arms just a couple of weeks ago. He had been ill for a very long time and was in a nursing home, and his wife called me and said the nursing home had called to say that this was the end. My friend was terrified to go to the home by herself to be with her husband and asked me to meet her there. I arrived and went into the room by myself. I had never been with anyone in their final moments, but I knew what I was seeing. I took him in my arms, and he was laboring so hard to breathe. He had been my surrogate father for so many years, and I felt like he was a part of me lying on that bed. Suddenly, his struggle to breathe became so hard, and I said, 'Let go, God has his arms around you.' And that was it. He did not draw another breath. I could not believe what had happened. And then I was frightened. I was afraid that his bowels would let go and I would not like the odor and all sorts of crazy thoughts. And suddenly the smell of flowers permeated the room from a breeze blowing in the open window. I laid my head down on the pillow beside his and talked to him in much the same way that you have in your after-death meditations in *Who Dies?* I told him to look around and to not be afraid and to go to the light. I have experienced the light in meditation in the last couple of months and know the validity of it, so it was so natural to tell him to go into it. I had an experience of being at one with the light last month during one of the meditations, and the knowledge has given me such strength in these past weeks of going through what seems useless treatment. I have a tough time acting from that space very often, but when it is there, it gives me a sense of healing. I don't know what is going on, but whatever it is it is OK too."

The work between Cassie and Mark became a profound influence in both of their lives. Each seemed to be opening more and more to their environment, including the potential death that each carried within them. It was a very rich time. A time of what Cassie called "a new loveliness."

On Thanksgiving Mark died with Cassie sitting by his bed holding his hand in the hospital. She called the following evening to say, "We had so much unfinished business that it seemed a year ago we could never really touch again in the way we had so many years before. But as I opened to him in love, as he let go of his past way of relating to me, his confusing sexuality, his denial of death, even his denial of life, something happened. You know, we could have talked forever and I don't think much would have been worked out. It would have been just more talking. More trading off for each other's approval. But late last summer when I found my heart just opening to him 'as is,' it seemed that our conversations changed radically. At times we almost had nothing to talk about because there were not so many differences between us. The love was just incredible. And though it didn't save his life in one way, in another way maybe it did. I don't know. But I miss him now more than I ever thought I would. And somehow our life together is finished. I don't know what I am going to do or what will happen with me, but I know I no longer need him to heal me. I am going to heal myself. And I don't know what that means either. Life is so incredibly unpredictable."

Two weeks later she called to say that her heart "was aching in the same way as before but deeper" and that she had never felt so alone and yet "so at one with things." We spoke of how she was experiencing the "grief of a lifetime" and that indeed she might notice this grief was not only for Mark's loss but for the years of loss between them. And too that she might be experiencing a kind of anticipatory grief for her own death. Her spirit was lighter though the sadness was evident. And just before we finished, she said with a laugh, "I have to tell you a story. I know it is awful to think this is so funny, but let me share it with you. A week ago my brother-in-law from Minnesota became so depressed that he decided to kill himself, and he took a shotgun and loaded it and went across his fields to go into the woods on the other side of the fence. But as he was climbing over the fence the shotgun went off, and as he puts it, 'I blew off exactly the leg I would kick myself in the ass with now if I still had it.' Maybe he got it out of his system. His attitude is certainly changed—although he is still in the hospital pretty badly wounded, he seems clearer and more heartful than he has been in some time. In a sense it seems he blew away his depression. He killed all of himself he really needed to and now maybe he can get on with it. I guess it runs in the family." She finished the conversation by saying that for the last week or so she had been working on a piece of writing about how this previous year had gone for her and would soon send it to us in a letter.

Just after New Year's I received a letter. "I wanted to tell you how my thoughts and feelings about dying and living have evolved since we started working together just over a year ago. When I first called you last Christmas, I had a rather coy attitude. I felt it was the 'in' thing to face mortality consciously. I remember I could only speak of my own death laughingly, in a joking way. It was somewhere off in the moderately distant future. I didn't have to face it directly, and neither could I foresee a long future in good health where I could live my life fully. So what it amounted to was that I was not quite dying and not quite living.

"When things began to 'come together' between Mark and me, something else happened which seemed to make life more acceptable. In some ways I was so unprepared for life. Even at fifty years old. And that is what made me so unprepared for my death, I think now as I look back at it. Life had so often been a struggle for me, how could my death have been any different. But then I began to let go of 'struggling' and in some ways I met Mark for the first time. His death was, if I may say it, one of the most remarkable experiences of my life. We had never been so close. How intimate it is to share in the dying of someone you love so much, someone with whom so much has been shared. In a funny way I felt as though we had gone through another marriage ceremony.

"In spring when I came to your Conscious Living/Conscious Dying retreat, I saw myself flirting with the idea of my dying. I tried to make myself confront it, and one way in which I did this was to emphasize to myself the way in which the disease was slowly disabling me. For example, one side of my body is numb and weaker than the other. I also have consistent lapses of memory and loss of concentration. I thought that focusing on this gradual form of dying would make me realize what was actually happening. But when one of the women at the retreat became so seriously ill that everyone thought she might die right there, I did not go to visit her. I felt frightened at coming that close to seeing myself in that bed.

"One thing that happened that seemed to make such a difference in my subsequent attitude occurred while you were guiding me through a meditation. You told me to let each thought arise and pass away, that it lasted no longer than a breath. I was trying hard (probably much too hard) to follow instructions, first by strengthening the breath, then by shortening the thought. After a while I sort of gave up and just let it happen by itself, and it got to be a very even process. Then for a breath-space, there was no thought. I had been weaving the world and suddenly I fell off the edge and dropped into the universe just long enough to see the emptiness before my mind resumed weaving the thought-world. Months later, as I was talking with Mark during a period of considerable weakness for him, he and I were able to have this same perspective. I understood that what kind of life I *do not have* is completely irrelevant. It only matters what kind of life I have when I have it. Mark and I shared this and it was a very precious moment. It made us both more willing to take risks. It changed our priorities about what was and wasn't important.

"I remember your quoting a few months after that experience some lines from the Third Zen Patriarch: 'The great way is not difficult for those who have no preference. To set up what you like against what you dislike is the disease of the mind.' Those lines kept ringing through my mind. The very nature of disease came into a new light, a light as bright at times as I had experienced in that meditation some months earlier.

"Then came the day you guided me through your variation on the *Tibetan Book of the Dead* meditation. I don't know quite what happened. I didn't hear any reading: I was just there. I can still see the place of my conception, which was the place of my dying, floating freely, light joining light above an idyllic pastoral landscape. That experience left its mark. After that I felt death is not so bad after all and life the greater difficulty of the two. Though I remember too the Zen Patriarch saying: 'To come directly into harmony with this reality, just simply say when doubt arises, "Not two." In this "not two," nothing is separate, nothing is excluded.' And remember on occasion that it is not life or death but *just being* in whatever state it finds itself. And I noticed in that meditation that it was much easier to die than to be born. I saw where my work was and that, perhaps as much as anything, motivated me to let go of the unfinished business with Mark, and to let whatever our potential for love was meet each other, as you put it, in 'don't know.'

"I have since worked with that meditation several times. And when I am able to get into it fully, something in me says, 'Don't think. Don't read. Just feel. Breathe and feel.' Though I often forget to 'just let thoughts think themselves,' as you put it, when I do, what a distinct experience of being fully alive happens within me.

"Now I can be in a room with a hundred people and know I am no less alive than the healthiest person there. My mind tells me: 'As long as I am not dead, I am alive. Fully alive.' No longer do I feel as I did before, that I am slowly dying, watching myself die, half alive, half dead. Now, for me, receiving chemotherapy is a moment of living. Hurting like hell is a moment of living. Being frantic with loneliness is living, living, living. Naturally, moments of joy and pleasure are moments of living—everyone knows that—but I am learning not to differentiate so much. Indeed, the great way is not difficult when preferences do not interfere and do not so automatically 'set up what I like against what I dislike.' As long as I am not dead—and who knows what that is all about—I am alive. Fully alive.

"Now I sit in meditation daily. Sometimes it is very short. Just five minutes. Sometimes twenty minutes. Sometimes forty minutes, and sometimes I lose track of time completely. But whatever it is, I tell myself when I get up that it was a good one, simply because I sat with myself with some compassion and awareness.

"Well, Stephen, that is the update. Maybe someday I will send you a note saying, 'When I am dead, I am really dead.' But maybe not. Who knows?"

Two Christmases have passed since the above letter. Every once in a while, we get a note about her continued healing. As her meditation practice deepens, she says she discovers "an increasing sense of being alive until whatever happens happens, and maybe then I will still be alive. It feels that way anyhow. I don't see an end to this sense of just being." And along with her questions about meditation, she tells us about her "dating," as she puts it. Her conversations are filled with life and a new meaning to existence. Indeed, often she speaks more of a new boyfriend, adding, "Ain't that cute," than of her diminishing disease. Her heart is full and her world seems constantly to be expanding into life.

Healing into Grief

KAREN

Karen called two days after her son had drowned during a family picnic at the seashore. While making sandwiches, Karen had looked up just as her twelve-year-old son was struck in the head by the log he had been floating on and pulled beneath the waves by a powerful undertow. All had dashed into the water but none could help. The injury to his head had been considerable. Hours of anxious resuscitation were to no avail. Nothing could be done.

Karen spoke at length with Ondrea about the "horror of the thing," seeing her son disappear beneath the water, the agony of her brother who had swum out to where Martin had been but could not find the body and somehow felt responsible for his nephew's death, the intense loneliness of losing her oldest child. They talked for over an hour, investigating the feelings and making room for the intense pain that Karen was experiencing. As they spoke, one could feel the levels that were being penetrated in their profound sharing. After the call Ondrea turned to me and said, "What a beauty she is. She seems like one of those who is going to use her grief as a healing. More power to her."

Three weeks later she called again and we spoke at length about the process of her grieving.

K: "It seems like I have done a tremendous amount of talking, a tremendous amount of reading, a tremendous amount of thinking in these past few weeks. And they have helped me some to deal with what is happening. But it has been a real intense morning. It has only made the loss more clear. I said good-bye to my sister who has been visiting for the last couple of weeks and who is going through some of the same things as I have been. We have been doing a lot of self-examining together. Exploring the parts of ourselves that have always been shied away from, the parts that aren't acceptable. If they peek out, they scare you, but my sister and I have been dragging out one piece after another. It seems like I have worked all my life trying to get those pieces out. They are coming out real fast right now."

S: "What painful grace! Most think of grace as something that descends from above, but in actuality grace is your original nature, and there is nothing like grief to tear us open to the places where we have bound ourselves to the mind, remained superficial, had little access to the depths of being. You are being torn open and exposed to yourself. There have been few moments in life when so much contact has been made with those areas that keep life rigid and confusing, that create the feeling of separation, that limit every relationship and filter every moment of life."

K: "I am going from being in the depths of despair to feeling sometimes a kind of exciting wonderment at life. One of the things that has happened since Martin died is that I only have one desire now. I just want him back. And that is a terrible, huge one and it keeps me miserable a good part of the time. But all the little wants have gone away, so underneath that miserableness there is a great sense of relief too. And sometimes I feel really pleasured, and when I do, I feel bad because how can I feel good when my twelve-year-old son, who I love more than I could possibly tell, is gone?"

S: "Because you are in the midst of the greatest healing experience of your lifetime. You have access to parts of yourself now that weren't available before. The 'escape mind' kept all of this suppressed before. But now there is no control over your suffering and it just presents itself as it is. Now these qualities of mind that may have made life unbearable at times in the past are available to your awareness because you are plunged into the depths of your wanting and fearing and your sense of no control."

K: "That kind of makes me feel nauseous. There is so much garbage coming up."

S: "Well, a lot of that stuff is not so deep. It only seems deep because it has been suppressed so long. The stuff you call 'garbage,' the wanting and fearing and self-consciousness, has always been there and now is just more clearly exposed to the light of day. Don't mistake all that stuff for who you really are. There is no need to gold-plate your garbage. And I use the word 'garbage' not as something horrible that must be eluded or discarded under any circumstances, but rather seeing it as old refuse that has been stashed away in dark recesses of the mind. It is only garbage as long as we fear it. But when it is brought out into awareness, it is instantly composted to a fine fertilizer that only further nurtures our growth. Growth is the process of letting go of our edges and limitations and expanding yet a bit more into our original nature. All those old desires may well be seen in a different light because now you have something bigger to work with. It isn't as though those leanings and holdings won't come back. But the way you relate to them when they rearise may be very different than in the past. That is the process of healing. Of responding to life with a new wholeness, with a balance of heart and mind that manifests compassion and wisdom instead of fear and hiding."

K: "Well, they do come back and I still catch myself wanting a new component for the stereo or something, but when this does arise, I look at it and think, 'OK. You really want that? Even though it really doesn't matter? It doesn't matter whether you get it or you don't. How important is it?' So it doesn't hang on to me this time and I don't hang on to it."

S: "Well, love has become the priority now as perhaps never before."

K: "I would like to think that I have always been a fairly loving person and I think I am, but now love is a real moving quality for me. It is as if because of my loss I have almost been given the right to love people. People can go up and hug a person to break through a whole lot of barriers that they might not have allowed or I might not have allowed before. I am feeling real overwhelmed with this love."

S: "Of course you are. And how amazing that we need to be so 'overwhelmed' to be as open and vulnerable as you are now, so receptive to love, so able to hug, to hold another to your heart. This is all natural. As is your wish to have Martin back more than anything else in the world. Of course the mind is going to reach out for him. But his work here is done for now. He completed the course. You know, we work with the parents of many children who have died—some have been murdered, others have died unexpectedly through a 'simple twist of fate'—and we have noticed that there are a number of children who die between the ages of eleven and thirteen. Perhaps—and it seems this way at times—they have finished what they were born for. And often just a year or six months before they have died, they will have blossomed."

K: "About two years before Martin died, when his little brother was born, it seemed to affect Martin deeply. In the last two years since Eric was born, Martin loved him so much that it seems to have opened him up."

S: "Just what he needed. Just in the way your love for him is opening you up."

K: "It is so hard to be without him. There are times when I desperately need to be with him. When I just hope that we will be together again. That there is some possibility of our being together again."

S: "Well, there is a possibility that you will be together again. Who knows? But you will have died, and perhaps when you die, you may get a whole different sense of what life was about and the urgency you feel now may not be the feelings you greet him with. Perhaps then you will just meet him softly and perhaps go for a walk together."

K: "You know, at times I want real bad to die."

S: "Of course."

K: "At the same time, I am still a little bit afraid. Especially at nighttime, in the dark."

S: "Afraid of what?"

K: "To die."

S: "Of course. It is all there. It is just beginning to surface. It was always all there underneath and now it is uncovered. It is not like this is something new to the mind."

K: "I know it's not. I mean, I am aware of that. I mean, all these things aren't new to me. My sister and I were talking today about that. And sometimes when we speak, it is not big sister/ little sister anymore. It is all just the same stuff coming out and being shared. It is really strange. Sometimes there is a terrible pain and then all of a sudden I am happy. It is hard to explain."

S: "Well, your heart is opening. Your experience is unpleasant, but you are also experiencing something deeper of yourself. Some place that exists beyond pleasant and unpleasant. Some place of openness and understanding. In a sense, the grief is causing you to go beyond yourself, beyond who you thought you were. And you experience not only the grief of loss of your son but also the grief of loss of your old securities, of who you used to think you were, of how you imagined you could make life happen. We have lived imagining life was happening *to* us when we were not getting what we wanted or *for* us when our wishes were fulfilled. But now maybe you are seeing that either stance is still just another separation from life. That it isn't happening to us or for us but that we are life, nothing separate from the process. An unfolding of magnificent complexity and almost unbearable simplicity in a strange sort of way."

K: "I know—not accepting life but still trying to enjoy it. To have that neat little being living with me. And when he died, I knew that I would never have that relationship ever again with anyone else. I'll have whatever I have with other people, but I won't have what Martin and I had. Know what I mean?"

S: "You might have the depth of love and trust with another, but the content, of course, will be different. You may feel the same about another person, exactly the same, but for a different 'reason,' as it were."

K: "I am working on letting go of a lot of things that in the beginning made it almost impossible to get through a day."

S: "It is still just the beginning of this grief. It is only a few weeks. You must be so gentle with yourself right now. There is no rush. In fact, there is really no 'doing it right,' there is just doing it in the moment as seems appropriate."

K: "I am really exhausted right now, you know. And yet I don't want to lose a minute of what I am feeling. This is the last of what I have shared with Martin. So even if I feel OK, I think, 'Are you really OK or are you hiding? Are you putting your fears away?' Sometimes I really feel OK."

S: "Of course you do, and then you feel guilty for feeling OK. The mind can be merciless. But it's OK to feel OK just as it's OK to feel lousy. Grief can be such a roller coaster at times."

K: "Yes. That happens. And it is happening for Martin's father, my ex-husband. You know, I often wondered if something happened to Martin while he was visiting his father, if I would hate him forever. But his father has come through like a shining light. He is a really strong personality. Has a huge amount of charisma and either he can lift you to the heights or let you go to the depths. For years I tried to make him see that I was OK. 'Cause when we were together, he used to say in total disgust, 'Look at yourself!' and every time he said it, I did. I looked at myself and over five years I decided, 'Well, you're not so bad.' And that is when I left. But I held onto enough of it that I wanted to convince him I was OK too. But somewhere along the line I quit needing to convince him. And when I did, things smoothed out beautifully. Occasionally, we bumped heads but really we did pretty well. And then when Martin died, he came over and we were at one in our feelings instead of separated by our thoughts, and there seemed to be a completion there as well."

S: "It sounds like even in the midst of this tremendous pain things are somewhat resolving themselves."

K: "Well, this isn't new in my life. It is just waking up. And sometimes I think maybe the learning thing for me is to accept my condition as an ordinary person and not feel that I have to be, well, I don't know what. That I don't have to be you or Ram Dass. Or have to go to the opera or do anything special. Like maybe the greater trial is just to be."

S: "Absolutely. To just be yourself, with no persona to hide behind. Grief tears away personas and leaves us exposed, and that may be why we find it so incredibly painful."

K: "Well, you know I work as a psychotherapist, and I meet people every day who are going through their life and can't quite find the 'meaning.' And I have always tried to help them 'decipher their lives.' To find some 'meaning' in it so they would be satisfied. But now I am not so sure that creating 'meaning' isn't just another way of eluding the work to be done, just another form of coping. Just another tie with life."

S: "When the mind is confronted with the unknown, the uncontrollable, as in grief or crisis, it has a tendency to create 'meanings.' That is a first response to the mystery of this continual unfolding we call life. It is reality disguised as mind. Somehow we find it 'meaningful' that the arrow which has struck us down has red feathers and an oak shaft. 'Ah, it is the red of destroying Shiva.' 'Ah, the oak of the Druid sacrifice.' Which leaves our pain unexplored. And our dying unattended even by ourselves. 'Meanings' at one stage are the response to first meetings with the unknown. Later these 'meanings' become stepping-stones for going beyond the rational apprehension of change into the spaciousness in which it is all unfolding, the essence common to all.

"In some ways this is 'grad school,' and perhaps when you re-establish your practice, you are not going to go in there in the same way you did: to give them a 'meaning' for each event in their life but instead to see it as process. Maybe you are beginning to see that no 'meaning' can hold it all, that there is more to us than mind can imagine. You may just go in there to share this 'don't know' wonderment at the mystery of life. There is an odd way the mind, particularly when threatened, attempts to find 'meaning' in life, to make some intellectual bargain with the unknown. And you may see that even this 'meaning' is just another barrier to the truth, something else to hide behind. You may even see that these 'meanings' slow down the process of letting go. In an odd way the attempt to create 'meaning' keeps Martin dead, maintains him as a separate object in the mind, while the letting go of trying to make sense of it all allows him to live in your heart as is. Allows you to experience the essence of your shared existence, the essence of being. You know, when we love someone, that feeling is not coming from them; they are just acting as a mirror for the place inside of us which is love. And when we lose that loved one, that mirror has been shattered. We have lost our connection, our contact with our original nature, which is love itself. We mourn the loss of our contact with that part of ourselves as reflected through that other being. We mourn for ourselves."

K: "Well, I have been doing as Ondrea suggested and keeping a journal. At first, I guess I thought the journal would uncover some 'meaning' in what happened to Martin. But a lot of what I was writing in the beginning was my pain, and it is changing a little bit, although some days it is like I'll have in my mind some idea, some 'meaning,' that I am about to write down, some quaint realization, but what comes out is pain and bitterness. And many of those pieces of myself that I have hidden away present themselves. My fears, my relationships to people, my doubts. I shared the journal with my sister, and she told me

some of the things I wrote were really upsetting to her and that
the parts relating to her made her feel like she was nasty. It
made us laugh really hard because it was so funny. But when
you hide those feelings away, they become terrible secrets."
S: "Then they become 'the secret mind,' the holding tank of
unworthiness and hiding that separates us from life."
K: "I don't want to live in the shadows anymore. I want to live in
life no matter what it has to offer, and it seems to offer just about
anything I can think of or am afraid to think of. Sometimes all I
can see wherever I look is pain, but at other times there is this
unique feeling of ease."
S: "You may even have moments of ecstasy, because on another
level you are in touch with the great mystery of life and something in you knows it and is ecstatic to be facing the truth. Just
watch these states of mind come and go. The full range of
emotions and feelings and thoughts are going to come through.
It is all going to play itself out in the mind. You can almost count
on it."
K: "I don't seem to have any choice. I am just doing it."
S: "Just let it happen and try to be as gentle and as soft and as
accepting of the crazy mind as possible. Even the crazy mind
that demands Martin back. The mind doesn't know which way
to turn in a moment of dissatisfaction, so it grasps at whatever it
imagines will make the pain go away."
K: "I gave his clothes away to a home for orphan children. I
didn't want to give them away to people I know, because I
didn't want to see anybody wearing them. But when I packed
them up, it was just terribly hard. I had to say to myself, 'OK. If
he comes back, you can buy him new ones.' And I knew that was
absolutely crazy, but it was the only way I could do it."
S: "You are just discovering how we bargain with the more
bizarre aspects of the mind and how we have been doing it our
whole life. It is just that things are much clearer now. Which is
one of the reasons you are in such pain. So many of the parts of
ourselves we have pushed away come up in grief. That is why
grief has this enormity of potential for healing."
K: "It sure seems like a hard way to learn."
S: "Terribly hard. But I see how ultimately this 'hard learning'
seems to benefit some people. And even though I know you
sometimes wonder, 'How is Martin right now? Is he doing all

right wherever he may be?'—in a sense, even a recognition or belief in an afterlife doesn't really matter. Even if there were nothing after death, the value of love and compassion in this life is only more obvious. In fact, death is not what happens when you leave your body. Death is what happens when we live our lives in confusion and closed-heartedness, in anger and fear. In a sense, we are all partly dead, and there is nothing like loss to make that evident, to make us see how unalive we have been, because it attracts our attention to the moment. Paradoxically, dying may be one of the few moments in life when we feel fully alive."

K: "Sometimes I wonder what it was like for him to die in the way he did. I have thought about it and about how at times when I have gotten hurt that it didn't hurt when it happened, that it mostly hurt afterward."

S: "Exactly. But he doesn't have an afterward in the body. Perhaps all it is is the shock of impact, which, because there is no physical afterward, may not at all be the way you imagine it to be. He got whacked. And then there was the shock of getting whacked. It may have been no different than if he had been hit by a baseball in the midst of a game. Whacked for a moment and then something else, then a spreading, a sense of dissolving. A peacefulness and letting go, a warmth. In fact, many people who have been clinically dead and then revived, have told about looking on impassively at people's urgent attempts to revive the body and thinking to themselves, 'Take it easy! Take it easy! What's the emergency?' "

K: "When these thoughts come up, I recall the story you told about your friend who had the automobile accident and told later of watching the emergency crews cut him out of his mangled car, hovering above the scene of the accident, noticing his body being carried to an ambulance and wondering whether he would get in the ambulance with his body or not, only to wake up in the hospital and know the decision had been made."

S: "All you can really do at this point is to allow that upsetness to come fully into your awareness. Not to suppress it. Not to try to talk yourself out of it or elude it. Your grief is like a bud, a very tight bud right now, but it will flower."

We spoke about the days to come, when she might see Martin go by a dozen times on his bicycle. Somebody goes scooting by on a BMX bicycle with the same color hair or same design sweater, and for an instant she may think it is him. How she might search her environment for him because the mind cannot be expected to be rational. How the emotional mind might seek his existence even though he isn't there because at a certain level the mind knows that only the body dies. But that his body is dead. And will remain that way for the rest of her life. That indeed in some ways her life will never be the same. But how she might open to the feelings as she may never have before and if it hurts, let it hurt. And if it feels like it is going to tear her heart open, to soften and let it happen. That there is nothing to protect. Our hearts are altogether too protected. To let her experience be one of great opening, as painful as it may be. Opening under the best of conditions is painful. That this is a very difficult situation but just to let it flower. How it is bringing her mortality closer and how she had an opportunity of facing it perhaps in a whole new way. "When you feel like screaming, scream, and when you don't feel like it, don't force yourself to do it." That different waves of feelings and thoughts follow one after another but none stay for long—all keep changing.

We shared that her mind may throw all kinds of debris up into consciousness. But just to watch and see how it is. To be very kind to herself and to treat herself like she were her only child— with great kindness. And when parts of the mind are severe or angry, to let them float to whatever degree possible. Not to contract around them. Nor to use force, because force will only intensify the feelings of confusion. And force closes the heart. That oddly enough, the highest expression of her love might be to begin saying good-bye, remembering that good-bye is not abandonment, but means "God be with you." Indeed, this expression of her heart might want to tell him to go with love into the light and to discover his new world with compassion and awareness. "All you can do is wish him well." That this time is like someone leaving on a train, and as the train pulls away from the platform, one can run along side yelling, "Oh, if only we could have had one more supper. Oh, if only we could have talked once more." But the traveler is irrevocably drawn away by the vehicle he is on. And he is left with a feeling of unfinishedness because of something you sought after the vehicle was already in motion. Or on the other hand, those things could still be in her mind, but in her heart, as the train pulls away, instead of intensifying confusion, she might say, "I love you. Go with God. Go into the perfect possibilities that are awaiting you." "All the 'I could haves' or 'should haves'—that is all done now. If there was ever a time to let go, this is it." Indeed, to let him go is the deepest expression of her love. It does not mean that she is abandoning him; it means a kind of trust in the process. "Yours as well as his."

K: "It is true. All I can do for him is love him now. I can't fix his meals or drive him to a friend's house. All I can do is love him. And sometimes this love changes and I see some of the separatism in the way I related in the past. And sometimes I feel a love of just total unity."

S: "In a sense, all you can do now is say to him in your heart something like, 'This is the work we all have to do. You may have died many times before and off you go again. And God go with you. May nothing delay your swift passage. Safe journey, my love.' "

K: "I talk to him a lot, off and on. Sometimes if I have a good day and I do all right, I sit and think and hope he can read my thoughts so he knows even if I am doing OK that I haven't forgotten him. And when I go to bed at night I say a prayer for his well-being. It is the only way I have of tucking him in."

S: "It sound like what you are doing is right on the mark, and your feeling good about it is not a sign that you are abandoning him."

K: "But it is such an awful feeling of leaving him behind, and is such a hard one when I think that in ten years I may not remember how he did things."

S: "He will be with you the rest of your life. In a sense, grief never ends, but the pain changes and moves from the mind, where we feel so separate from the loved one (and often did even while they were alive), into the heart, where we feel our essential connection with them. Love never dies. You will in years to come, perhaps in a flash, see him as he was in the way he did things."

K: "A lady called me who had lost her daughter seven years ago in an automobile accident. Ten years before, she had lost her husband and was left with five children, and the girl who was killed was the youngest. And she had this same thing of having this bright and happy young child and then having her gone. She told me, 'It was like holding a hot pot and it was burning me, but there was nowhere to set it down. Nowhere to get rid of it.' She said eventually she found a place for it but it never cooled off. And occasionally she still burns her fingers on it, but she had such love and good humor about her. It happened to her too."

S: "I think that your talking to Martin will probably be useful for a while. Just don't be too rational about it. The mind is going to say this is just the mind answering back, but let the heart listen as deeply as it can. You will hear perhaps the wordless sound of his voice in your heart. It may be so simple and easy you won't trust it. But it will be there."

K: "When I talk to him sometimes, I feel sort of crazy and that blocks my receptiveness, I guess."

S: "Just speak to him as though he were calling long distance from a foreign country. You can even ask him how he is doing or 'what's up?' Let it be a kind of play, don't make it too serious, it is just more of the same healing.

"We don't know what happens after death but it seems to me, without a doubt, that consciousness survives the body. This much I know through direct experience over many years of meditation and working with the dying, though I have no idea what happens after this remarkable dissolving. But just remember with that kind of lightness, that if you are telling him to wear his rubbers, he might playfully say something in return like, 'Mother, I hesitate to tell you this, but my real nature is ten feet tall and I have four arms and four legs. Which pair of feet do you want me to put the rubbers on?' "

K: "We are funny, aren't we?"

S: "Yes, we think in very narrow terms. The mind can only think in its own realm, but there is so much more to us than mind."

K: "I haven't laughed with him in a long time. I might have to practice a little."

S: "Practice trusting your intuition. You won't have to create it. It will just be there. The mind may distrust what is there but your heart won't have to create it. It will just be there. The

distrust may be, 'Did I create that?' But if you look at it, you will
notice that it is his tone, his attitude. That in a sense it is him, no
matter what reflection of yourself or what contact with the
unknown that might be. Just trust that 'don't know' openness to
the mystery. Just don't become mystical or occult about it, because it's nothing special. He is just no longer in the body but he
is still in your heart. And it doesn't even matter where it comes
from. Only that communication in your heart is established and
you can finish up whatever needs to be said and a lot of loving
good-byes. Because there may still be a place within you where
you haven't said good-bye to him, although giving his clothes
away was quite a step toward that. But there is no rush. Don't
push yourself. Don't try to be someone who is 'doing it right.'
There is no doing it right. Just wholeheartedly as is natural to
you in the moment. In fact, what is right for one person may not
be at all so useful for another. For one person it is appropriate to
go out and go jogging and scream and yell and kick the earth
and that is the expression of the energy around their hearts.
While for another they need to speak to a person softly and sob
and be held. Clearly, it's all the braille method, just feeling our
way along moment to moment, and nothing makes this clearer
than grief."

K: "I think I'll do more of that for a while."

S: "You may experience a lot more warmth and laughter when
talking with him than you imagine. Because he is not caught in
the same way you are right now. He knows he isn't the body."

K: "He was such a character. I always enjoyed talking to him.
He had such a good sense of humor."

S: "Well, he may have lost his body but I doubt he's lost his sense
of humor. Just feel him there in your heart as love."

Karen, in the last months during the preparation of this
manuscript, has called occasionally, and on each occasion a
greater depth seems to be exposed. It is difficult to know at this
point "what she will get out of it," but clearly her intuition and
her acceptance of her grief have opened her in a totally new
way to the world. She is undergoing the most difficult purification of a lifetime, but there is an appreciation of the process
which allows her greater trust and willingness to "just stay with
it."

Attending a Dying Parent

TOM

Tom called during Thanksgiving supper. "My father had a stroke some months ago. And then other complications came up which include cancer and various problems with his liver. Then he went into a coma three days ago." Tom's father was a history professor at a major university and had left a living will: a document which some months before detailed his desire not to have any "extraordinary or heroic means" employed to keep him alive if indeed his body should fail further. Now his father was in a coma and had developed a respiratory infection which might kill him if the appropriate antibiotics were not applied. "The doctor insists that I allow the penicillin to be given to correct the respiratory condition. The doc says it is not "extraordinary means" but is instead "the most common pharmaceutical applied in the most common way." I really don't know what to do. I want to keep to my father's wishes, but there are so many people around who say to give it another chance. Who knows if he won't come out of it, who knows what new treatments might be discovered?"

Talking to Tom on the phone about his dying father, I hear our children in the background whooping and hollering their adolescent war chants of virility and vociferous confusion. I am father to those children, who might some day be required to make the same agonizing decision that Tom is presently faced with. Clearly our linkage is full cirlce. We are each the other.

S: "Did your father say to you that he did not want to live if he had to rely on artificial means?"
T:"Yes. He said, 'I have had my life and it has been a good one. I don't want to end up with a bunch of tubes sticking out of my

nose and gut. When my time has come, let me give up the ghost gracefully.' But my mother, his wife, insists we should do everything we can to keep him alive, and now that he can't speak for himself with his usual academic eloquence, it's all on my shoulders. How do you let your father die?"

S: "How do you not let him die if the process has already begun? How strongly can you pull against gravity to keep something airborne when its nature is to return to earth?"

T: "They say he could go on like this for years. Maybe every few months getting pneumonia or some such infection that a dose of antibiotics would eliminate and allow him another six months of involuntary suffering. I know I wouldn't want it done to me, particularly if I had asked to be relieved of that situation."

S: "Well, it's a difficult one for sure. And there really is no 'right' answer. There is just what your heart indicates is appropriate. Your mother, of course, wants her husband to 'be well.' But that seems not to be given, so she feels the next best thing is just to keep him alive. She has, of course, this deep commitment to protect and take care of her husband. For many, to protect someone means, at the very least, to keep them alive. It confronts us with the great riddle, 'What cost survival?' Our common notion of 'survival at any cost' conflicts with our desire for a 'life of quality,' particularly when the present quality of life is unbearable.

"It is not a question one can answer for another. But if one has spoken up and requested that no 'extraordinary means' be used to prolong life, it seems it is his moral and spiritual right to make such a decision. The law even indicates by the very existence of the 'living will' that one has the legal right to make such a decision."

T: "But the doctor insists it's not 'extraordinary means' and has even threatened that if we don't give him the antibiotics, he will withdraw from the case and my father will not be able to stay in the hospital, because we are not giving him 'the treatment that is called for' and therefore he has to be taken to one of those convalescent hospitals. They are really putting us in a vise."

S: "Will they allow you to take him home?"

T: "I don't know, but they are really pressuring me to 'help your father.' This thing is making me crazy."

We spoke for some time about how Tom's two brothers and one sister felt about their dad "being allowed to die as he willed." One brother and his sister had said they felt "Dad would be better off dead." While the other brother had said, "How can you let Father die when there still might be some hope?" Tom went on to say that he thought his brother who felt his father should be given treatment was perhaps more concerned with their mother's well-being than with the extraordinary predicament they were all in.

S: "But in either case it sounds as though your mother has lost your father in the way they have known each other. It might be useful to encourage a family sharing of the grief so that the predicament can be yet more clearly acknowledged. It may be that the idea of allowing him to die as he wished is confused with the idea of his dying at all. That the very desire to keep him from dying, from even being sick, is being projected into the 'logic' by which life at any cost is preferable. It seems like it is time for a large family meeting, to sit down and really explore each person's feelings about your father's condition."
T: "That's not a bad idea. It's just that we all live in different parts of the country and haven't really found it possible to be together with Dad at the same time. . . . But as I think about it, I must admit that even among ourselves, we are really not talking about it in the way that's needed right now. When Dad first got sick, he told me what his feelings were, but that he was concerned about 'protecting' the rest of the family. I am the oldest, so I am left with this burden of carrying out my father's wishes and also having to explain his decisions to the others. I am becoming a salesman for death and I don't like it at all. I don't want to be the middleman. If it were up to me, I would take him home and care for him as long as was needed. My wife is up for that too and although it might be hard at times, we could work it out. His grandkids love him and I'm sure they'd get into helping too. But how can I do that when he has said he doesn't want to live in this condition? A lousy shot of penicillin has become the greatest moral crisis of my life."

It was decided Tom would call a family meeting. That all would be present with their mother to "try to take this thing a little deeper and as soon as possible."

Later that evening Tom's mother called, irate: "What the devil did you tell my son? That he should kill his father?!"

Her anger was a natural dumping of the last month's frustration and confusion. It reminded me to soften and listen with the heart, to hear the being behind the pain. We shared for some time the predicament of letting go of a loved one while honoring wishes they might have and the dignity of allowing them to live out their illness and decide for themselves on the means of dealing with it. Her anger soon turned into a deep sobbing. She too was "getting burned out by having to figure out what to do," caught between models of being a good wife and being a helpmate that allowed her husband to go as he chose. As we spoke more of how her sons and daughter were responding to the situation, she said, "Well, you know, I talk to one and then the other. We haven't all been together as you suggested to Tom. At least not in the way we may need to now. I don't know if we can wait a week or two to get everyone together, because my husband's condition won't stand much delay. I don't want him to die just because we couldn't make up our minds what to do."

S: "I know there is very little in life that prepares us for this type of situation. At least nothing has been very evident. But the love between you tells you in a soft whisper there in your heart, to the degree you can open to it and just listen, what is right for this situation, for this moment. A new truth arises from moment to moment, from condition to condition, from situation to situation, and all we can do is allow our heart to respond as it feels appropriate. Even though a moment later the merciless guilt voice of the mind may insist that we 'should' do it another way—"

M: "Excuse me for interrupting you, but as we talk now, I look out the window across the lawn and the first snow of winter is falling. How Frank loved the first snowfall. He often would go for walks in the birch forests behind the house. He would come back elated at what he called 'the fantastic beauty of it all.' But now Frank will never walk in the woods again. In fact, he can't even see the snow and I wonder what life is like for him now.

What are we doing by keeping him alive. What other birch groves might await him." S: "Well, whatever you do, let that be a conscious decision. Listen to your heart, and let the mind's angry and frightened voice just be acknowledged for what it is. It is completely natural under the circumstances that anger and confusion, guilt and frustration should run rampant at times. It's not even surprising. But in a sense, it is the same momentum you were met with at the hospital when their guilt and confusion about life said, 'If you don't do it our way, you have to leave.' Compassion is not simply talking away someone's pain. That may be pity: the fear of pain in ourselves and others. Compassion is the ability to allow your heart to remain open to another's suffering in whatever manner they find suitable. There are no guidelines for this decision—just to trust the heart's sense of what is right. There really is no wrong in this situation. There is just love meeting the impossible in whatever way it can."

At noon the following day Tom called, outraged: "During the night someone took it upon themselves to give Dad the antibiotics. They don't give a damn if he suffers or not, they just want him to do their bidding."

We spoke to Tom for some time about our work with patients in coma. (See "Working with Comatose Patients.") We suggested he sit by his father and speak softly to him from his heart and to listen to the "deepest whispers." Just to allow his heart to receive the moment without any need to label where it is coming from or seek reasons for what is going on. "Just let the heart share the moment."

Three hours later Tom called back to say: "I was sitting with my dad talking really quietly to him, telling him how much I love him and of my confusion about what to do, when a social worker came in the room to tell me how lucky we were that 'your dad is better now,' which really popped my lid, and I became angry as hell at her and the whole damn place. They don't give a damn for him, they are strictly into their medical thing and can't see beyond their nose. They are as screwed up about what life means as anyone I have ever met. They are like a bunch of mechanics who insist on keeping the engine running even though the car has been totaled. All they care about is keeping the motor kicked over even if the car will never go anywhere again. It is just their ego. That social worker was really off the wall.

"But what was funny was after the social worker left, as I turned to Dad again, I could almost hear him laughing and say, 'Look out for that one, the next thing she will be suggesting is cryonics' (after-death freezing of the body to wait for medical advances in the future and eventual defrosting for further treatment). I was a little bit surprised to hear anything in return, much less that, and I felt my mood change almost instantly. I know what our job is now. My wife and I just decided over the phone a few minutes ago to bring Dad home and allow him his own way. When I sat down and talked to Dad in my heart about our decision to get him out of the hospital and take him home, all I could feel was a great soft 'yes.' In fact, if it is possible, I would say that I could feel appreciation. It is all so strange. I have never experienced anything like this before."

S: "It sounds like you are tuning in to that place where decisions can arise from 'the appropriate' rather than from old thought and old ways of being. All you can do is proceed step by step with love and a deep listening, not making the kind of decisions that are rigid or based on fear or guilt. If you are bringing him home out of love, then he is in the best possible environment; but if you are bringing him home because you think you should or because you are frightened that you are not doing what is right for him, that may not give him all he needs right now. Let your love make the decision."

A week later we received a call from Tom saying, "Well, I brought my dad home five days ago and I think he rested easier than before. But what is funny is, they didn't give him enough antibiotics, so the respiratory condition just came back more virulently than before. And we let it go. He died last night, and all I feel right now is a kind of relief that he is no longer 'trapped in the body,' as he might have put it. And I also feel good about doing all we could under the circumstances. These last few days with him at home were good ones. All of us were taking care of him and I feel as though somehow he knew it. We were all with him on the last day.

"At times, it seemed that he was having some difficulty, but mostly it seemed that it was just one step after another as he went on. And my wife, who is not particularly religious, for about the last hour or so, just wept and wept and said over and over again, 'Praise God! Praise God!' Afterward she said she wasn't even crying out of sadness; she was just blown away by the intensity of what was happening. And later she said, 'Dying seems so easy. I am so glad we brought him home to be with the family.' I don't have any question that we did the right thing."

About ten weeks later Tom's mother called to say how beautiful Frank's death had been, surrounded by loved ones. How she had stayed upstairs at her son's house during those five days and how much she had appreciated being able to be with her husband in a warm, loving home. "It was like our marriage had always been before he got so sick. Just being there with each other, allowing each other his day, just being there for each other and letting things that we had talked out pass away with a good night's sleep and a good-morning kiss over the breakfast table. It just felt so much more comfortable to be with him in this way and even to be there when he died. As scared as I was at times, there was so much of a feeling of being together that I didn't have when he was in the hospital, when people were fighting over him to make him live. I miss him so, but I feel we have shared a whole lifetime together—thirty years of marriage —and I have no regrets."

The Only Work We Have to Do Is on Ourselves

NANCY

One evening we received a phone call from Nancy, a psychotherapist from Los Angeles who had attended several of our workshops offered by a local hospital. She called, quite disturbed that a client she had been working with for some time had "shot his wife and the man she was with and then went off and shot himself." "I am grieving for the loss of a child. My client was my child. I really loved the man. He was beautiful, and the fact that this part of him took over and blew away all these people is so incredibly shocking. I remember what you said, Stephen, about things like this tearing your heart open (allowing a kind of profound vulnerability, a new readiness to receive the world), and I really feel like this is what is happening."

We spoke some of "the edge" at which all growth occurs. How growth is really a letting go of those places of holding beyond which we seldom venture. That the edge is our cage, our imagined limitations, our attachment to old models of who we think we are, or *should* be. It is our edges that define what we consider "safe territory." While it is the willingness to explore the vast unknown and to meet our natural fear of the unexplored with compassion that allows us to take each ministep beyond ourselves into who we really are, into our true healing.

Clearly, Nancy was going through the therapist's version of the "therapeutic crisis." The edge at which the therapist often finds themself unable "to help." It seemed that the great teaching of helplessness was approaching. And although she was attempting to stay open to it, still the power of old conditioning might once again close her down by trying to "find a way out" of this unaccustomed vulnerability and sense of connectedness with change, by treating this vulnerability as a problem to be solved, gotten rid of, submerged.

S: "I wonder if you aren't grieving not only for the loss of your child but also the loss of yourself as a good mother?"

The silence on the other end of the phone was answer enough. You could almost hear Nancy's breath stop as she went deeper to examine where she might have been holding. And then the breath resumed with a deep sigh.

N: "Emotionally, it felt like I just couldn't help. I tried to help him but it just wasn't enough. At least not the way I wanted to, although I did help him in some ways."
S: "You sound like a parent who has suffered sudden-infant-death syndrome. You are saying, 'There is nothing I could have done about it, but couldn't I have done something about it?' The feeling that you just can't do enough. It is that wanting 'to do something' for your patients that cuts you off from them, that causes expectation to limit the possibilities of their own intuitive path of healing. That causes your mind to become the navigator instead of your heart. Can you see how that may be so?"

Although it felt as though what I was saying was self-evident, we have come to learn that often the obvious is enough to begin the deeper investigation of the hearsay of the mind. I asked if she was trusting her intuitive sense. "All you can really do is sense what is appropriate for your patient. Perhaps it will arise as a sudden wordless understanding from which will flow insight and compassion for the patient. And of course, he also will only receive this as he is willing and capable."

As we had done before, I encouraged her to open, to investigate. To sit with herself and explore her edge. To see the anger, doubt and fear. And even allow that inner voice of fearful negativity: "How come you call yourself a therapist when people come to you for help and you just can't help?" To become more distinct so that she could examine the edge at which she withdrew into self-doubt and a feeling of powerlessness. To watch the moment when frustration flipped over into anger or fear and she met the moment with aversion instead of insight. To notice the moments when her fear of not being enough displaced her intuitive wisdom and natural love.

N: "That is really scary."
S: "It is scary, but it is exactly what you want your patients to do. You really can't ask them to do anything you are not willing to undertake. You may come to a place where you feel impotent and frightened and not want to go on. There may be a moment or ten of just wanting out, of just wanting to pull back from that feeling, that edge of self-protection. That edge comes between you and all your life's work. Your feelings of impotence have to be acknowledged so they don't block your love and reinforce the idea of 'having to be right.' Otherwise, ever so subtly you may transmit to a patient that your way is the only way, and that can be devastating for both of you."

One could almost feel the old conditioning surge across her mind—a wave of fear and self-protection, afraid to die into the intuitive, becoming one with the patient rather than remaining separate and hidden behind old theories and a hackneyed confidence of "knowing what you are doing." It really meant for Nancy to die into each patient she met. To sense in her own body, mind, and heart what might be the next appropriate step, to explore the pain of the holding mind, recognizing it as the edge encountered in others and herself.

S: "When you are giving a therapeutic suggestion, if you think you possess 'the right way' you close your patient to access and exploration. You have given them 'the answer' and encouraged them to stop asking the question. Some therapists have a considerable confidence in themselves. They have a couple of instances where a few patients are quite ripe and break through and the therapist experiences a kind of pride that infects with confusion all the clients they meet. The therapist has become God (which of course he is, but in this case he's right for the wrong reasons) instead of just another pilgrim on the path. All the therapist really is is just another oarsman rowing toward the other shore of freedom, another being in the same old boat, willing to continue on his or her own deep healing. If another in the boat has a weak pull on one oar, all the therapist can do is offer his strength and commitment to help stay on the intuited course, to bring the boat back to midway in the common stream. Not overwhelming the other being with your confidence and strength, but exploring together how we hide behind our strengths as a means of disguising weakness, as a means of not surrendering into the vast healing and natural balance within. Accompanying another as you would a beloved, gently into the light of awareness. All this work of investigating your fear and powerlessness is the path to wholeness.

"What you transmitted to that fellow may have been precisely what he needed on some level. He apparently had lots to do, couldn't hold it all, and exploded."
N: "Yes, I know. I feel a kind of anger too at him. Sort of a, 'Shit, you didn't give me a chance to do my thing. We were just starting to get somewhere and then you split and you didn't give it a chance to finish or complete some kind of process.' "
S: "Right. Now you have become the patient. Instantly, you are someone with confusion in the mind, with some lack of ground. It is a very valuable experience if you don't close it up too quickly. You can explore the hearts of all those you are working with by exploring your own feelings at this moment. It can be a very fruitful time for you, painful as hell, but very useful."
N: "I know my own tendency to be 'mature' and on top of it all and just coping with things just fine and all."
S: " 'Coping' makes one long for control. It may make one attempt to appear 'very together' as a mask for feelings of powerlessness. Indeed, it is the remarkable power of letting go that creates balance instead of a need to maintain control; it is trust in our vast 'don't know' that allows room for the truth, that allows the next intuition to float to the surface. In a funny way it is your models, your knowing, your training, that keeps you from becoming the healer you have always wished to be. All training is a preparation to go beyond training. It is the effort we make to reach 'the effortless.' There are no rules. There is only a sense of the appropriateness that floats in the heart, changing from moment to moment."

N: "I don't want to give in to this tendency to use my strengths to maintain control and I certainly don't want to transmit that to the beings who call on me for help. But there has been very little in my life that has encouraged me to surrender, to let go of my knowing, or look for a deeper truth."

S: "This ancient desire to control, this need to heal, stops you from joining in the healing, in healing yourself as well. Just notice this deeply imprinted desire for control. You have to accept it, otherwise it will always be something in the shadows, white knuckled, with the reins tight in its hands. You will just be 'letting go' as a disguise for what is really suppression. Letting go means letting be, accepting the moment 'as is,' which is a very powerful means of opening to the next unknown unfolding. But you can't let go of things you haven't opened to fully. I would sit and be quiet and let all these feelings of powerlessness come up and investigate them. It may be very painful, and perhaps in the middle of it you may think, 'How the hell could I ever be a therapist?' and it is that 'How the hell could I ever be a therapist?' resolved that I see in the eyes of the most loving, skillful therapists I know, because they are right there in their heart listening to another. They are coming from the great 'don't know.' They let each patient be a mirror for their own immense nature. For such therapists each patient they meet is a collaboration in healing and growth. Go to the truth beyond the mind. Love is the bridge."

N: "My first reaction was, 'I think I will just chuck this whole profession.' "

S: "Of course—salesmen and plumbers don't have these problems. But this may be why you got in to this work in the first place."

N: "Well, yes, I guess so. I knew that sooner or later something like this might happen. I just didn't think I would be involved in a murder and a suicide like this."

S: "If you are going to do this work, nothing can be excluded from possibility. When you work with suffering, things can go any way at all. It is not always going to reinforce the feeling that you are 'Captain Karma' come to the rescue. It is all work on yourself."

N: "That is the impotence. How could this happen? I didn't have any idea this could happen. I knew it was possible that he could commit suicide, but I didn't have any idea he would shoot anyone else. . . . I think a lot of it too is just tuning in to his pain, the anguish I know he experienced."

S: "That is the awkward place where you really don't want to examine your own pain. You say, 'Oh, God, I don't want to go into all that shit,' but actually you can't get by it until you allow it to come to bloom, to fully flower in some quiet safe place so that you can lose control and just be as crazy as anyone you have ever met. But when you do this, somehow, because you are not looking at it in a judgmental way but simply investigating it with a kind of 'don't know' lightness and wonderment at the perverse workings of the mind, there is a heart quality involved and all the fear, anger, confusion, and even outrage have room to come and go—there is a willingness to see it, an openness to it, that your patient probably never allowed himself. And awareness itself will melt it, will allow it to heal.

"In a sense, he has now become your therapist, your doorway to yourself. He is putting you in touch with all the places of fear and holding, all the need to be someone in the world, to be right, to be in control, to be good. And now you are just experiencing yourself as being in this great 'don't know,' in this great collaboration of the truth that we each meet in another's eyes."

N: "I hear what you're saying and that's probably what I need to do, because I'm almost in shock about how he killed these people. You know, I had seen him just a few days before, and then on Friday he walked into a room where his wife was sitting with a fellow in a wheelchair. He may have thought this fellow was her lover, but actually he was another therapist trying to help. She was shot three times in the chest. It was the kind of thing that could have been fatal but somehow it wasn't. And this fellow he thought may have been her lover but wasn't is dead. She was crying on his shoulder and the husband thought there was more going on than there was apparently. It is all pretty confusing, but the reality is that she is injured and that my client and this other therapist are dead."

S: "You know, it sounds as though your work with him may not be finished—for you, anyhow. What are you doing to finish your business with him?"

N: "Well, the next night I dialogued with him. My partner in psychotherapy acted as my client, and I talked with him and

wailed and cried, then I used my partner to act as his mother
and I talked with his wife and all kinds of people. I haven't done
it since then. It is real hard for me to do anything on my own."

Nancy and I began to explore together how that was "the
clinical way of sorting things out" and how that would probably
be useful to get in touch with some of her feelings. But as we
went deeper, I suggested she try something a bit less rational.
Something on a more "don't know" level. Just picturing him
and wishing him well. "We don't know, any of us, what happens
after death, but it seems as though nothing can be lost by your
wishing him well." To make him the object of a forgiveness
meditation. Starting by sending him forgiveness. To feel him in
her heart and encourage him to open and forgive himself.
"That was just a painful moment, my friend, and it is gone now,
completely gone now." Encouraging him to open his heart to
himself, to go into the light. How he needn't force himself to
suffer anymore. To let go of it and try a little to forgive himself.
And for Nancy, to listen in return to what he might have to say.
Not to be too rational about it. To become part of the therapy,
not the therapist. Allowing the healing to penetrate to the marrow—forgiveness of himself, of herself, of this often incredibly
painful level of existence. To play "this fantasy" out for both of
them to heal in whatever ways they might. Seeing that in a
sense, he is still her client, but her work is no longer to "social-
ize" him. Her work is to remind him of his own great nature.
Another level of "mutual therapy" not perhaps so available as
when he was sitting in her office. If she said to him in her office,
"Go to the light," he would probably say, "What light? What the
hell are you talking about? Are you just another crazy person?"
But now, although it may sound very weird, how very important it might be to understand that the more he thought he was
the body, the more he thought he was the mind, the more
confused he might be right now if death is what it appears to be,
a going on beyond the body. And even if this were completely
mistaken, it could only be a healing for her, a deeper moving
into grief. Sending him on with her heart, from her heart, in
light and care for his well-being.

I could feel how this might be more than Nancy was request-
ing. And I asked her if this was a bit much, whether we were

going beyond what she cared to hear or if this in any way
seemed useful to her. To which she responded, "It sounds crazy,
but it feels right. Let's go on with it." I suggested to her that she
picture him in her heart, to concentrate on him clearly, taking a
few breaths slowly and deeply into the heart so as to make
contact with the sensations there in the center of her chest, and
then with each inhalation to draw in her love and with each
exhalation to just send that love out to him, encouraging him to
open to the next moment in love and forgiveness for himself
and all others, even using his first name. Just allowing it without
locking into it being any particular way. "You've got nothing
better to do a few minutes a day than to encourage him to
understand that he is an evolving process. What you share with
him now may be as important as anything you have ever offered
him. Remind him to be kind to himself, and take that advice
into your own heart as well. I would talk to him as though you
were talking to your only child."

Nancy went on to explain some of the genesis of her client's
illness. The death of his son two years before in an automobile
accident that he could never fully open to. She mentioned how
the process I was suggesting might have been useful for him to
make contact with his son and finish business beyond the mind's
incredible self-cruelty and guilt.

S: "Well, just do it for yourself and see what happens. See what
you hear back. You may feel confusion or nothing happening at
all and then another day a sense of real emptiness and peace.
You may be able to help him as much as you ever have. It sounds
strange, I know, but it holds the possibility of healing. As we are
talking, I hear quite a bit of sadness from you."
N: "Yes, I am feeling sadness and fear and a lot of things. As you
said, I am feeling the 'full range of emotions' and I am feeling
more in touch with it all."
S: "Good. Cry for him if that feels right, and cry for yourself too,
because in some way you think you have made a mistake, but
you haven't, you have just followed your best intentions. No
blame. You have done what you can, and the mind will go on
with its guilt trip as it always has and probably will for some
time. So since the mind is probably going to feel guilty a thousand times more, why not take each opportunity to make a little

space around it, to see what the nature of guilt itself is, to explore that edge. So that when you are working with another in guilt, you are not coming from some therapeutic text, but from the very heart of the matter, from your own experience."

N: "That sounds right on. You know, I have another jealous husband I am working with at the same time, and my reaction was, when I heard about my client's actions, that I would refer this other fellow to someone else. But now I am realizing that maybe I am the best person for him to work with."

S: "If you are working on yourself to examine jealousy and fear and self-protection, then you are the best therapist for this fellow who is feeling these same confusions. It's all just the braille method—until we each participate in our wholeness, we must just feel our way along moment to moment, practicing deeply the forgiveness and investigation that brings us closer to our true being. Speaking more and more from a sense of what is appropriate in the moment, letting go of attachment to 'results,' to that 'appropriateness' working. You just do what you do as work on yourself, deepening the compassion and love, letting go of the fear and knowing that keep us so isolated."

N: "This has been useful, and thanks for the feedback. I will get back to you soon to let you know how it is going."

In the years since this event Nancy has grown greatly as a therapist. Her style has changed considerably; she has become more a *kalayana mita,* a "spiritual friend"—a concept used by southern Asian Buddhists who find the idea of a "teacher" or "guru" or "knower" as somewhat missing the point and subtly reinforcing separation and a feeling of not being enough, of being a student or patient rather than just another being on the path meeting his edges and teachings, with each step joining in the collective healing of us all.

Once Healed, Now What?

KELLY

Last spring we heard from Kelly, a thirty-two-year old cancer patient whom we had been working with for some time. As he deepened his meditation to let "the healing in," he came to several workshops and would call occasionally to share the changes he was going through. In midwinter he had called to say that the "meditations and treatments, or something anyhow, is working" and he had great confidence a complete cure would soon be evident. In March he had written, "It has been a long haul, or should I say hall, but it looks like I will be home free very soon."

Today he was calling to say all had gone well, that indeed his radiation treatment had been completed a few weeks before, but now he was "feeling sort of empty."

K: "It was hard. There were a lot of side effects and things—nausea and diarrhea, stuff like that. I got really tired but I think I tolerated it pretty well. They said that I did, and they seem to work, these treatments. They had discovered another tumor in the lymphatic system that was about the size of an egg, but when they completed the treatment last Wednesday and I went for a follow-up X ray, they said it was completely gone."
S: "So there is no longer cancer discernible in your body?"
K: "That's right. So right now I am clean."
S: "Right! All the holdings in your life are gone now." (Both laugh.) "Gee, who was that radiologist, anyhow!?" (More laughter.)
K: "Well, my lifework is not all finished. In fact, the emptiness I feel is really telling me that. But my blood marrow, which was so depleted, and my white blood cells are all back to normal

now, which means the danger of infections and such are gone and I can be back in the world around people again. So now maybe I have to face whatever my real work is going to be."

There was just beneath Kelly's voice the wavering conflict of being pleased at the healing yet longing to replace the intensity of this past year's connection with life. It was an identity crisis that we had seen occasionally from those who found themselves healed after a long period of self-exploration and new openings.

K: "You know, I was feeling so good. I was offered a job teaching scuba diving and was all set to do that, but then I found out I had injured one of my lungs and that it had deflated about ten per cent and would take a few weeks of rest for me to allow it to heal. That is difficult for me right now, because I was ready to blaze off and go diving. But apparently, the message is to spend some quiet time and to reflect on what all this has been about and where to go now."
S: "So the treatment is over now. The symptoms are gone. And now the causes must once again be dealt with. The world. What comes next?"
K: "Well, it is odd, because all during the treatment I was pretty active. Still doing some running and a little diving. But now I really have to take it easy and just let up for a while even though cancer is not the problem any longer."

We spoke some of what his alternatives were in the months to come, as he would only be convalescing for a few weeks with his lung healing and soon would be out in the world as he had not been in some time.

K: "It is kind of a letdown, kind of an empty period now, because I don't have the structure that going to radiation provided. It offered daily contact with some really wonderful people."

We talked about how "now that the nausea from the treatment is gone, another kind of nausea has arisen." He said on the one hand, now that he didn't have to maintain a special diet, he could eat whatever he wanted, but at the same time he was upset that his relationship to food now was "mostly in a craving for sugar and junk food."

K: "It is almost as though I am looking for something to fill up this emptiness now that the cancer is gone. This craving for food has a force about it which goes beyond just wanting to eat. It kind of scares me. It seems like the choice is either to go through a period of just allowing myself to eat the sort of things I wish and to work with it in that way, or to continue pretty much just cold-turkeying any kinds of sweets or crap food. It seems like I am looking for something to replace what is missing from my life. It is difficult. There are times right now when it seems that life is real empty. Yesterday I thought, 'I don't have a family, I don't have a home, I don't have a job or even an all-consuming passion.' I just don't know where to go now. I don't know what happens from here on."

S: "Well, no need to judge it, just notice it as it is. No blame. Just the mind moving toward other satisfactions. Maybe food represents the world to you now, represents that which was beyond your reach and is now readily available. Are you afraid you are going to stuff too much down? Do you fear the world is just going to give you more diarrhea, just make you sick again? This is your relationship to a brand-new world, a world of no longer being a cancer patient. The world of being out there without having to be 'someone with cancer.'

"The cancer patient has died and left you red-handed with all the longings and confusions that the illness temporarily distracted you from. You are newborn and wobbling in the world once again."

K: "Well, it is almost as though McDonald's is my father and Dairy Queen my mother." (Laughter.) "And I am not sure if I want to go home again."

S: "Maybe you will have to adopt new parents. Or perhaps just learn to love your old ones without expecting them to give you all the nourishment you require." (More laughter.)

K: "It's odd when you say 'to adopt new parents,' but I do have a feeling of kind of being orphaned. I should be so happy because I just found out my cancer seems to be gone, but I sort of feel bored and directionless."

S: "Have you been orphaned by your cancer? Have you lost your identity as a 'cancer patient'?"

K: "This winter was really difficult but it was also really high. Going down there and seeing those other patients was just wonderful, and seeing this one little girl down there broke my heart. I saw her week after week as she went through her treatments, and then one day she wasn't there and I found out a week later that she had died and I felt something tear in my chest. It was like all the resistance broke in me, and a few days afterward I had this feeling of going beyond my life, of going into something more universal. Some part of my fear of death died with her. But now it is almost as though that fear has returned. But now I see maybe all along it never was a fear of death but living which frightened me."

S: "Maybe you don't need to have cancer to be 'someone.' Perhaps you can let go of that one now. You don't need your cancer anymore. You told me a couple of times in the past how much you have learned from this experience and how you feel in touch with people as never before. Maybe eventually you will do some volunteer work at the hospital—your new direction may be to serve others. Perhaps you will serve the next little girl waiting for radiation a bit too. Your experience is invaluable. In the midst of all that isolation and fear, the least little bit of love has such power!"

K: "That sounds right, but I don't know where the direction will come from. I feel like a demagnetized compass."

S: "The urgency in your life isn't there anymore. Sometimes when people find out they are no longer 'terminal,' they feel lost—something of great importance at one time is no longer present in their life. Some people two or three years after being 'terminal' have told me that the intensity of their life has gradually diminished as their 'dying receded into the past.' The intensity of being in touch with things each day is no longer so present because death is no longer acting as a mirror for life."

K: "This winter in radiation the people there, the technicians and everyone, were really wonderful, and so were the doctors. It was a really good experience in a lot of ways, and at one point I got to talk to a group of nurses. They had heard I had done a lot of alternative treatments, and asked me if I would come and talk to them and I did. And it was just wonderful, because it gave me an opportunity to reflect on it and put it into words. I have an inkling this might be something I would like to do."

S: "Well, Kelly, you told me how in the past you had looked 'everywhere for a teacher.' How all your years of doing yoga had not, as you put it, 'broken you through.' That you had prayed to find some teaching that would bring you more into yourself. Then cancer came along and you could no longer elude the way your mind held, the way your heart closed. It tore you open to life. But you know, you don't need hell any longer to put you in touch with your heart. Hell is just resistance anyhow. Cancer was your teacher for a long time, and perhaps now you feel a kind of grief at your teacher leaving. But you don't need that teacher or that teaching any longer. Cancer isn't the path. You are the path. Always you will be coming to your edge, to the place where you hold, and notice whether you are meeting life in fear or in that vast 'don't know' compassion that that little girl's death put you in touch with when you 'went beyond your life.' Let the teacher go. Let cancer be a well-respected teaching of the past and go on to the next unfolding, this unity with other beings that you so often feel."

K: "You know, when I was with those nurses just trying to be available to them, I really didn't think too much about what I was going to say. I talked two hours and then answered questions for another hour. And they really thought it was great. I wish there had been someone like myself who I could have talked to two years ago when I found out I first had cancer. Someone looking at alternative treatments and someone who was willing to experience this whole thing not as a tragedy but as some great learning situation. It would have changed my whole attitude from the very beginning. The nurses came up to me after the talk and asked me if I would come again in a few months and speak to a workshop they were going to have for other nurses. While I was talking with the nurses, that feeling of unity was very strong."

S: "It sounds as though you have gotten the teaching. I feel there is very little more I need to say. It is just time for you to settle into your new life and integrate all you have learned over these past years. I can hear how much more of you is available each time we speak. How much more present you are."

K: "Yes, I guess I have learned quite a bit. At first when I went in for treatment, I didn't see it that way because I was confronted each time that I went in there with the word 'cancer' and the big machines and big buildings. And they gave you a permit that says, 'cancer patient,' park in the 'cancer patient parking lot,' and you go into the 'cancer building,' and they give you a credit card that you charge your treatments with that says 'cancer patient,' and I became quite comfortable with the word 'cancer' in a very short time. At first, it was really scary and dehumanizing, but I worked on it from those first days we began speaking some time ago. And as I was commuting to and from the hospital, I would just watch my breath and notice all the thoughts that came between me and all those sensations. Watching my breath was almost like looking into a crystal ball. I could see all the distractions in my mind. All my fear and doubt. At first, the technicians seemed cold and inhuman, but soon I saw that if I was really going to do this thing fully and integrate it and not see it as something separate, I would just have to open to it. And one day I just let go of my old way of seeing it and went into the place and was visualizing the radiation as you suggested, as just another form of universal love, of universal energy, and the technicians set me up and then left the room and gave me the treatment, watching through this special glass, and I was sort of working on this sense of connectedness I had, and they came back in the room and they all seemed very changed. They were asking me where I was from, and it ended up there were about four of us in there, the technicians and myself, just smiling and laughing. It was just incredible, and I had to get out of there, because I was so blown away that my openness was so clearly being manifested in this place that I thought was filled with nothing but cancer and sickness. That love could be there even in the midst of that depressing environment. And from then on that is the way it was down there. I made so many good friends. They are doing really intense work down there. Just the most compassionate, wonderful work."

S: "You were just open to their wonderfulness. You had gone beyond being the person who had cancer. You were just touching being itself without any need or ways of doing attached to it. You were touching on your essential nature, which includes all others and is experienced, for lack of a better term, as love or unity."

K: "You know, I have been a jock all my life, thinking of myself as a strong body and a person who could endure hardship. But when I got this cancer it made me hate my body, so maybe now I am starting to learn that there is more to me than just muscle tone. Maybe I don't need this cancer anymore! Maybe it is just time for me to get on with it! It feels as though part of this teaching I have received seems to be for me to share what I have learned with those who are struggling through the same experiences."

S: "In these next few weeks while you are healing your lung, you might just want to contemplate what your next steps might be. What form of service or play might be appropriate for you. In fact, you might want to practice being an undercover Buddha for a while. There is an invisible job you could do that would be of great aid to many beings. If it feels right to you, you might go into the lobby of the hospital down the street where you used to go early on in your treatment and just sit in the waiting room with all the people who are waiting and worrying about loved ones in the emergency room next door. There is no need to say a word. Put a magazine in front of you and close your eyes and just start sending those feelings of loving kindness and compassion to all around you. Fill the room with your deep caring. See how that feels. Speak silently through your heart to those around you. Let them know that what seems a tragedy at this moment may prove to be a great teaching in the future. No one knows it better than you. How many people could say it as genuinely from the heart as you can. Just allow the loving presence that you feel so often to be sent out, to be radiated to all those in need around you—the fellow smoking his tenth cigarette, the woman staring at her hands. If there is any place in this town, in any town that needs calm, loving care, it is the waiting room outside intensive care or the emergency ward."

S: "I have been thinking about some kind of sharing, but I didn't quite know how to go about it. With those nurses it wasn't like I had some kind of knowledge I had read. I just told them what I had done and how it was for me. It seems like there is such a need for someone to be able to give that permission to people, to be with what is going on as an investigation of their fear and a going beyond the question, 'Why is this happening to me?' "

Two weeks later Kelly called back to say that he had been laughing a lot to himself lately after his regular visits to the waiting room. He said, "I guess the only thing I am good for is loving." And then he added with another laugh, "It is a hell of a job, but someone has to do it." We talked about the possibility of his taking training in respiration therapy so that he might be with those who were in the most emergency like situations— the panic of not being able to breathe or catch one's breath—so that they could both "breathe easier." The love in his voice was palpable. He was no longer "being loving," he was just being, and the love that was there to be shared was flowing from him in all directions. "You know, I guess even this punctured lung had something to teach me about how deeply I could breathe if only I let myself be." And he finished the conversation by saying, "You know, it's true I don't need my cancer anymore. But still I call it 'my cancer.' I think the teaching now has become to simply let go of suffering, to stop making hell mine."

One meditation retreat and two lovers later Kelly called to say, "I have found my direction. I am going to set up a 'listening post' for those waiting the long hours for radiation treatment in the hospital. Yesterday I went down there and was leaning on a gurney (a wheeled metal stretcher), talking to a fellow about the photography and articles in a *Life* magazine he had, when it hit me what was going on—plain and simple, I was him and what was being talked about was a hell of a lot more than a magazine. Just two people alive. It sounds so simple—but we were Life itself, we were all of it. We were appendages of each other—my half of our body had already gotten its radiation, his half was about to. I was just precisely where I was supposed to be. I have already talked to the hospital administrator about hanging out with the people waiting for radiation and he said, 'Let's give it a try.' "

Now, some months later, he continues his work with the many patients waiting anxiously for radiation. His "undercover Buddha-ness" ranges from offering magazines and playing checkers to reading to the more seriously ill—or yet further, sitting quietly stroking the brow of a fourth-stage cancer patient, singing silently to her of the power of love to heal. We have come to refer to him as "the X-ray gremlin of the heart."

Even Pain Is Workable

ANONYMOUS

One day we received what was obviously a long-distance call from a woman who refused to identify herself. She said she was "contemplating suicide" and didn't want anyone to stop her. "But," she said, "I want to die with as much finishing as I can muster. Can you help me? Will you help me?"

She told me that she was suffering from very advanced cancer that had spread to her lungs and lodged in her bones.

S: "How are you feeling about dying?"
A: "I am ready. I want to die soon."
S: "Why?"
A: "Because I can't take it anymore. The distress. Everything seems to be getting worse."

We spoke for some time about the alternatives available to deal with her pain. She had at one time used Brompton's mixture, an extraordinary compound devised in the Brompton's Hospice in London which contains a mixture of morphine, cocaine, alcohol, and a chemical to reduce nausea which might result from opiates contained in this mixture. Being an oral medication, many have found Brompton's mixture useful in diminishing pain when a patient has decided to come home and shots and the like are no longer as practical. But the Brompton's mixture, which has been helpful to many, "never really touched my pain." She had used it falteringly and without the continuity that seems necessary to maintain the pain-suppression level that this compound is capable of for many. We went on to talk about the necessity for regularity in the taking of these compounds and about the recent, much wider use of a precisely

balanced regimen of oral methadone or straight liquid morphine compound, used now by so many dying at home, which
diminishes pain to an extraordinary extent.

A: "But I don't want to be knocked out. I am afraid I could go to
sleep and wake up in a hospital plugged in to a machine that
would force me to live through all this awful pain. I would
rather die now. Why go on with this any longer? I have difficulty
talking or even breathing because of the tumors in my lungs. I
can't walk because my hip is half eaten away. If it weren't for
this pain, I might be able to see this to the end, but it is just too
much for me to bear."

Although it was clear that her resistance to pain might make
it difficult for her to hear ways of working with her predicament
—how she might make use of the pain meditation (see "Five
Pain Meditations" in *Who Dies?)* that so many have found skillful—I felt that since she had asked, we had to offer all that was
available. "Let's go for broke. Close your eyes and let's try a
little experiment. It will only take a few minutes. We may never
speak again so let's go for it." To which she replied, "That's what
I called for."
S: "As we are talking now, can you feel the tension in your body?
The place that resists this impossible situation?
    "Let your body soften. Bring your attention to the area of
pain.
    "Let the tissue soften all around it so there is sensation clearly
received but all about it the body begins to let go of its clinging
to the pain.
    "Feel the sensation beginning to loosen.
    "The tissue, the flesh, all around the pain—let it begin to open
and soften.
    "Don't push the pain away, let it be felt as it is. Let it just
begin to float free, not even trying to change it, just soften.
    "Soften all about it. Let go of the tightness, the hard holding
to the pain. Soften.
    "Let the fist that grasps it let go lightly.
    "Let the fingers of the fist that have closed around it slowly
begin to open. Softening. Let go of the holding to the pain. Let
it begin to float free.

"Let the body which has tightened so around the pain begin to loosen. Let it soften—the flesh, the muscles, the ligaments, the tissues beginning to soften and let go.

"Begin to open to the sensation, cradle it in the body instead of grasping it.

"Just let that feeling be as it is. Let go of all resistance and just let it float free. Feel the sensation as change. As movement. See its constantly changing form floating in the open space of the body.

"No resistance anywhere. The body soft and open. Sensation changing moment to moment.

"Most of what we call pain is that intense resistance to discomfort."

After a long silence she said softly, "Yes. I can feel that. But why is it like that? I have always thought that if I pushed it away there would be more of me without pain, but when I push against it, it feels like that pain and resistance is all that I am and it is so damn wearying."

S: "So much of what we experience is our fear. If there was a single definition of hell, it would be resistance. The pain is there, the cancer is there, your body is there, but I think if you will look, you will see that most of what makes it almost impossible to put up with, that which makes you want to die, is the mind's long accumulated resistance to the unpleasant.

"Just noticing the difficulty in softening and opening so that the pain is allowed to float just a bit more gives us insight into how we hold onto our pain, magnify it, gold-plate it, become it. The very difficulty in letting go of our pain shows us how long we have held to our suffering, how long we have tried to push it outside of ourselves, not noticing how each moment of pushing pain away has formed another bar in our cage, another resistance to life. And we are just left within our cage, locked into the pain.

"But we are suggesting that you open to it instead of being so harshly crushed by the mind's resistance. By the fear experienced as pain. The mind is taking the sensation and turning it into an emergency. Indeed, as unpleasant as it may be, this is really another moment in your life."

A: "But when the pain is strong, I don't want another moment of life, I want to die."

S: "Your dying is not different than your living. This is it. Right now. And if you let it, there may be a point where the resistance begins to melt and you are able more gently to let go of this painful body at so many levels. The way you can do that to make it easier for yourself is to gently soften. Softening is a key word. It is almost magic. To soften so that what you are going through doesn't become hellish but instead becomes the moment of the body's falling away.

"Right now, let go of that body. Indeed, your willingness to kill yourself puts you in a unique position. If nothing is worth living for, there is nothing to lose.

"Make everything that arises an experiment in truth.

"Let go now. Without the pills. Without the suicide. Right in this moment. Don't wait for death to come. Open to death as a means of opening to life.

"In a sense, what I am suggesting is that you practice dying. That you give your body permission to die right now. That you let go of your mind and just feel the softness of the heart.

"Let the body soften. Let it melt.

"It is very understandable that there is pain at times as the body falls away. But you aren't that body. That body is sick, but the nature of being is not sick. The awareness that understands these words is not sick. The awareness that feels the pain is not sick. It observes sickness and even because of a long-conditioned case of 'mistaken identity' has a tendency to identify with the sick body and the painful feelings and imagines it is sick, but who you are, who you have always been, even before you were born, is not sick.

"If you can soften and settle back the least millimeter so there is just the slightest space, the slightest floatingness of that pain, you will get sort of a sideward glimpse of the awareness which is experiencing it all. Because the awareness of the pain is not the pain, it is the awareness, it is that which existed before you entered a body and which will exist afterward. It is the deathless.

"Even with such pain there is on occasion access to this place of boundless spaciousness.

"I know this may all sound very strange and even impossible

considering the discomfort, but yet there is a place within you that is beyond the cancer, that is beyond the pain.

"When you are asleep, the body may still be in pain, but because the awareness does not touch it in that instant, you are not in pain."

A: "True . . . I have no pain when I awake."
S: "The pain comes as you start to think about your condition?"
A: "Yes. My body seems to become hard as a rock, like a molten stone, the longer I am awake. Each morning as I awake, within a few minutes I think again of how much easier it would be to be dead, to just be out of all this."
S: "It is like the sensation is there, but as you start to think about it the fist of resistance begins to tighten. The tension around the sensation starts to intensify. It is like tightening a fist around that burning ember. The tighter you grasp it, the more deeply you are burned. But if that hand somehow could be encouraged to open, even visualized and softened, there would be just one touch point where the ember makes contact. There would be only one point of pain instead of your whole experience imploding around that discomfort. When you close the fist about the glowing ember, your whole life is pain, not just one aspect of your experience.

"Your awaking and your fear of the situation cause you to contract, and that contraction greatly amplifies your pain.

"I don't mean to minimize the reality of your discomfort in any way, but what I am saying is that it is not unworkable. I am not saying your pain is imaginary, but what it has within it is perhaps much less difficult to deal with directly than the tension that surrounds it and magnifies it so. The fear that turns that sensation into hell. There is the sensation and then there is the closing around it which intensifies it and makes it into an emergency. As I am talking now, are you softening? How is your pain now?"
A: "Less. Or maybe it is the same but not such a problem. Keep talking."

We went on for some time with the next stage of exploring the pain in meditation. As the softening seemed to penetrate deeper, I could hear her breath becoming longer and softer, the

tension diminishing from her voice. After about twenty minutes of sharing in the meditation, softening, opening and investigating the nature of this pain, this cage which had come to
crush her into thoughts of suicide and "any way out possible,"
her voice said, "Ahhh. That is much better. I even feel as though
my lungs are more open. I haven't had a deep breath in so
long."

Having spoken for a bit more than an hour, we ended the
conversation speaking some about suicide. Of the possible "un-
skillfulness" of acting on aversion, even one so real as this long-
conditioned resistance to pain.

S: "I can't say what is right for you or for anyone. But my sense is
that to react to this aversion only increases it. When you leave
the body, you will see that you were never the body in the first
place and that somehow we have cultivated more of that resistance, more of that hellishness, by killing ourselves, by closing
our heart to life, again and again out of fear and pain. How many
times may we have to come back into a body to learn to open to
our fear and resistance?

"It is not that there is any moral indictment against suicide, it
is just that it seems unskillful. Every moment you can spend
opening and softening to this burns away years and years of
holding. It is at a moment like this when opening and letting go
is most difficult that the least softness, the least release of our
pain, the least letting go of our suffering, is so incredibly valuable. Each moment now is so precious though perhaps more
painful than any experience in your life.

"You are at the very edge of the work that we all have to do.
No one can say what is the appropriate response. No blame. No
judgment. But now seems to be the time for the work of a
lifetime to come to completion. Each day is so precious. Not in
enduring the pain. Not in being 'strong.' But in opening, in
learning, in softening for even a millisecond, the preciousness of
letting go of our suffering becomes very evident. Letting the
body and mind float free. Letting the heart open to even this
impossible situation."

A: "Well, the pain is not so bad right now, but I know it will
come back, and when it does, I just want to die. Can I call you no

matter what's up with me? I mean, could I use this softening to help myself to die, could I soften around my suicide?"

S: "I hear that fearful expectation that so intensifies our suffering. But this softening, this openness will help you with whatever you do. And whatever you do, we are with you. Whatever you do, know there is no act that excludes your real nature, that excludes God, even suicide. All things float in this oneness. You can, with the same openheartedness that you would give birth, allow death in. If you are going to kill yourself, you can still do it with a great deal of love and self-forgiveness, for how hard it is to be born into this world with a body and how difficult it is sometimes to remember to soften when it is painful. Not with a self-pity but with an accepting compassion. The more conscious your decision, the more conscious the outcome.

"This dying is so much like being born: We are safe for so long in the womb, but the time of birth approaches and we can't stay any longer no matter what we think or imagine is going to happen afterwards. When we are expelled from our warm placenta, out we come into the truth that is waiting there for us. It is my experience and understanding that as the body falls away, awareness separates from that old carcass, and in that moment there exists the possibility to see this awareness as your real nature. Who you really are shines like a great luminosity before you. It is a time of great potential merging with your true nature. It may be a time when you discover the power of forgiveness, the value of seeking the heart's way. You may experience the most intense openness to life you have ever known just after you die.

"The more that you can open to this whole process, the more smoothly it will go, whatever happens. But what I am suggesting is that you can let go of your body now, you can discover the light of your true nature now. Indeed, your willingness to kill yourself gives you a special quality of going for broke, of nothing to hold to. Die into life. Die out of your fear so that when the body dies, you will be that much more present for whatever opportunities arise afterward. You know, in the Hindu holy book the *Bhagavad Gita*, it says, 'If you think you kill or if you think you are killed you know not Me.' That is a manifestation of God, of your true nature, saying that no one is born and nothing dies.

"To the degree that we think we are born and believe that we die, something like suicide becomes a potential lens for seeing how often we have attempted to escape life. I am not even saying that if I were in your situation I might not do the same thing. I don't know. I am only suggesting that you use these days to deepen your awareness, to open your heart, to soften, to finish business with yourself."

We finished the conversation with a loving, soft good-bye. Clearly, her decision was still in the process of clarification. I could only wish her safe passage in whatever path she chose.

Five days later she called back. "Well, I am still alive." She laughed.

S: "How have the last five days been?"
A: "They have been different. My pain is still there, but I have been doing that meditation three or four times a day and it seems to have helped a lot. My breath is a little bit smoother, my pain a bit less of a difficulty. But I am still afraid of what is to come. I think you are right—my greatest problem is not the pain or even the difficulty breathing, it is the fear of what will come next."
S: "That has always been our edge, our fear of the unknown, our wish to hold onto the seemingly safe present even if it is hell. Why should our dying be any different? We die the way we live. Fear is even to be expected. Big surprise! Here it is again. But we can meet it with softness and acceptance. Fearlessness is not the absence of fear. Fearlessness is our willingness to allow fear its ancient momentum without closing around it. To explore it. To stay open to it is real fearlessness. Then there can be fear in the mind but you are not at all frightened.
    "How long have you been sick?"
A: "Two years."
S: "When your voice cracks, is that because of pain or emotion?"
A: "Emotion. I think it is both fear and anger. Anger that God should leave me in this situation. Everything was coming together so beautifully in my life. Things were looking up. At last I thought that life would become good, and then the cancer hit."
S: "Of course you are angry and that is perfectly natural. Nothing to judge or tighten around in that one either. Just to be

aware of how this anger and this fear cause you such pain, such a sense of isolation. In a sense, you relate to the anger and the fear in the same way that you do the pain. You open to it, you acknowledge it, you soften around it. You let it begin to float free as it is without even changing it. And you begin to sense some of the space in which it is all happening."

A: "Yes. In the last couple of days I have had a few moments that I have been so surprised about. When everything was just OK, when I felt such peace. In those moments I don't even know if I was in pain or not. There was pressure, there was intensity, but somehow I was OK. Is that what death is like?"

S: "In a real way it doesn't matter what death is. You will meet it then as you meet this moment now. Just as when you wake in the morning and the fear has not quite formed yet, before the pain arises, how do you relate to that openness, that spaciousness of being which is contactable right now, which is accessible even in this bewildering realm of pain and cancer that you experience. If you grasp back at your pain now, what are you cultivating as a response to the unknown realms to come? In a sense, I think that death is not what happens when you drop the body, death is how we respond to life with our heart closed and our continual resistance to the unpleasant. In a sense, many have died long before they leave their bodies, while others seem, in a manner of speaking, to outlive death, to remain conscious and aware as they navigate the waters of their true being."

A: "There have been moments when I understand this. Sometimes when I am really able to soften, I feel more alive than ever. I feel like I am melting. Not such a solid thing as this pain. And the new medicine helps too. Although it makes me groggy sometimes, I am 'playing the edge,' as you put it. And strangely enough, I feel closer to the world, to my children."

S: "Are you still thinking of killing yourself?"

A: "I don't know."

We spoke for a moment more, ending the conversation in a fifteen-minute softening meditation, once more exploring the pain, allowing the awareness to open all around it so that it begins to reveal its hidden nature, so that there is more space in which to make any decision that seems appropriate.

For the next three weeks we spoke every two or three days. Her ability to work with her pain was impressive. Her openness to life deepened. She told me that her name was Cynthia. A few days before our last conversation she called at four in the morning, her voice compressed with pain. As we sank into the meditation together, expanding awareness beyond the body, opening all around it so that the pain floated, once again I could hear her breath soften and deepen. After about forty minutes of her not saying a word but just our moving together beyond our holding to pain, she said, "Thank you. That is much better now. I am glad I stayed around long enough to experience this kind of letting go."

About a week later her daughter called to tell me that Cynthia had died naturally two days before, holding her hand. Her last words were: "I love you so. Be good to yourself."

Resolving Death

GAIL

Some of the patients and therapists we work with on a regular basis have entered into a depth of commitment to the investigation of what is happening in the moment that we refer to as "a contract toward truth"—an agreement to "push to the heart of the matter." Those with whom we have this agreement have, in a manner of speaking, asked to break the old social mores and intricacies of etiquette and instead "to go for it." To work toward letting go of aspects of the self-image which might be threatened by this direct investigation or commentary on what is being discovered in the moment. Not that we know what truth is—or that truth can even be expressed—indeed, one cannot *know* the truth, one can only *be* it. Rather we have entered together into a mutual "experiment in truth" where feelings are not guarded but rather uncovered and investigated as a means of transcending those qualities of mind that block the intuitive wisdom of the heart.

This "contract" has been agreed upon by a relatively small percentage of the patients we work with. Although this "truth" is the basis of our most profound relationships, still there is within most that place which wishes to remain disguised and protected. Few are willing to "die into the truth," though that indeed seems the work to be done by us all. So often the "defensive mind" rises to our supposed protection only to incarcerate us in our fears, to make more solid our sense of separation and isolation. This commitment toward the truth is for each of us the hardest work we have ever done.

One with whom we have such a contract is Gail, a nurse we had met while offering trainings at her hospital some months before. Gail called to say that one of her counselors who had been an early teacher for her was now dying of cancer and she was finding it a very difficult time. Many of the people around him were encouraging him to hold onto life when in actuality "there was almost nothing left for him to hold onto." Her mind was boiling with confusion.

G: "This fellow I am working with was such a light to me a few years ago. And now I am dumbfounded by how he is approaching his death and how everyone is telling him to grasp onto life. His friends and doctors are always holding out hope, and they put him through one miserable thing after another. And things get more and more miserable, and they keep talking hope, and what is there hope for? I think I am angry with the doctors. I am angry with that whole process of 'let's grab one more miserable day.' And he's really going for it."

S: "Well, when you have cancer, that will be your decision to make. But this is your teacher's death now. This is his decision. Do you think you may also be trying to show him what a good student you turned out to be? You may be wanting his approval some way."

G: "I think what is happening is that I want him not to hold on so, I want him to let go and try to be peaceful."

S: "Well, why don't you begin now to do exactly what you want him to do? I don't hear you letting go and being peaceful about it. So where does he have a model of someone who is doing that? You can't express love when you are filled with anger and frustration. You are blocking compassion by holding to your frustration. In an ironic way you may be transmitting a clinging to life by your own aversion to how life is not the way you wish it were. Maybe your frustration with people's medical models and insensitivity is just creating more agitation in the room. If there is war within you, how do you expect there to be peace around you?"

G: "I just want to make it all right."

S: "I don't know that you can make it all right. All you can do is open to those qualities in yourself and acknowledge them so that when they arise they won't suddenly cause your heart to contract. He has his own unfolding to be with. You know, it is a bit like the passages you were working with last year in the *I Ching*, the Chinese Book of Changes—in the chapter called

'The Army' it says one cannot really ever overcome the enemy until one has rid oneself of that which is found despicable in the other. This is your peaceful death right now. To allow yourself to die into this moment, to be that space into which your friend can surrender as he wishes, if he wishes. Don't make him die your death for you."

Gail's attitude was, "Yes, but . . ."—a constant wrestling with the facts to try to make them fit her model. Each push against the flow of how things were unfolding caused her to retreat more into the mind's incessant strategies of "how to make things better." Each push against how it was caused her heart to close to the perfection of that moment. Clearly, there was a way she thought "dignity" meant dying in a particular manner. We spoke about how dignity was allowing a person to be who and how they were, that to allow a person to die in dignity includes allowing them even the choice of denial. The only work to be done in that room was work on herself, to open her heart past ideas of how things could be so she could experience events as they presented themselves with care and compassion.

G: "It is just all so unfair. What I mean is some people just seem to carry so much more of a burden than others. Nothing is evenly distributed in this world."
S: "I don't know why it is that way, but I see some people get certain teachings and lessons that seem to be more intense than others. If there were nothing to learn, then perhaps there would be no suffering. It is said that one might even be born a blind leper in a ring of fire, and if your mind was focused only on the truth of the vastness of being, you would always be in heaven. Suffering can only be attracted to that place where we are grasping or pulling back from the world. When an event floats through the stillness of being, nothing closes around it and there is no suffering. I see how much some beings have grown, how much more present and loving they have become from situations which most would call a tragedy. This 'vale of tears,' as the poet called it, seems to be the plane of reality where we learn compassion. Perhaps heaven could not teach us what this plane of suffering teaches us. I am not trying to rationalize it, I

just see an openness that some move toward when suffering becomes intense. Why some come to the edge of their suffering and break through while others curl back into an embryonic cinder is impossible for me to say. For some, fear teaches about fearlessness, anger teaches about the depth of love, self-hatred teaches about how merciless we are with ourselves. The question 'Why?' strangles us. Only the questions 'What is happening?' and 'Who is this happening to?' seem to set us free. 'What am I feeling? What is this experience? Who is experiencing this? Who is the experiencer?' These give some insight. They take us into the pain to discover its real nature. These put us in touch with the scintillating suchness that our holding painfully blocks us from receiving."

G: "But how can I help?"

S: "If you are just who you are, that will be enough. If you are giving from a feeling of not being enough, of needing to give more, you will not go beyond the small holding self, beyond the sufferer into the deathless spaciousness of being that exists as it is without fear or anxiety for it has nothing to protect, nothing to be. It is just as it is—edgeless and ever present. You are still giving from your mind, from your personality, from old thinking, from the density of being 'someone in control.'

"To the degree you want your old teacher to be who you think he ought to be, that is the degree you lament not being who you think you should be. Your distance from him is your distance from yourself. Don't try to be enough. Just be. Explore who you really are in order to know who another might really be. 'Being enough' does not mean that you are able to change things, it means opening to the enoughness present in each moment. Sometimes we receive that enoughness with new clarity: 'Oh, look at the difficulty he is going through, but look at how preciously he is receiving life now. . . .' All these teachings seem quite paradoxical. Allow them to take you behind the mind, beyond reason, into the very heart of the matter."

G: "I feel as though each word you are saying is like a challenge thrown at me, like a ball coming across the net that I must bat away from my home ground. My mind is struggling to prove you wrong. The harder I struggle, the lousier I feel. Something in me knows you are right. But my anger and frustration scream you must be wrong. That we must be able to help."

S: "I am not saying you can't help, just that help doesn't mean changing something or being attached to the outcome of your labors. It means doing what you do because there seems nothing else to do but not getting hung up in its results. Help means being an available space. Around your teacher are people encouraging him not to die. But you can create a sense of peace in the room. Make room in your heart for him to die. That will be the depth of spaciousness in the room. If you insist that he die as you think he should, you will just be another insisting mind, more tension in the room. Another offering of fear to one who is about to melt out of the body, who needs to trust the process of letting go, of the OK-ness of things."

G: "I hear you, reluctantly, but I hear you. I certainly wouldn't want him to get into the same frustration that I am feeling right now, but it is so hard to give up these feelings that people should leave him alone and let him die. But you're right that I am not leaving him alone either."

S: "It is like Mother Teresa's attitude when she is picking up some fellow dying on the sidewalks in Calcutta where he has lain for days. As she gently eases him to a stretcher, his skin sticks to the pavement and peels off as he is lifted. She says she sees such beings as 'Jesus in his distressing disguise.' Now if you can see your teacher and your coworkers, even your own suffering as 'Jesus in his distressing disguise,' you will start receiving life not as something to wrestle with but as a merciful teaching within you. You will start experiencing a deeper opening to your own death, directly entering into this moment of life. This world, this whole plane of reality, as it were, is the truth in its distressing disguise. Life is not an emergency, though it's often painful, because we hold to its being other than it is. You know this teaching in helplessness may tear your heart open, but it can take you beyond what you think into who you really are."

G: "You know, as you speak, I hear what I first said about how everyone was fighting his death, and I guess I see how in a way I have been fighting it too. I am trying to make his death suit me."

A week later Gail called back to say: "I think that I am at last able just to hang out with him. I think now maybe I can just 'let' him die. And it is odd, because as I have fewer notions about how he or the people around him ought to act, it seems like he is more comfortable with me in the room than he was before."

S: "Could be."

G: "You know, but it's still damned hard, because those old thoughts about how things should be are still real strong at times, but now they seem to listen a little closer to what I have to learn from all this. And what I am learning is how much I insist on having things my own way, not only from him but from everyone I have ever met, how much I want them to do my thing. You said in one of the workshops that to love someone you had to let them be 'as is,' and maybe that is what I am getting from all this. To let him be as is, to let me be as is. Someone once told me they had been 'should on long enough.' Me too."

S: "Yes. And enough is enough. And that's the teaching in mercy, in letting go of judgment, to just get on with it a moment at a time. When did it begin to change for you? When did you notice you were just letting things be as is?"

G: "Well, you know what I've found. My sense of it started to change a couple of days ago. I noticed as I was going in and out of his room my mind was just saying over and over and over again, 'Thy will, not mine,' and I just repeated it over and over again. Each time I would come into his room I would feel that old hankering, and I just left it at the door. And every time I left his room, as I felt myself start to analyze, I would just notice the old scramble for control and I would let it fall away with 'Thy will, not mine.' I think I am learning what surrender is. I guess I was taught by my machismo father that surrender was defeat, a kind of weakness, sort of giving up. But now I am seeing how much heart muscle it takes, how much courage to let go of the 'infernal dialogues' and open into the love I have for the other being. I'm even starting to care for those overworked doctors and nurses that I called you so angry about. I think maybe as I am finding myself, I am finding others too. Things still aren't the way I might wish for, but I appreciate what I am getting from things the way they are."

S: "When Plato was dying, it is said that he went into something of a coma and then came out of it again, and all his students around him asked what was his last teaching before he died. And he said, 'Practice dying.' You know, Gail, it feels as though that is what you are doing, opening to the next unknown moment with awareness and love. You are starting to die out of the mind's barriers to life. It is not easy, but how fruitful. Both of you are learning to die. What greater gift could you give your teacher than to be the example of the teachings? Someone once asked in a workshop, 'What is death?' And I found myself responding, 'Death is the space between thoughts.' Now that answer exists on several levels, but in one sense it sounds like you are starting to practice dying into that space between thoughts. You are beginning to trust that 'don't know' which allows everything to come and go without judgment, without fear. Just let yourself continue to die out of the mind. Don't even try to understand it; let understanding arise by itself. Just try to be there with the enoughness of the present moment, with the care and love you have for his well-being."

G: "It seems over this last week as I have come into his hospital room with just that feeling, 'Thy will, not mine,' that things are better between us. He seems less restless and more open to talk about his situation. He really seems quite all right with it all. I will call again when I need to. Thanks for the push."

Some weeks later Gail called to say that her teacher had died in considerable peace. That in the last few days it became clear to her that he was not buying into all the emergency strategies. He was just being open to those around him, not pushing them away or trying to change them. And it felt like he had been doing his own work just as he needed to all along. He just wasn't talking about it. She said, "I guess the problem was all mine, and I think that for just a second I saw Jesus through his distressing disguise. And you know, the morning of the day he died I got into reading the words of Jesus on the cross when he turned to the others being crucified and said something like, 'Fear not for tonight we shall dine together at my Father's table.' Ted died at two-fifteen in the afternoon, and that evening I went home and was about to sit down to eat alone when I thought of him and placed another plate on the table, and then all of a sudden I 'knew' how this whole world is 'my Father's table.' And that what I have learned will always be with me if I can only hear it. Maybe I am just learning table manners. And table manners means just to look for God in it all. Just to listen with my heart."

A Teaching in Surrender

LOBELLIA

Over the past few years we have worked with several people in their seventies and eighties who received a terminal diagnosis. Some received their dying with a sense of completeness. Their approach to death followed a well-worn path and often had an ease and moments of considerable humor. For these it seemed that all those years of living made death less an enemy, less an "interrupter," more an old friend due for a visit. Most had experienced the death of many, if not all, of their closest friends. Death was not unfamiliar though still somewhat entangled with long-conditioned fear in the mind. For some that fear was met with a lighter acceptance. Many of the older people who have come to us to "see more about dying" seemed to have made peace with death and entered the shadows that lead to the light with a certain grace.

But of course, that was not the situation for all we worked with. Some of the strongest "denial" that we have encountered came from people in their later years. Obviously, for some a longer life has just left greater remorse and deeper traces of unfinished business.

One woman to whom we were introduced by her physician was Lobellia, an ex-alcoholic who had turned toward God through her twenty-five-year association with Alcoholics Anonymous. She was "afflicted," as she put it, with lung cancer and emphysema. She was having a hard time of it. Deeply committed to her work with Alcoholics Anonymous and said by many to be "a fine counselor," she was approaching the end of her life with an intense feeling of incompletion. Though many thought her to be "very together," her life was a tangle of loose ends. Her relationship with her two grown daughters was indicative of the intensity of her unfinished business. One married daughter was a "real nice girl" who fulfilled Lobellia's model of how a daughter was to be. The other daughter, an artist living in a commune in California, was "not to my taste, a damned rebel" and was very straightforward in her communication, which often left Lobellia feeling angry at not getting her own way. "She just won't behave."

Though she had been ill for five years, she had opened to it very little and said, "The cancer came upon me too fast." She found herself approaching death with no foundation. As we spoke over the months, it became evident that Lobellia's relationship with God was more in the mind than in her heart. She knew the right things to say. She was well read and had wanted to be "the Perfect Teacher" to many of the younger people she counseled. "But my life is quite the mess at times."

S: "Well, to be a perfectionist is to be constantly dissatisfied, to always be looking elsewhere for perfection, to always be in pain. Much less that a perfectionist is someone who seldom sees the perfection of things."

Lobellia came to many of our talks at the hospital, and we noticed afterward as we spoke with her that quite often she was quoting what we had said without really understanding it. Being so greatly loved by so many for her years of service and kindness to others, she was surrounded by several who wanted to "sit at her feet and get the last teachings of the great woman." But what came through her was more a conglomeration of things her mind had overheard in its seeking for knowledge than a real willingness to penetrate her long-held suffering, to let go of being a teacher, and instead open to the teachings of the moment. This pattern led to a "secret life." So attached was she to her self-image, to exactly that which she feared she would lose upon dying, that she pushed the possibility of freedom away by building greater posturings and self-protections, which only made life more unbearable and death more frightening. Although her cancer caused her to sip water every few minutes and her emphysema made breathing difficult, when no one was around, she would "sneak a smoke," unwilling to expose herself in front of others. It was this unwillingness to let life in that was holding death out. For the last several years she had lived a shadowy kind of separate existence, turning off the television when people entered the house, waving away cigarette smoke, "eating meat behind their backs," hiding ash trays. When her mood was cloudy or confused, she would tell people that she was "busy that day" rather than share her process. This left her with very little stability as she lost more and more control over her world, over her life.

Several months after we met, we came to visit one day and found her surrounded by many young "disciples." She was pontificating on the "ease of dying" and said in a dramatic tone, "I have chosen not to continue this travail. Eating is very difficult and so I shall no longer take food. I shall give myself to death." Later, in the kitchen, she turned to me and said, "I have begun to think that I have to let go of whoever the hell I thought I was." To which I replied, "That sounds good, Lobellia, but it sounds more like your mind's mutterings than your heart's song." Because by this time we had developed "a contract" we encouraged her to examine yet more deeply her motivations so they might be coming out of the heart's sense of what was appropriate rather than the mind's posturings and holdings to self-image. Pointing out to her how she was closing in response to our encouragement to open, we reaffirmed that we supported her in whatever decisions or choices were made.

We didn't hear from Lobellia for a week and imagined that perhaps she had died. But we soon heard from one of her bewildered students that "she has panicked and insisted on a gut tube and special feedings. She chose to take nourishment after all. This 'humanness' at looking for a way out of death has just endeared her even more to us all." But Lobellia did not recognize this "humanness" as a moment of truth which could be lovingly accepted and shared from the heart and instead angled for some intellectual rationalization of her act. "My work isn't finished as it should be. I just need a moment more." Soon afterward a number of her students and friends offered to form a "healing circle" to try to soothe the emphysema and cancer but when asked to participate, Lobellia simply shrugged. Some took this as an "equanimity with death," but in reality it was Lobellia's unwillingness to be put in the position of being the "helped" rather than the "helper." Her unwillingness to be vulnerable was causing an even greater distancing from life.

Often we would speak about the power of the quality of surrender, of a willingness to be open to the present, to be naked before the truth. "How will you die in wholeness Lobellia, if you live such a fractured life? A life of such self-protection and seeming togetherness. You know, most of the people I have met who say they have their shit together are standing in it at the time. Perhaps you should wiggle your toes once in a while to test the ground on which you base your appearance in the world.

To which she would reply, "Why, yes, Stephen, that is a good one." Her reply was another shrugging away of the possibilities of greater freedom, a closed-heartedness to herself and the world. She wobbled between denial and self-hatred. Her self-judgment at times so intense that it blocked her ability to hear others, much less the subtle whispers of her heart. When she was open to it we often worked with the investigation of guilt and the quality of self-forgiveness as a means of softening that "tight-assedness that I sometimes feel."

But she had her moments. There were times when Lobellia was the "picture of serenity." But because she had made so little preparation to allow herself to enter her heart, these moments did not last long and were often followed by periods of dissatisfaction and extreme weariness. There was a way in which she pictured herself as Christ on the cross, and when that image would arise, I would ask her, "Lobellia, isn't it enough just to be the sacred heart? Must you be the whole body as well as the cross-members of the crucifix and the nails as well? Does all this control and knowledge have to come between you and your living/dying? Wouldn't love be an easier path? Wouldn't forgiveness, the very essence of Jesus on the cross, be a clearer path to tread?"

When we would speak of being "locked into old ways," she would just say, "Hmm. I see what you mean. . . ." But clearly she did not. And once again it was time to take our own advice and just be watchful of any desire to "force wisdom" when it was not what was asked for. Obviously, our work was just to manifest the way of the heart, just to love her as she was and to be open to her in a way she seemed unwilling to open to herself.

About a year after we had met, Lobellia dropped by one day displaying a much softer mood than usual. It was the fortieth

anniversary of her mother's death. Another patient in her seventies also working with cancer was visiting that day, and we
introduced them, thinking they might have much to talk about
and create some mutual support. But as it turned out, they
scared each other, because each saw the other as dying while
seeing herself as somehow eventually to be healed. Each said
that she "didn't plan on dying" and found the other too harsh a
mirror of her own condition. Indeed, some months later when
the woman we had introduced to Lobellia died, Lobellia's jaw
set in a line of resistance upon hearing the news.

Before leaving that afternoon, Lobellia told us she had come
upon a letter one of her mother's best friends had written to her
at the time of her mother's death forty years before, and she
would like to share it with us and anyone else who would find it
useful because it had meant so much to her upon rereading it.

As her cancer slowly increased its deterioration of her body, a
certain vulnerability arose infrequently that allowed her to explore her difficulties with her daughters. One night she called to
ask, "How do you do it? How do you let it all float? I understand
it in my head and can even teach it to others but then, but then,
but then . . ."

S: "You have to let life be before you will be able to let life go. To
let it float you must become one with it. Work gently and consis-
tently with the letting go meditation. There can be no pulling
or pushing, no grasping or retraction, no posturing or wishing it
to be otherwise, just a loving watching of those old holdings in
the mind which try to create the world instead of meeting it
with love as it is. It is just allowing the moment to be as it is. You
can't let go of anything you do not fully accept. In a sense, it is
your willingness to be human that takes you to God. It is the
acknowledgment of the mind that lets one see the mind for
what it is, just passing show, just old momentum running off. It
allows you to live in the heart of things, in the very moment in
which being is present and death is just a dream. Do you think
you have acknowledged your suffering at that level? How much
acceptance have you given yourself to be as you are?"
L: "I don't know. I have been working at it and working at it.
But then it hits me that I am not getting anywhere and doubt
moves in like a big black cloud."

S: "Are you working to let it be or are you trying to change it? Fighting with the natural doubt as though it needed to be slain only creates more tension and more doubt. Can you let life in? Watch the process unfolding. Even your trying to change the moment limits your ability to participate directly in it. Allow it. Stop pushing it all away. Investigate it. Indeed, you could experience great insight by just watching that doubt. If you open to it, if you just let doubt float in the mind, recognizing it as 'doubting, doubting,' then you won't become the 'doubter.' You will be instead just awareness focused in the present. Indeed, a moment of seeing doubt as just another state of mind, just an impersonal process passing through the vastness of your true being, can allow you release from the painful shallowness of the mind. The mind insists it is so solid, and yet these thoughts are just bubbles, fragile impermanences passing through, constantly arising and dissolving, instantly replaced by the next uninvited arising. The mind is happening all by itself. Doubt arises uninvited."

L: "I try to talk myself out of it but it just doesn't work. I tell my mind there is no reason to doubt but it just won't stop."

S: "It is your resistance to that doubt that makes you think it is so real. In your situation doubt is perfectly natural, but you analyze it, you become 'ever so reasonable' about it, and it just gets a deeper foothold. Ironically, insight into doubt can breed exactly its opposite quality: confidence. Confidence means trust in the process. But you have often cultivated very little trust in the natural process of the mind and body because you have fought with it so often, thinking you have to be someone else, and it reinforced the quality of doubt in your mind. No blame, just something to notice. Big surprise that there is doubt in the mind. Who doesn't have it? But the way in which we meet it can create an even deeper faith within us that all we are experiencing is simply a passing show. Nothing you need to fight. Just something to soften, to acknowledge, to open around, to let go, to let be as it is and to greet with more interest and less fear. You have pulled back from this natural process so often that now you are left with very little sense of its perfection or the possibility of peace that is always present within. This trust you seek seems to arise when we let the process be as it is and watch from the heart the mind's meanderings. Remember, the mind creates the abyss and the heart crosses it."

L: "You know, I tried last week to just let it all go. Just 'enter into it,' as you put it, and it was awful."

S: "Why was it awful?"

L: "It was frightening. I thought if I really let go of the mind, my body would dissolve too and I would just die. I must keep hold of what I think to keep this body functioning at all and that means effort."

S: "Perhaps there is too much force in the way you are approaching this practice of opening. What you need is to surrender into it. Let go of the trying and just be. It is the trying that is making it so hard, so tense. Perhaps it is time to have a truce with life. You have been at war with life and with yourself for so long that the gunshots are still ringing in your ears even though in a sense both 'sides' are willing to make peace. The one 'side' is frightened and grasps at life, imagining the body its only priority. While yet another aspect of you knows better and senses the value of opening in love to the present moment, and even to the agonies of the past. But the second voice is the weaker and is given little nourishment because of the well-fed fear that beneath it all is just more shit, that indeed there is no 'true nature' which will be revealed when you let go. Something in you has come to distrust itself so much that you distrust the process as well and fear if you step off 'the known,' letting go of your old ways of thinking, of your ideas of who you imagine you are or should be, you will disappear into some great void, and nothing will stay your fall. Not recognizing that the void, the vast edgelessness of being, is your true nature. It is the holding to the attempted solidity of a self-image, which makes you 'someone' separate from God, someone to protect from death, which is making it so difficult, as it has always made life such a struggle."

About a month later the cancer seemed to have metastasized to her brain and she was displaying some of the effects of disorientation and aphasia (scrambled speech). One morning Caroline, one of Lobellia's support team, called to say, "Lobellia had a real tough time last night. Today she is a little better. But last night and yesterday she was totally out of it. Nothing she said made any sense at all. She is still a little out of it today, but she is at least in the reality of the present."

S: "And what reality is that? Your reality? This is probably the most she has ever allowed herself, if allowed is the word, to just be. If you let go of your image of her as being 'the teacher' then you will just be able to be with her in your heart no matter what she is going through and these things won't be so frightening because they won't be so different. Be gentle with yourself and with her and let her go through what she needs. Meet it with love instead of fear. Does she have any remembrance of what it was like last night?"

C: "No. She was making statements which bore no relationship to anything. They would be very disconnected and pretty weird. She was making connections which didn't exist and her time sense is all screwed up. She thought it was another day and that something had happened five minutes ago that had happened two weeks ago. It really frightened us."

S: "Why did it frighten you?"

C: "If I had to put a label on it, I would say that she was insane for a period of time."

S: "Well, the cancer is in her brain now, so this is your teaching in nonexpectation. And it is her teaching as well. Just let her be 'as is' without need to be anyone or anything else. I guess you will just have to let go of your models of her and of yourself as her student and just be with her as an ongoing process, not as a solid person. What was her emotional state during her experience last night?"

C: "At times, she was angry, particularly if anybody asked her anything, or tried to clarify anything. If they asked her a question, she got furious with them. But along toward the end of the day when I realized that she really wasn't with it in a real sense, I just started playing with her and she got into a very good emotional state, she was quite happy."

S: "Your intuition is leading you perfectly to the mark. How wonderful for her to be displaying some anger before you all who think her such a saint and perhaps do not love her or yourselves deeply enough for being just what we are, human beings on a path with a ways to go yet. How are you going to love yourself when you are angry, if you can't love her when she is? It is time for her to stop all forms of protection, of her students as well as herself. She is dying on so many levels. She is actually quite fortunate to be 'losing it.' It's quite a teaching to let go of our much overrated 'lucidity.' "

C: "She is beginning to get a little spacy again."

S: "Well, just start to play with her again. Let it all just be the good old theater of the absurd."

C: "She is coming to the phone now and would like to speak to you. It will take her a moment to get over here. . . . Ahh. Here she is."

L: "Hi, Stephen. How are you? I am a little weird myself."

S: "Well, it's about time. Just let yourself be. I know it feels strange but the final initiations often do. How are you feeling?"

L: "I am all over. I have no center in a way."

S: "How wonderful! No control. No way to be separate from God. Nothing to obstruct your safe passage."

L: "Is that all right?"

S: "It's not only all right, it's perfect. You've been altogether too rational your whole life anyhow. Time to let that perfectly irra-tional part of you emerge as well. Now you can start writing French surrealist plays."

L: "Oh, good. I'll start doing that immediately." (This was one of the first times I heard Lobellia laugh.)

S: "It is all right to be confused too, you know. That is just another state of mind. No need to struggle for clarity. Or even understand what I am saying right now. This is the teaching in surrender that we spoke of so often—to just let yourself be as you are and to meet yourself anew.

L: "Well, that seems to be what is happening. I don't have any choice. It is just passing show as you say. And I see that somehow now more clearly than I usually do."

S: "Right now the mind contains confusion. In the next moment it will contain something else. In fact it sounds already as though there is some clarity in your willingness to be unclear."

L: "That's right. Whatever."

S: "It sounds like other people, though, are having a bit of trouble keeping up with you."

L: "Yeh."

S: "That's OK too. Does it make you feel a little alone?"

L: "Yes. It does. I guess this is the aftermath of playing the teacher for so long."

S: "Oh, nothing to judge. That is all to be expected. You are sort of walking down a different road than you have before. Perhaps the people you have taught are still walking down a path you have since diverted from."

L: "I think that is so."

S: "That is fine. That is one of your last teachings to them. And it is a wonderful teaching too, because you're teaching your friends to trust the moment as you learn it yourself. To open to the process."

L: "I have felt that a little bit. But as you said, it is all right to be any way that is the way of the moment."

S: "That is right. And there is no need to protect anyone or be anything for anyone."

L: "I am not at the moment trying to. In fact, I couldn't be a teacher now if I wanted. Every once in a while my minds gets all spacy and screwed up and my words come out all crooked and lopsided."

S: "Are you saying things and not understanding what is being said?"

L: "Halfway."

S: "Ahh. Time to let go of meaning."

L: "I guess so."

S: "When you let go of meaning, you hit the essence."

L: "That's lucky." (This was the second time I heard Lobellia laugh.)

S: "Let go of 'meaning' and only the truth will remain. It might be a truth you can't even express to yourself, but it is the truth of being. All this precious 'meaning' that you have tried to transmit and that you have attempted to make your life appear as, is just more suffering. What is there to say, anyhow?"

L: "It's all right then that I am sort of weird, huh?"

S: "The mind may be weird, but who you really are is just edgeless awareness and peace."

L: "I am?"

S: "You know, I've never heard you so open, Lobellia. On you delirium looks good. It's just the perfect balance for your 'knowing.' Your connections with the world are diminishing. Trust that. It is a merciful aspect of this process of letting go of the body."

L: "I suppose so. It seems that way anyhow."

S: "One of our greatest requirements and strongest attach-ments to the world is being 'understood,' that our words and thoughts have meaning. But it is time to let go of being under-stood and enter the place of understanding."

L: "That seems to be what is happening."

S: "Ahh. Wonderful! Do you think death is approaching?"

L: "He has been coming for a long time but he is shuffling his feet."

S: "Well, it sounds like he is around here somewhere."

L: "Perhaps so. I wouldn't be surprised."

Over the next three weeks as Lobellia went in and out of what a few of her more frightened students considered "tempo-rary insanity," the qualities she had bred in her students began to close in on her. Once again she found in herself little trust in the heart of things and more force in the mind to struggle for its survival, its old way. Once again her denial became solid and obdurate. The confusion of her helpers and students resulted in many phone calls trying to get some sense of who they were in the midst of this confusion. It was a time of great learning for all. A time for considerable recognition of holdings and old fears.

Her nurse friend Caroline called one morning "because it looks like Lobellia is going to die in the next few hours." We made the drive to her home and met her assembled family and friends in the crowded living room beside the bedroom in which she lay. One of her nurses said that they had asked her this morning if she thought she was going to die, and she had responded once again, "I don't plan on dying." When we heard that, we laughed and said, "It looks like she is just right for the wrong reasons. She is not going to die. But it certainly seems as though her body is going to be left behind."

We spent some time talking with her students. Their hearts were wide open to her. It was only their thoughts that were in conflict with the moment. As we encouraged them to see their thoughts as simply old ways of being, hindrances to the clear seeing of the flow, the tension in the room seemed to diminish.

Moving en masse into her large bedroom, we approached her

bed as she slowly opened her eyes from the intermittent sleep of a body preparing to let go of itself. "Hi, Lobellia." She looked up, a bit surprised to see us there, and said, "What are you doing here?" To which we replied, "We just came to say good-bye." To which she responded with some surprise, "Oh! Where are you going?" We couldn't help laughing aloud at this almost quaint denial. The room rippled with laughter. "Oh, that," she said, turning her face slightly toward the wall. Hugging her good-bye and giving her a parting kiss, we left the room as her students gently rolled her on her side to give her a massage.

Later that evening we received a call from Caroline, saying Lobellia had just died and that "she went in and out of these weird states for a few hours and had pretty much stopped talking to everyone." She went on to say the last week had been a purification for everyone, "letting go of Lobellia," and that Lobellia had died about an hour after going to sleep. The nurse added that Lobellia had left us the letter her mother's best friend had written her at the time of her mother's death.

Because the letter was so pertinent to Lobellia and her heart's sense of the world, of the soft voice which struggled so for recognition during her life, the letter was read at her memorial service.

"Dearest Lobellia:

"If a certain strength did not utterly fail me at times like these, I would have talked with you before this—calmly, evenly, earnestly—offering the solace which only words between friends can foster when the one has been hurt and the other longs to help.

"But it does. All my earnest thoughts and humble convictions well up in me like a wave, then recede because I have not the strength to gaze into the eyes of any stricken person whom I love . . . and I do love you. You are one of my few friends.

"I could not honorably minimize the fact that your mother has been taken. I could not say, 'Lobellia, we must all go through this, lose loved ones, take up life again, be brave. . . .' Knowing inside that when the time comes for my own to part with me, I will be gripped by a stark, blind rebellion, not bravery. There are some griefs that cannot be shared, and the soul left lonely by the gesture of a loved one's removal cries inside, 'Oh, how can you pretend you understand! It is my sorrow, my mother, not yours!' There is in those first dark hours of realization even a faint, strange hostility toward the most tender offers to help. One's world seems to shrink, excluding light.

"But I can try to say this to you. Lobellia: I can say, 'God's planned life very beautifully, hasn't he? To conceive us, then to break our eternity into great movements which surge and change as rhythmically as the seasons themselves, working toward the climax of some super scheme. You know, I take parts of those grand symphonies and play them sometimes—as separate moods subtracted from their whole they can make you weep, sigh with awe, sink in ponderous sadness, expand with hope, smile with fine delight in the sufficiency of beauty unto that moment. But it isn't until you relax completely and hear the whole from first note to last, it isn't until your eyes cloud with the profound, too brilliant visions summoned from nowhere by the epic sweep of movement on movement, that the splendor of a thing complete floods through your consciousness. Perfection, completion—life, death—their movements too, synonymous with a whole which cannot be judged in part. Isn't it strange, Lobellia, how we struggle against the cosmic outlook sometimes, how we try to isolate death as if it were discreetly foreign to life instead of an integral movement in an infinite succession of moods progressing toward the godhead. The grandeur of that vision almost blinds our souls, I guess. We have to grow up to that connection; we have to deny a defeatism which says, 'Because I can no longer hear it, this piece of music that I loved so much must be ended.'

"Your mother and my mother can never leave us: the temple of their lives may change, but the theme of their vast love, still throbbing in us, will only be continuing somewhere, and it is my simple, strong faith that we are never, never to lose contact with that love motif. Somewhere again our hearts are to stand still in ecstasy as we recognize those familiar, lovely notes of our beloveds and find them—a little farther along in their scores than we, perhaps, but intrinsically the same fine symphony."

Opening the Heart in Hell

MARCIA

Marcia first called at six in the morning. "My daughter was viciously murdered about six weeks ago and I am just having a very hard time. I am calling because someone told me of the work you did with the Gregorys when their daughter was abducted and murdered. I don't know if there is anything you can do to help, but I have nowhere else to turn."

S: "How are you feeling?"
M: "I don't know how we will ever possibly survive this, but somehow it helps to talk to someone who has some understanding of what has happened."
S: "In a sense, understanding is not what is needed right now. That might come later. What is needed right now is to have the mercy on yourself that somehow allows the pain to be acknowledged. When the Gregorys lost their daughter, their heart was torn open as yours must be. And there is a place in the mind where it just grabs at its security, but there is just no security to be found because, in a way, there is just no way we can be protected from any of the changes that happen in the world. All we can do is allow ourselves to be open to the moment, to allow what we feel to arise, to honor the pain in our heart."
M: (After a long silence.) "What we have found, and this is very strange, is that she has come into us so much. We were so close to her that she has become a part of the four of us who are left here. More than just the four of us, because there has been an outpouring of so many people who knew her—so many of her friends—and she seems to be such a part of us that that seems to make it possible to survive for a while, and then suddenly the loss—it's just such a cavern. . . ."

S: "Well, you know, when the Gregorys' daughter was abducted and murdered, there was another fourteen-year-old girl that was also killed, her best friend, Sarah. Both disappeared and were later found tortured and strangled. As you can imagine, this has been an incredibly difficult year for both families. But the two families responded very differently to the event. The Gregorys allowed themselves to be torn open to their daughter's murder and of course suffered greatly, but somehow, because they allowed the pain to enter their heart, their heart seemed yet more in touch with their other children and with the spirit of their daughter. She became, as you have said, more and more a part of the family. The other family, the Spinells, had lived their life in a stiff kind of orthodoxy that they expected would protect them—a bargaining with God—and when Sarah was murdered, they lost their faith. Their hearts closed to each other and the world and they have become more and more destroyed by this experience. They raged against the universe. Their relationship is in tatters.

"Meanwhile, the Gregorys have never been so close. They shared the pain. They met her death in love. They allowed their rage. It burned through them. It may never be completely gone, but still there is a sense of unity with life that has been the legacy of their daughter's death. The Spinells' younger children feel abandoned, frightened. The younger children in both families felt strongly the doubt that the world was a safe place to be. In each case the older daughter had been murdered and the younger children felt that they were completely unprotected. The Gregorys' children have come more and more into the heart of the family, of their parents, of their friends. The Spinells' children have become depressed and very unsure of themselves. Marcia, undoubtedly this is the most difficult experience of a lifetime, and in many ways it has just begun."

M: "I know. I get sight of that. I know that we are going to have a time that is going to be very difficult."

S: "You may also have a time where for some reason beyond anything you can put a finger on, your heart is more open and you feel more love than you have ever felt. That is what happened with the Gregorys. The other couple closed and became outraged with God."

M: "We went through that when it first happened and we have

been going through that for years with what is happening in the world. But what happened with our daughter somehow opened us up. She was working after school at the local newspaper, just a few blocks from where we live. She was a young girl who seemed to have everything. Just sixteen years old. She was so very beautiful, she was like the sun. She had sort of a classic Renaissance face. She had very long blond hair and she walked so proudly and beautifully."

S: "You know, her face is gone and her walk is gone, but her beauty will remain forever."

M: "I know. Believe it or not, I know. She was like sunshine and we have been having a lot of that lately. And she was walking home when two men got her, raped her and killed her—they beat her and finally stabbed her. When she wasn't home at the time she usually arrived, I started worrying. After a short time I walked to the newspaper, but she was nowhere to be seen and they said she had left some time before. And then I knew. Because she wouldn't ever go anywhere else without letting us know. That just wasn't the kind of relationship we had.

"So we went through the whole horror of trying to get the authorities to go out and look for her, and they did. We were out looking all over for her. I was out looking for her and I couldn't find her. She was only three blocks from home where they found her. They came with a priest. They didn't know we were Quakers.

"We have had letters from people all over the country that we have never met. Their support has somehow helped us live from day to day. Some of the letters were from parents who had lost a child through violence. Those letters seemed to be helpful."

S: "Well, you know, nothing I can say is going to be very helpful right now. In a sense, this is a time when you touch your powerlessness and your fear of the world. As a Quaker you have the long-established practice of 'listening to the small voice within.' But that voice is going to be difficult to get in touch with sometimes, because the mind naturally is going to be agitated and in such a spin."

M: "Yes. We go on and off. Right now I can function."

S: "Can you allow yourself to not function?"

M: "Yes. I do what I have to do."

S: "What would be useful right now is to allow yourself to feel all that you are feeling."

M: "I don't seem to have much choice."

S: "Well, there are many kinds of feelings. The full range of emotions are going to arise. Just have the mercy on yourself to leave them room to happen."

M: "Well, this just happened about a month ago, and now the men have been arrested who killed her and we have to appear at their trial. I sense this is going to be very difficult for both of us. But anything that is hiding under there will most likely be brought out by this awful trial. I feel anger toward them, of course. I feel like the whole world has been hurt. I feel like it is some mindless, senseless evil that she fell in the path of. What I feel is this horror for my child. She used to be frightened sometimes, and I would go in when she would have nightmares and say, 'Give it to me.' She would tell me and then go to sleep, and I would take the nightmares—and I am trying to take this nightmare . . ."

S: "But you can't take this nightmare for her. It is your nightmare now. Her nightmare was just a moment long and has long since dissolved behind her. Yours continues as you repeat it again and again in your mind. For you she is accosted and raped a thousand times. For her it happened only once. For you, each time she is beaten and raped, at the end of that rape she is once again beaten and once again raped, over and over again. But for her each moment was followed by the next. Death only happened once, for a moment, and then the next moment arose. Her experience is different from your imagination of her experience, than your fears, than your feeling of impotent rage because you could not protect her from this 'senseless evil' that she was touched by.

"Feel the love, the anger, the fear, but know that what you feel exists only for a moment and then becomes the next moment. In a situation like this there is a tendency for the mind to replay the incident a million times. But you know, if you thought right now about breaking a leg as you walked across the lawn, there you would be, walking along the lawn, tripping over the sprinkler, falling down, breaking your leg, and then you would start thinking about walking across the lawn again, falling again, breaking your leg again, walking across the lawn—

again and again it repeats in the mind. But in actuality when that happens, you walk across the lawn and the lawn is past. You trip over the sprinkler and the sprinkler is past and there is a moment when the bone breaks and that one is done, and then the next moment comes. But in your reflection about what happened to your daughter, the next moment never comes. You always go back to the beginning again. She did not suffer what you are imagining. She went through it only one time."

M: "I know. I go through it every morning."

S: "You go through it a million times. Your fear of what happened to her, in a sense, is worse than what happened to her. As you know, when you hurt yourself, you are right in the midst of that pain. Everyone else around you is trying to help and there is confusion in their mind and fright and all kinds of feelings that may not be in your mind at the time. At that time you are just with what is happening, just with the broken leg, just with the pain of the moment trying to figure out what the next step is. What she experienced is perhaps a moment of incredible fright, but then, as we have been told by many in similar experiences who lived to relate the tale, because the imminence of the danger is so great, something else seems to occur. A kind of disconnecting. Not a dissociation where you are pulling back and have gone mentally catatonic, but a displacing of the mind from the body."

We shared with Marcia the stories we have been told not only by those who had been violently attacked, but also by those who had experienced the violence we imagine occurs to the mind and body during the process of drowning. One might think drowning would be one of the most terrifying deaths that could happen, but having spoken with several people who had nearly drowned and were on respirators and in treatment for some time thereafter before recovering, this apparently was not the case. Each said there was a moment when the water was above their head and when there was no chance for escape, when there was a burning in their lungs and the first recognition of what was happening—that they were going to die—when all of a sudden what came over them was an extraordinary peace, that though they saw their body thrashing in the water gasping for air, their experience was not the experience one would have imagined looking at that body wildly struggling in the water. Their experience was a peacefulness that "this too was somehow perfectly OK."

S: "Yes, your daughter may have been very frightened. But that was not the only quality in her mind during that experience. When the body recognizes that it is so thoroughly threatened, something else seems to happen, so your daughter's experience can only be imagined. For her the experience was only a few moments long, and then it was over and the next moment occurred: the dissolving out of her body, the going on which apparently is in peace, without fear and without pain."

M: "Yes. It is the mind replaying it that is the greatest difficulty right now. Like today. I saw her hand in my mind. It was very difficult, it was very hard for me to see her hand, because she was an artist and her skills had taken some enormous steps forward just in the last few months. I could see her hand with a knife cutting the paper, and with the sureness of the pen she was using, and this whole thing has just been very hard for me this morning because of that hand."

S: "Because of who she was in the world."

M: "Yes. And I held that hand so many times. We walked together all over. We had been so close—all of us."

S: "How old are your other children?"

M: "One is just a few years younger than his sister was, the other is in second grade."

S: "One of the things you might want to be aware of is that a child, even one who is in his early teens, still has the feeling that his parents can protect him from anything. Now your children see their sister killed, and somewhere deep inside they may be saying that there is no real security in this world."

M: "Yes. The older boy says it isn't safe for him to walk the streets."

S: "And that is one you may find you will be working with off and on for some time. The death of his sister has probably had a very strong affect on his view of the world right now. But with all the unity and love that your family feels, his sense of security will re-establish itself in time.

"I have seen many younger siblings become the 'oldest child' with a kind of strength and courage and pride, taking the position of the eldest in a new kind of responsibility toward life. "All of it will change just as your feelings are going to change. Indeed, you couldn't make these feelings stay even if you wanted to. Because they are all part of a process, the process of grief. You are experiencing what comes next just as your daughter did."

M: "For a long time I couldn't go upstairs into her room. I would pass by her door and it would make me feel so sad. I guess I am still worried about her well-being. At first after she had died, the house was filled with people and there were so many distractions, but then when everyone left, every time I would walk past her door, I would feel my heart just burst. It was almost as though I was waiting for her to come out that door all shiny and bright, ready for a new day.

"But then one day her boyfriend, who had been almost catatonic for the first couple of weeks after her murder, came over and asked if he could go up into her room and just sit there quietly by himself for a while. Of course, we said that was fine. After about an hour he came downstairs and asked us all to come up into her room. And when I went upstairs and went into her room, there was an incredible peace there. It wasn't so much that I was avoiding her room before but just that I didn't know what to do. But when I went up there, it was just incredible. I sat there for a long time and since then I have sat there several times with her friends and we have talked and laughed about her. Now and again, I am so filled with joy, with the beauty of the life she lived, for the love of the people she knew."

S: "And that joy will be there on and off. As you experience the grief less in your mind, as you experience her less as her separateness, as her form, as a being who had come into life as your daughter and instead just begin to experience her as being itself, the grief will sink from the mind's incessant agitation into the heart and you will just be with her in oneness, in your essential connectedness. And then the form which seemed so important but is now denied you may be seen through as an illusion which in some ways always kept you separate. Separate from the most profound, silent, inner penetration of each other. In an odd way now you can go beyond the forms that always kept you separate, of mother and daughter, of elder and child, of someone who knew and someone who had something to learn. Then the essence of being is shared in love and the grief will burn its way to completion. She is gone now into her next perfect evolutionary step, just as the unbearable pain you feel propels you toward your next stage of life and being."

M: "I so wanted her to be old and me to have grandchildren and for us to laugh and talk."

S: "Well, that is not going to be given, but what may be given to the degree that you can stay open to it, as it seems you are, is to let your heart be torn open. She had quite a basis for love and self-acceptance in her life. Two hundred thousand people die every day on this planet. Of that two hundred thousand, how many do you think approach death with their hearts as clear and open as hers was, with a life so full?"

M: "In the last six months she opened up in an astonishing way. Her friends had great confidence in her and often confided. She was, as some of her friends said, 'an old soul.' She had really been coming into her own in these last months. The last six months of her life had been just incredible, so full, so complete."

S: "It sounds like she was finishing a lot of business with herself, with the world. She was very fortunate to have those last months."

M: "When I talk about her being there, I mean she is in me, her brothers, her father. . . ."

S: "And you have the same lessons to learn that she did, that we all do. She may have learned those lessons in an instant six weeks ago, I just don't know. It may have been given to her to learn all that she had come to learn in just those few moments of life she was granted, much less those sixteen loving years."

We spoke for some time more about how the family, including grandparents and cousins, were relating to this sudden loss. Her loss had brought the family together as never before. The grief was being shared by all in a deep caring for themselves and each other.

Over the next year, we spoke to Marcia, her husband and oldest son on various occasions and watched as the pain sank deeper and as they slowly again surfaced into life with a new commitment to compassion and mutual support. The healing was slow and profound. Her younger brother began playing the piano as she once had. As he started slowly to take the position as the oldest child, he began babysitting for his younger brother in a way he had never wished to in the past. And his playing piano too as he feared he never could because "she was always so good at everything and now I am too."

It is not that Marcia's family's grief will ever be completely gone but rather that it has caused them to open to life in a way they may never have imagined in the past. In a sense, they have allowed themselves to die into life, to appreciate the precious moment in which this sharing is to be experienced, letting go of the fears and worries that may have in the past kept life somewhat stiffer.

There are a few dozen families with whom we have shared over the past few years the healing that accompanies the grief of a murdered child. In most cases we have seen a slow reorientation, a deepening to life, while for a few, talking to us has just become too painful and they seldom write or call.

Often as I am talking on the phone to the parent of a murdered child, our children will come into the room filled with the urgency of adolescence, "We can't wait, we're off to town, what time are we supposed to be home?" And though the mind may be momentarily frustrated by the distraction while I am on the phone, the heart opens to the preciousness of each sharing, of each moment we are allowed together. The priorities become clearer and clearer: to honor each being as they unfold without holding them back or pushing them aside. Each day we learn a bit more and let go of the pain that keeps us separate, the isolation of father and son, of mother and daughter, and continue to merge in the one being we all share.

Healing into the World

ANTHONY

We met Anthony, a twenty-year-old Oregonian, about two years ago when he showed up at a workshop, the left side of his face greatly distended from tumors of the cheek and lip. His appearance instantly caught one's attention, but it was not simply the distortion of the left side of his face that was so striking. His eyes were like the green algae pools that form in the cooling lava after a volcano has destroyed all in its path, the spark of life regenerating in these pools—still quite in jeopardy, life on the edge of rebirth or extinction.

Occasionally, he would call and ask if we had a "moment to chew the fat," a phrase that always made us laugh since both of us were verging toward vegetarianism at the time. Our first work together had been a deep listening to the "unburdening mind" as it dumped the pain of a lifetime on the table between us. For the first few months our work together seemed to be an allowing of a shedding of the past more than the use of any particular techniques. It was a while before Anthony asked what meditations he might use to "unlock my cancer."

Making it clear that I didn't have "the right answer," I shared with Anthony how one could apply the practice of sending love and forgiveness into an area of sickness as a means of healing. That many found it useful to direct their attention to the area of discomfort and begin sending it love instead of a kind of fearful rejection. I explained to him how many had learned to focus their awareness on the area of illness and go directly into the sensations there. To concentrate on the physiological spot where the cancer or disease was and funnel love into it, which, oddly enough, for many meant accepting it for the first time by just letting it be there, letting it in, where their natural healing could have access to it. Focusing the awareness on the moment-to-moment change in sensations there. Bringing deep awareness to that spot. Noticing any emotions there or even "if it has anything to say." Listening to the illness, adding nothing, just opening to however it might express itself. Meeting the illness with forgiveness and mercy. Even visualizing the sickness there as outlined by the subtle variation in sensations. Once the contact with that area slowly becomes established, to then begin the second step, to bring the attention into the heart center. Taking several deep breaths directly into the heart as though it had an invisible vent right through the sternum. Beginning to open into the warmth and care that is there just beneath the mind's incessant ramblings. Letting the attention be focused in the heart. Then with each soft, natural breath to spend some moments cultivating a feeling of that loving-kindness and a wish for the well-being of all sentient creatures everywhere. Perhaps using some words like, "May all beings be free from suffering. May all beings be healed of their pain." And as the loving openness to life begins to be cultivated, to use the connection with the sensations like a conduit between the heart and the illness and to begin sending, with each breath, as through a tunnel or river, loving-kindness directly into the area where sickness is perceived. To soak it with love. "None have said it was easy at first, that it may have even felt kind of mechanical but as the heart opens more and more it seemed easier and deeper. Several have told us that sending love regularly into their illness, and especially when they felt discomfort, healed them in a way that nothing else seemed to."

As Anthony worked with sending love into his cancer, it seemed to cease its insistent progression. There seemed to be the possibility of remission. As is often the case when a patient feels better, particularly when the healing meditation is working well, there is a much decreased need to call us. As a greater degree of self-acceptance began to emerge, in one of our conversations Anthony said, "I have felt like a five-year-old my whole damn life."

S: "Well, it's time to be six. Let's have a surrender six party—a rites of passage out of helplessness celebration."

After the rites of passage party at which Anthony blew out
the six candles on his birthday cake, there was much singing and
laughing and sugar indulgence. Anthony continued with his
meditations, even consciously directing his treatments precisely into the affected area. It had been some time since we had
heard from him when at seven o'clock one morning the phone
awoke me to Anthony's trembling voice. He said he had been
"going through endless changes" and told me how he had
started to lose the sensation in his arms and legs some days
before, adding, "Strangely enough, it was just when my father
came to visit."

A: "I was bugged that I couldn't even lift myself out of bed. I
was losing control of my arms and legs. I thought it was in the
spine, but when they took me to the hospital, the neurologist
looked me over and said it might be in my brain. Not a tumor
but that something in the course of the disease had affected the
cerebellum which controls balance and coordination and I
might never get it back. My arms have almost become totally
useless. They are so cramped I can't even use my hands, and the
lumps under my arms have started to get bigger. I am not even
five. I am helpless as a baby."
S: "You know, as I listen to you, I wonder if it is the cancer or
your father who is making you as helpless as an infant right now.
Perhaps something is blocking the love that seemed so healing
before. Are you giving your power over to the cancer and perhaps eventually death, just as you once, and still seem to, give
yourself over to your father? Has cancer become your parent
after all these years, telling you when to go to bed, what to eat,
how to dress, how to spend your days?"
A: "It got much worse when my father came. I just couldn't do
the meditation. I was quite sure I was going to die."

When I asked him if he was frightened, he said that he wasn't
but that he just felt sad. But exploring the feelings in his body
and the repetitive "tape loop" in his mind, it became clear that
there was considerable conflict and confusion. Although he had
said it was all right to die at that moment, it seemed otherwise.
Considerable unfinished business was intensifying his fear and
dread of "leaving things half-ass." That somehow he couldn't

die in wholeness because he felt he couldn't die the way he
wished to—not only the lack of control over his body, but the
inability to be who he wished to be in his father's eyes. His
father was insisting he be "someone in control and able to beat
this thing." When I asked him how it was to have his father
there, he said: "Terrible. He is going to leave. He is going to go
back to Miami where he says he has a new job waiting for him."

S: "Did you make a decision with your father that he would
leave today?"
A: "No. He decided he would leave last night. He thinks I should
go for more chemotherapy and radiation for a while, and if I
don't want to do that, he doesn't want to be around me. He says
I want to die and I say I don't and he says, 'Yes you do, because
otherwise you would do the "rational thing." ' It is my life and I
have to make the decision for myself. The more I get this sense
of it being 'my life,' the better I feel and the more love I can
send myself. But the more I live for myself, not just to be
'independent' but because something in me is getting stronger
—that heart voice we spoke of—the more he says I am pushing
him away. He does not feel I show him respect and love. He
thinks God is something to wrestle with, to fight against, that
God is dying and that we must finish off the job. I think actually
he fears God. But I think God is love, is my support. For him
God is The Most Fearful and you have to wrestle every little
thing out of him. We have very different attitudes toward life.
My feeling is that I have the right to live and die as I choose. It is
his right to believe in what therapy he wants, but I don't think it
is his right to say that I am wrong and keep pushing me if I don't
do it his way. He is with this beautiful lady he met a while ago
and she doesn't agree with what I am doing, but I never feel
from her this sort of 'I am right, you are wrong.' My father says
because I am his son and he loves me I must do what he says or
else I am very selfish."

Anthony said that he was feeling considerably better in the
last few days since he decided to trust his feelings about how to
treat his illness. He said, "I am just allowing myself to be sick
and to feel out what might be the next step for me." I asked
Anthony, "How much of your pain do you think is resistance to

this unexpected reoccurrence of your illness?" To which Anthony softly began to cry. He said that part of him felt that his
acceptance of his illness was a betrayal of his father and the love
he wished existed between them.

A: "He says I'm giving him 'too much lip' and not obeying his
wishes and then I look in the mirror at how distended my face is
and I wonder how much lip I have to give before it kills me.
How can I be there with how I feel when I think I shouldn't feel
this way? When I am told by the person I most want care from
that I must care for myself in a different way than I feel is right
for me? And besides that, my pride is really pushing on me
because all of a sudden I need so much help, so many people to
take care of me."
S: "That is all part of sending care to yourself, of opening your
illness to love. You are receiving the great teaching of helplessness, of allowing another to be there for you in a way you need
to be there for yourself. To serve and heal yourself as though
you were some lost child you found shuddering in a dark doorway.
   "And yet you doubt you should give yourself that help. You
think it's the wrong path. You are receiving the great teaching
of helplessness, of allowing another to be there for you in a way
you wish you could for them."

   When I asked Anthony about his support group, he said that
there were many beautiful people loving him in a most tender
way and that the more they loved him the more guilty and
confused he felt about not being able to help himself as his
father insisted he must.

A: "In a manner of speaking my father is insisting that I be
independent, but in his way, not mine. He says that I must 'fight
for life,' but I just want to allow it instead of warring with it. I
want to stop this struggle. I just want to help others in the same
way they have helped me."
S: "How much easier it often is to give than to receive. How
much more control one has when one is the helper instead of
the helped. But this is the teaching of this moment. Because
when you are helping, when you are in control, your places of

holding may never really get exposed because you are involved
so much in your doing and receiving so much gratitude for your
actions. You don't notice the places the mind feels guilty or
insecure or self-righteous—the self-hatred that lurks just behind
your good deeds. Everyone is giving you strokes and telling you
what a good person you are, but always you know better.
Though sometimes when you can't maintain who you wish to be
in the world, when you don't get what you want, your attention
is drawn inward. You see safe territory is not to be found outside
of you in all your doing. That it is the heart which has to do the
work, cultivating a willingness to let go of the mind in its various
posturings and manipulations. To begin to let the mind sink into
the heart. Indeed, even our months of talking about 'opening
the heart' is not quite on the mark, because in a very real sense
the heart is always open. All we need do is let go of the mind,
which blocks access to the heart's deep acceptance of the flow.

"Acceptance is not in the mind. It is in your heart. When you
experience the natural openness of the heart, you find the mind
naturally accepting. In essence, acceptance comes from letting
go of who you thought you were, to open to the vast connectedness, the universal compassion that lies just beneath the grasping at separate thoughts of a separate self. Opening right now to
this great unknown moment unfolding as it will instant to instant."

When Anthony asked how he might more deeply open the
heart energy to healing, it seemed appropriate to offer a practice called the "warmth and patience breath." It is a centering
of the attention on the sensation in the chest area. Breathing in
and out of your heart. With each inhalation drawing in warmth
and kindness. With each exhalation slowly breathing out the
tension and holding, cultivating that quality of patience.
Breathing in warmth, breathing out patience. Each in-breath
deepening a kind of warmth, a nurturing quality that increases
confidence in the process and allows the seeds of self-awareness
to germinate. Each exhalation deepening the patience that allows room for that deep growth to take place. The patience
generated on the out-breath is not the patience of waiting for
something to happen, for that is actually impatience; it is instead that allowing quality which opens to things just as they

are. It is not rushing anything. The warmth of the in-breath
nurtures that germination. The patience of the out-breath gives
it space to grow as it will. It is one of those deceptively simple
practices with which many have found comfort and insight. In
an odd way, sending this love directly into your tumors is not so
different from sending love to your dad.

Ten days later Anthony called to say he had experienced
"something inside me breaking open like a cyst—blood and pus
everywhere, love and fear as far as the eye could see." When I
asked him what his experience was, he said, "Yesterday was an
exceptional day for me, sort of a breakthrough period, an emotional day, something I often don't allow myself to have. I am so
busy keeping it together. At one moment I was sitting listening
to some music and the effect on me had me wanting to cry. So I
did. When I looked inside I found the tears were about joy and
thinking the music was beautiful. When I looked under that, I
saw a lot of sadness, it was all sorrow and pain. It seems the pain
is the years of closing off, of manipulating life. Lately, I am
beginning to see there is *nothing* to hold onto. And yet that is
what I am doing every moment of my life. Closing tighter
around pain. Shutting down to the uncertainty of things.

"So yesterday I began to see what that sadness was about, and
how I create it. So as the day ended and I reflected on my
emotions, I let the sadness come up and I lay there crying. I
noticed how I would not let myself surrender and how much
more pain that was. I saw how I don't cry because I am frightened by that part of me. I feel part of me is dying a small death
right now. The part of me which holds to what I thought 'a man'
is supposed to be. That act isn't me. Part of me is dying maybe to
let the rest of me come to life."

The warmth and patience breath seemed to be giving Anthony more confidence and strength in which to grow. As he
examined the conflict with his father and the conflict with himself, he saw more deeply how he had been pushing away his
healing. Now with the breathing in of warmth and the expansion of patience, he felt there was "room to heal, even to die" if
need be, but without an urgency, without a fight against life. In
a real sense, by allowing his illness to be as it was, he now had
access to it as never before, and he could work on it deeply with
a new trust in something essential in himself. He was beginning

to take responsibility without blame. In the past few days the sensation was slowly returning to his arms and legs as he felt a new sense of being in the world, a new wholeness which came out of entering directly into the predicament without dragging along the mind's reflections of others and fears of itself. "You know," he said, "God is my friend, though I don't understand all his ways." Sensing it might deepen his "don't know" trust in the process, I shared with him the story of St. Teresa at the time she was dying of consumption in her monastic cell, when, as the story goes, she called to Jesus of the immense discomfort in her body as she slowly moved toward death. "Jesus, why have you stricken your faithful servant? I have loved you so much and you have given me such pain." When in return she heard the soft voice of Jesus saying, "But I give pain to all my friends." To which Teresa replied, "Perhaps that is why you have so few."

Anthony and I laughed together for a moment and set a time to be together in the near future.

Over the next year Anthony undertook what he called "some new, radical delights"—acupuncture, herbal medicine, special dietary disciplines—and deeper levels of self-acceptance, of the warmth and patience meditation, directed into the cancer seemed to aid in a remarkable healing. The swelling of his face and lips decreased, his energy returned.

A: "So now I am my own parent and my own healer and it all fits just right. In fact, I spoke to my dad the other day, and instead of the old hassling there was a feeling of protectiveness for him. I wasn't afraid of him. I just loved him. And I must say, it sure shut him up. He started out the same old way; then when I told him how it was going for me, he just stopped and broke down and cried. It was the first time I have ever seen him cry. I was his father there for a while. I just loved him. And you know, all of that feels OK, but now that my energy is back I have another problem. I am horny!"

S: "So what else is new!? All the old ways of being in the world will present themselves once again. But you can meet it all in a new way. In the heart's way. This healing, this love you have been sending, goes deeper than just the body. It is all new now, no need to force goals. And the sexual thing is a very common way people who have been quite ill notice that they are re-

entering the world. It's the same for people who are quite ill on
and off and between symptoms occasionally notice a little dusty
lust floating through. It means the body is ready for action
again, so to speak, and you know, it is the same on every level.
Just as with your illness you had to break the 'struggle syndrome,' so too now it may be well to remember the old adage
from the sixties, 'Make love, not war.' Let even your sexual
energy be one of healing instead of the old control fears—no
panic, no urgency, just the sharing of love and delight. Or if I
want to be really corny, I could say 'de-light,' the light.''
A: "Well, I'm real open to that, but right now I have no lovers
and I'm feeling real lonely and pretty unselective. I was talking
to a friend about this recently and told him I was praying for
understanding, and he said facetiously, 'Forget all that, pray for
sex.' And I had to laugh, but lately I must admit I have thought
about it seriously.''
S: "Whatever works! But I am not sure how the heavens receive
prayers from the groin. Just do it with a bit more humor and a
bit less frantic lust. Warmth and patience, patience and trust. As
a friend of mine said, 'God is a hell of a matchmaker.' And
remember when you ask for something in a prayer you are
really just praying to yourself, but when you sit in prayer with a
willingness to listen, you receive God, you receive deeper and
deeper levels of yourself—you may even discover that there is
no such thing as 'strangers' but only a oneness that all share.
Imagine making love from this oneness instead of the fearful
grasping at satisfaction with which we so often approach sex.
And enjoy. Let go of the struggle. Make love, not war.''

As Anthony returned to the world, to a new job, to new
friends and lovers, the healing continued on many levels.

Anthony called several months ago and I asked him how
things were going. He said, "I am just doing my life." His cancer
has completely disappeared. "Now the trick is not to lose all that
I have learned. To let go into it. To get on with it.''

Who Dies?

STAN

Late one evening we received a call from Stan. "I am sorry to be calling so late, but I have been struggling with this all day. It is so hard for me to ask for help. But it seems that I am going to die from this lung cancer."

Stan went on to say that he was a plumbing contractor who had found out three months before, during a regular checkup, that there were spots in his lungs. In the last months his ability to work and play had been greatly diminished by the pain and the short-windedness of his condition. "You know, in these last months I have looked back at my whole life and found nothing that really helps me to face this. Actually, the only thing I have done that seems to prepare me to die is a weekend workshop I did twelve years ago with Ram Dass. Somehow something I learned then still whispers in my head. That helps some but I feel as though I am on a treadmill of 'me, me, me, me.'"

When I asked him how all those "me's" felt, he said, "frustrated, completely frustrated." I asked him what was he not getting from life that left him feeling so frustrated, to which he replied, "I guess it is fear and being so completely unprepared to be so sick, much less to die." When I asked him, "Does your frustration come from a feeling of incompleteness?" his response came back in an angry howl: "Complete! Nothing is complete! Everything feels like loose ends. What the hell was my life all about? Where has it gone? Why is this happening to me? But most of all I feel so alone, so unprepared . . . my life feels like a failure. I have a sense of an endless hall with numerous 'me's' at different levels." I asked him, "What do all these 'me's' have to say?"

Stan said with great frustration: "Everything! Sometimes I am

so confused I just wish I could die right now and get it done
with. It doesn't seem like I will ever see any light at the end of
that endless hallway. I am lost in myself."

When we first speak with someone, we are often somewhat
surprised at the particular technique we hear ourselves offer.
The process is a very intuitive one. Stan's connection with the
weekend workshop some years before indicated a deeply spiritual tendency, particularly since this seemed to be the only
frame of reference that gave him any kind of support. Though
Stan was manifesting the anger and pain that anyone might in
his predicament, there was somehow, through all the anger, still
a sense of some deeper potential for "breaking through." A
sense that perhaps he might be able to use the "Who am I?"
technique of self-investigation that several of those we have
worked with had found to be of immense use.

S: "Who is this self who is so lost?"
St: "Huh?"
S: "Bear with me a minute. Let's just share a moment of investigation. You say that you are suffering, frustrated, doubting existence itself. And I am asking you *who* is this that is frustrated?
Who is suffering? You are saying, 'Well, it's me,' and I am simply
asking you to whom does this 'me' refer?

"If you try to fight the frustration, to fight fear and confusion,
it will tighten around you like a noose. So instead of being
strangled by the confusion and frustration, let's investigate who
or what this noose is tightening around. Just for a moment let's
investigate the mind with its 'endless halls of me, me, me.' How
often have you listened quietly to its different voices and attitudes, just watched its conflicts and frustrations, instead of
opening every door and straying down every corridor? Let's
stop for a moment and try to get some sense of 'who' is experiencing all this rather than getting lost in the experience."
St: "What good is that going to do me?"
S: "Perhaps instead of getting lost in the fear, you may be able to
get some space around your predicament. Is there even some
satisfactory answer, some 'me' that is always the same? Is the
'me' of the forty-five-year-old fellow who is dying the same 'me'
as when you were six? Or do you just find incessant change
whenever you look for some solid 'me' on which you can plant

your flag? Isn't the 'me' you are trying to protect just a title of the imagined solidness you fear you will lose upon dying? But who is this precious 'me' that you fear losing?"

St: "Do you think this will help?"

S: "Well, right now you have no space, no peace, because every voice of every conflicting aspect of mind fills you with tension and confusion. Can you just listen to the voices? Can you just begin to watch the different personas rise and pass away in the hallway of change? One voice constantly replacing the other. A moment of frustration, a moment of fear, a moment of doubt, a moment of understanding, a moment of pride, and lost once again in the flickering lights of the dark hallway of the mind."

St: "I am not sure I understand what you are saying. Are you saying that there is no 'me'? Because if you are, that is just a lot of bullshit. I am suffering!"

S: "No. I am saying that who you really are is not what the mind is calling 'me.' And that if you begin to let go of all those imagined 'me's,' only the truth will remain. And perhaps beyond the separate 'me' you will find something universal, some inseparable quality of being. You may discover the deathless. Anything the mind says it is, know that is not the whole truth. When you are in pain and you ask yourself, 'Who is in pain?' sensations are experienced, but who do they stick to? In pain, for instance, it is that sense of 'me,' of 'someone suffering,' that seems to intensify the anguish. Indeed, the stronger the sense of 'me,' the more difficult it is to deal with pain. The more there is a 'me,' the more there is someone to suffer. 'Me' is the name of our resistance to life, of our constant angling for satisfaction. It is precisely that 'me' which fears death. The idea of being someone with something to lose—attributes, reputation, family, security, safe territory. Who is this 'me' who is suffering? Who dies?"

St: "Well, I hear what you are saying, but it still feels like *me* who is dying from cancer!"

S: "Which 'me'? I know this sounds strange but lets stay with it a moment more. It's sort of like learning algebra. At first, it seems impossible that x will ever become decipherable, that it will always remain 'the unknown quantity.' Then after hanging out with it all for a while, it suddenly becomes self-evident. We have nothing better to do right now anyhow, so let's play with this one.

"When I ask you which 'me,' I am not trying to trip you. I am simply asking, that with all these acknowledged voices, with all these different 'me's,' which one is the real 'me'? You have always called yourself 'me' from two years old on until now. But that 'me' always referred to someone different. Or is there some constant 'me' behind it all? Some unchanging 'me'? If I should ask you 'Who is dying,' how would you respond?"

St: "I am!"

S: "Well, Stan, when you say 'I am,' to whom does that refer?"

St: "Well, I guess I mean Stan, the owner of a plumbing business, the father of my children, the protector of my family . . . some poor asshole dying of cancer."

S: "What is this sense of 'I am' that is behind all the guises? You know, when you say, 'I am this' or 'I am that,' there is always something to lose and somehow it is never the whole truth. There is always some feeling of being an impostor whenever there is a 'this' or 'that' attached to the pure sense of being, to that experience of pure consciousness which the mind refers to as 'I am.' But with just this 'I am' there is a very different experience. There is just a sense of being, of presence. But in all these 'thises' and 'thats,' there is the basis of all the confusion and conflict, of every holy war, that the mind experiences. Go into the 'I am' itself. Investigate this open space. Just consciousness. In fact, if you stay with it, the 'I' dissolves and only the 'amness' remains. Just being itself, another opportunity to touch the deathless.

"It is the 'I am this' that suffers when you can't support your family any longer because you are too ill to get out of bed. Who is the owner of that plumbing business when your lung capacity is so diminished that you can't work for more than an hour a day? Who is this father and lover, husband and protector who can't husband his family, father his children? Our 'I am this' has been so well-cultivated that when you can't maintain your *doing* you feel like a failure."

St: "Well, that's what is so frustrating. I just can't be who I have always been. My body is getting weaker and thinner and I hardly have the energy to climb the stairs sometimes. I just lie there in bed sometimes and listen to the kids in the next room, and I am just so damn frustrated that I can't get up and help. What is happening to me? How come I feel so lousy? Not just in

my body but everything. Everything feels so lousy to me. I feel so cut off, so alone. Why is this so damn hard?"
S: "There are a lot of ways we could approach this. But it is my sense that for you the simplest and most direct way is to begin examining who is sick, who it is that is going to die, who it is that is so frustrated. That may sound a little bizarre right now, but my sense is that you have the capacity to break through this pain and holding that is keeping you so locked away from life and trapped in your fear and frustration."

We finished the conversation with a few stories about others who had used this technique with some success. Success being some sense of greater space around all these things that are happening. Not that the happenings change so much but that the space in which they are experienced is very different.

S: "The attitude toward the illness can change radically and allow whatever the next perfect step of healing may be, whether it be the displacing of cancer from the body or the displacing of 'you' from the cancer. I don't know what is right for you. Only you can find your way through. You must lead yourself gently and with great awareness. That the weekend twelve years ago should have so much importance for you makes me sense that there may be a way through your predicament. That it is the investigation of the spirit, of the experience of being, which may be your deepest healing, your greatest freedom. 'I' is just an *idea* of who you are. It is not who you really are."

Three days later Stan called: "Well, as bizarre as this investigation all sounds, somehow it feels like it might be useful. I will do anything."

S: "When you say, 'I'll do anything,' who is this 'I' who will do anything? Or is it just the mind continuing to pretend to be someone?"
St: "Well, I don't know. I guess it's still some idea of some 'me.' "
S: "Good. Keep that 'don't know.' It has room for the truth. Let's take it a step deeper. Which 'me' in that hallway are you

referring to? Is it the frustrated 'me'? the frightened 'me'? the
anticipatory 'me'? the angry 'me'?"

St: "I guess it is the willing 'me.' Go on with it. What comes
next?"

S: "Perhaps you might want to take some time to investigate
these states of mind like willingness, fear, frustration, doubt. See
what their nature is and see who is experiencing these states. Or
do frustration, doubt, joy, the full range of emotions just float in
some space? Investigate, ask yourself, 'Who is willing? Who is
frustrated?' Go to the vastness of being beyond the mind. Behind the voices, what is the throat of the truth?"

St: "I can feel my brain heating up just trying to answer this
question. It almost gives me a fever. But I've got no other place
to turn to."

S: "You may be trying to understand all this with the mind.
Instead, just listen with your heart, with your intuition. Don't
try to grasp it, just allow it to soak in. When I ask you who you
are and you say, 'Don't know,' you say it from frustration, from
confusion. But actually, in that 'don't know' is great peace. The
reason there is fear and tension around that question is that you
are scrambling for an answer, which just creates more of 'someone to protect.' Let go of your 'knowing' who you are, of who
you think of as 'me,' because this 'me' seems to be the sufferer.
Ironically, the mind is scrambling to hold onto its suffering, to its
fear of death. What I am suggesting to you is that you begin to
investigate who it is that is experiencing all this. The way that
you do it is to ask, 'Who am I?' Don't fight the experience,
explore it. Don't fight the mind. 'Who is experiencing this?'
'Don't know.' 'Don't know' arises and is met by resistance and
becomes confusion if you demand an answer. Just stay with the
question. If you just allow that 'don't know,' there is the possibility of freedom. You become vulnerable to the truth. Your mind
only knows what it has been taught. It has never learned who it
really is.

"When you investigate this sense of being, that to which you
refer when you say 'I am,' does that sense of being, of suchness,
of endless presence seem to have a beginning and an end, or is it
just 'is'?

"It is the 'me,' the content of the mind, the different thoughts,
the self-image, the models of oneself, the self-reflections, the

self-pity and fear that create a barrier to allowing life in, that
cause you to feel trapped by your predicament. Who is trapped?
Or is it just that all these models and all these self-images have
always been a trap that now becomes evident when you can no
longer fill it with your doing? The self-image is like a balloon
with a few pinpricks in it that you have to keep puffing up or
else it deflates and becomes flaccid and pitiful. Maybe it isn't the
illness that is the cause of your suffering, maybe the cancer is
just putting you in touch with your holding to old ways of being
in the world. Perhaps it is your self-image, no longer constantly
able to be reconstructed, that is causing your suffering."
St: "When I ask myself, 'Who is listening to all this?' my mind
has a dozen answers. But none of them help. When I ask myself,
'Who is thinking?' I just get more thoughts. Stephen, who is
thinking?"
S: "You know, Stan, it is not so much that you receive an answer
but that you keep asking this question so that it will take you
further and further behind the sufferer, the 'me,' the 'I' that has
something to protect and is scrambling for safe territory, behind the mind itself. The 'I' that is having the rug pulled out
from under it by cancer, by no longer being able to maintain its
persona, its mask in the world. When you let go of that mask,
what face is beneath? It is a bit like the classic Zen question
'What was your face before you were born?' Under that mask of
your doing, your name, your body, your attachments, there is
just the space that it is all floating in, just awareness itself. Are
you other than that? Who are you? Who is thinking?"
St: "Well, when I am thinking, if I am real quiet and watch it real
closely—like you suggested the other day—I mean the
thoughts, I see that, at times, anyhow, I can see that, thoughts
are just moving around. If I am sitting in my chair looking out
the window and I watch myself looking out the window, I notice that in a funny way the eyes are doing the looking and that
the 'me' who I say is seeing it all really comes afterward. It is
another thought and it is a little scary sometimes cause I am
almost not there. It is just as though this 'I' is just more thinking.
It is almost as though 'I' comes after it all."
S: "Yes, where is this 'me'? Or is it just an afterthought? Does
this 'me' just follow us like some lost dog begging for a home?
And we keep throwing scraps to this idea that constantly de-

mands feeding, that whines for recognition, that demands attention. Be gentle with this lost beast, be kind to it. Make friends with it, come to know it well, see that it is not you, that it is just another voice in the hallway, another growl behind closed doors. A whimpering in the shadows. Watch fear crouching in the dark corner, unsure whether to attack or run away with its tail between its legs."

Stan and I spoke for some time of the technique that the remarkable Indian teacher Ramana Maharshi called Vichara Atman, whereby one investigates one's experience by constantly asking "Who am I?" constantly investigating this sense of self around which all fear and doubt accumulates, asking the great questions, "Who is it who is alive? Who is suffering? Who understands? Who investigates?" Until it all goes back and you find yourself behind the mind experiencing deeper and deeper levels of being. Until there is no one separate from life or from death and just being unfolds moment to moment. It is the experience of the deathless, the investigation of being, the exploration of our original nature beyond our identification with the body or the mind.

S: "As one teacher put it, 'When you let go of everything only the truth remains.' It will take courage and perseverance to let go of the holdings which cause you suffering—to find out who it is that experiences all this. It may be difficult at times and luminously self-evident at other times, but still that keen, openhearted watching, that mercy with our self that is willing to hold nowhere, that is willing to let go of its suffering, will take you through. It will take as much courage to investigate this sense of being, to let go of the sufferer, as it will to confront the illness in your body, to be eye to eye with this cancer, with this process of degeneration in the body."

Five days later Stan called again, his voice filled with excitement. "Wow! This is the weirdest. The other night around four in the morning I was having a lot of trouble breathing, and I found myself coughing a lot and becoming very frightened, and I remembered what we had spoken about and I asked myself, 'Who is coughing?' and the mind had all these things to say, but when I just focused on the sensations of the coughing, as you suggested, I found that the coughing was just happening in the body, and in a funny way the body was just happening in the mind. It almost felt as though I were watching someone else cough. The coughing was there, the sensations were there, even the fear was there, but somehow I wasn't suffering. There seemed no 'me' to be frightened. It was the weirdest experience I ever had. Here is all this coughing and sputum but there was no tension. There was just this constant hum in my mind that kept asking, 'Who is coughing?' And the only answer that came back was, 'Coughing is coughing.' I don't know what is going on but I hope it continues. Now I have to ask myself, 'Who is excited by all this?' "

S: "Who is excited by all this?"
St: "I don't know but there is excitement. There is a sense of getting into something that is actually going to be of some help. I thought there was no where to turn. Now I ask myself, 'Who is turning?' It is the weirdest."
S: "It looks like this technique is just right for you. You see that everything is workable, even pain and fear. It isn't always easy, because the content of the mind is so seductive. The content keeps saying: 'I am what you are. I am pain. I am confusion. I am the real thought. All the others are just dreams.' But they are just more bubbles, more milliseconds of thought constantly changing in vast space. In the space of pure awareness. You know, the last time we talked, I asked you who you were, and you said you were a father, a plumber, a bread winner, a sexual entity, but each role you added only seemed to create more frustration, more of a separate 'I' to suffer.

"Maybe you can see just a bit more how whenever you say, 'I am this or that,' there is some feeling of frustration, some feeling of incompleteness that the whole truth somehow just can't be articulated in a single breath. There is no 'I am this' which remains for very long. One moment we are a frustrated 'I am' and the next moment an excited 'I am' and the next moment a pained 'I am,' but all these 'thises' and 'thats' that we attach to the 'I am' are just the names of our suffering."

We spoke about how if you made a list of all these "thises" and "thats," they would be our fear of death, our distance from our original nature. They would be our holding to our superficiality, our constant creation of the universe in our own image and likeness. We investigated again how whenever we say, "I am this or that," there is always some feeling of being an impostor, that somehow we cannot say all of who we are. "It is time for you to let go of being an impostor, to let go of the mind's constant posturing and hiding. Indeed, Stan, it may be time to die out of your limited idea of yourself into the great 'don't know' out of which will arise the truth of your real nature." Exploring together his recent experience of not being "the cougher" but of just being—with no "this" or "that" attached— he saw how there were no endless halls of "me's," but just content floating in the vast spaciousness of awareness. Just thought floating through who he really is. How by not grasping at any of the objects, and not pulling back, his experience just began to float in "don't know," in the vast investigation of be-ing, of who dies, of who was born.

St: "These last five days I have experienced some of the most interesting moments of my life, and yet oddly, I can't really say 'I' experienced them. They were just experiences that seemed not to be so dense, or actually they seemed very dense, but they didn't seem to be experienced in much denseness. What is the next step?"
S: "When you say, 'I am excited,' to what does that 'I' refer? That is the whole practice. When you say, 'I am excited,' it means that you are noticing excitement, that excitement is being experienced. It means there are states of mind arising and dissolving all by themselves.

"As we speak, close your eyes and just investigate that 'I feel excitement' feeling. Feeling is there and there is also a sense of 'I.' To what does this sense of 'I' refer? There is a presence, a sense of just 'I am' which when you follow it back further and further will turn more into 'am-ness' than 'I-ness.'

"Let thoughts come and go as they will, and begin to focus on how each just arises spontaneously, then disappears, so fragile, so impermanent. Then you get some sense of the space in which they are happening. Just the experience of being, of your suchness, the vast space in which all life is unfolding. You know, in an odd way your whole life you have acted on the assumption that if you can see it, you are not it. Right? The reason you know you are not a tree is because you can see it. It is seemingly outside you or other than you. The 'reason' you think you are not a rock is because you can feel it, see it, kick it. Anything you can see you feel is not you. So why after a lifetime of seeing thoughts, do you still think they are you.

"Look at thoughts as you would a tree. Examine their branches and leaves, their foliage and root system. See how they grow and change all by themselves. Do not mistake what is watching for that which is being watched. Do not mistake yourself, your true nature, for these ever moving bubbles in the mind.

"So who is this 'you'? Is it simply the object of observation? Who is the observer? Or does observation occur all by itself in pure awareness?"

St: "Well, all my feelings and thoughts just seem to come and go, but 'who' is watching it all flashing through I can't define. It's not one of the things I can 'see'—it is where seeing is coming from—it's sort of like not being able to see my own eyes 'cause I'm looking through them at the time."

S: "Language doesn't hold it too well at this point. Only the investigation that goes behind the mind, behind the source of language, can directly experience itself. Beyond language or any need for definition lies the deathless peace of your true being.

"Experience is happening but you are not the experience."

St: "That one I'm getting! Yeah, yeah, I know, 'Who is getting it?' Right!"

S: "The mind is conditioned to relate to each object as the knower knowing the known. But in reality, is your experience of the known or the knower? Or is it just the experience of knowing itself? Just an ongoing process?

"Stan, you are not a noun. You are a verb. A constantly changing process ever unfolding into its next open moment.

"The knower and the known dissolve like bubbles in the mind. Just more ideas, just old mind floating in the ever-newness of pure awareness.

"Let the knower and the known die into the knowing itself.

"Let the 'someone' dissolve into the underlying reality. Let experience be seen on the screen of consciousness and maintain the vigil—Who am I? Who experiences?"

We spoke for another half hour, Stan telling me how this investigation was for him and how hard it was to let go of all the things he had learned to be, to which I replied: "Can you notice what the mind is doing? It is sort of playing its top forty. The mind is going to throw up 'oldies but goodies' again and again. All the ways of your being, all of your doing that you identified with, that you attached to the 'I am,' is going to reassert itself again and again. This is the investigation of life itself. It goes beyond even someone dying. It goes to the very heart of the matter. Your mind is going to take certain themes that it is particularly conditioned to play out. Very deep conditioning that 'I am the body,' 'I am what I do,' but you are not measurable by what you do. You are the very essence of truth. Not as an idea but as a directly experienceable essence of being. We keep thinking that we are the contents of our mind, but actually we are the space in which those contents are happening. That space doesn't really care what the contents are, but we keep losing that space because we think, 'I am the content.' All the other tunes in the top forty insist on recognition, so you say, 'Well then, I am that,' which also has a feeling of partial truth about it. But when you simply say, 'I am,' just 'I am,' the whole truth seems accessible. There is no question to be answered and no answer to be questioned, just the wholeness to be experienced.

"You can just sit in the 'I am,' and your mind will become quiet and your eyes will close and there will just be the presence of being, and somehow that presence of being, because it is not so lost in time, has a feeling of timelessness, of deathlessness about it. 'I am this' is going to change. 'I am that' is going to move. Everything, all content in the mind, in the world, is in motion, is constantly arising, existing but for an instant, and dissolving. But in 'I am' there is just pure being. Investigate again and again to what does this 'I am' refer? What is that feeling of presence? Examine 'I am' and you will come to the screen of consciousness itself.

"You will watch awareness meet object after object of the

senses, a moment of seeing, a moment of hearing, a moment of feeling, a moment of thinking, constantly changing. A flow unfolding instant to instant in vast boundaryless awareness. All is happening within that sense of presence. Focus on presence itself, on being, and see if there is anyone left to be afraid. As one teacher said, 'If there is anyone in there to suffer, they will.' "

Over the next three months, as Stan found his body becoming weaker and necessitating more days of bed rest, we continued our investigation. Clearly, it was the appropriate technique for his temperament. As he said one day, "You know, the more I investigate 'Who am I?' the more alive I feel. The easier it is to just be where I am, even if I feel pretty lousy that day. The less I am fighting life. In some ways this is the most fascinating thing I've ever done. I wish I had gotten going on this one sooner, but I am thankful that I've gotten into this as soon as I have. I am nowhere near being liberated or any of that stuff, but in some ways I have never been more interested in my life. I've never given more attention to what is going on around me or inside me. In fact, goofy as it may sound, I feel as though I have never been so here. What a miracle! It's just remarkable to not hold on to my suffering and just be. In some ways I see what you mean when you say I don't have to be anything or anyone to be of value. Just being itself is so full. My body may be falling apart but I have never been more whole."

About five months after we met, Stan called to say that his doctor had told him, "There is nothing more we can do for you.

"I have received my final death sentence today. No reprieve. No court of appeal and although I am frightened, it's OK. It feels weird, but my sense is that although my body is probably going to die, whoever I really am will continue this investigation until it just is what it is all by itself. But you know, that's just part of it. I don't always feel so at peace with dying. Sometimes I feel a lot of self-pity, and when I ask myself, 'Who is pitying?' the mind is so full of doubt that it just doesn't want to investigate. It calls me an asshole for not trusting it, for abandoning it."

S: "Well, you know, when the mind has a lot of self-pity, it is very seductive. In fact, doubt is perhaps our greatest obstacle to a deeper investigation, because it says, 'There is nothing to investigate, don't bother, this is all a scam, how could you be so foolish?' But these are all just old thoughts floating, if you can see them as such. The mind is liable to spend a lot of time reflecting with pity on itself instead of getting on with it. All that you are experiencing is mind. What if the mind continues to create as much after death as it does now? What a wonderful opportunity now to open to self-pity, to doubt, to not be drawn in.

"Who is experiencing doubt? When you say, 'I don't like it,' or 'I need a way out,' to what does that 'I' refer? Who is it now? Or better yet, who has it always been? Go behind the mind. You are looking to thought for an answer, like a drunk in the lamplight searching for the keys lost around the corner in a dark alley— but the alley is too dim to explore, so he stays in the pool of lamplight where the looking is easier though the keys are not to be found. The thinking mind is like that. It searches itself for the truth which it does not contain in its entirety.

"Be very gentle with the mind now. The least force will close your heart, will cause confusion. Trust that great 'don't know' of the investigation. Who pities himself? When the mind says 'I,' what is the sense of 'I'? Is the 'I' of this moment the same 'I' that pitied itself hours ago? Or is it just consciousness itself? There is confusion because the mind thinks it is the confusion, but you are not the mind.

"As you relate more and more *to* the mind instead of *from* it, the various 'thises' and 'thats' which often obscure the 'I am' of pure being are just noticed as the comings and goings of the passing show. Awareness, which creates consciousness in the same manner that light allows images to be projected on a movie screen, never changes, though the objects on the screen of consciousness are constantly changing. Touch the eternal now.

"You know your mind is listening to what is being said now and interpreting it, but behind the mind there is a vast stillness, there is just being. In fact, everything you call 'I'—all the 'thises' and 'thats'—float on the screen of consciousness. Focus on that screen and all the objects just turn into motion, constantly aris-ing and dissolving, and only the nonclinging spaciousness of pure awareness, just the light by which they are seen, is experienced. Self-pity dissolves when there is no sense of a separate self to pity.

"As your confidence in this process of letting go into 'don't know' deepens yet further, I sense that self-pity will not catch you in the same way that it does now. Just listen to the top forty without choosing favorites. Just notice all the mind projects, all the 'me's' in the corridor, and keep moving toward the light by which all this is seen. Don't mistake the seen for the seer. Don't mistake the known for the knower. Just see, just know. Allow yourself to rest in the act of being. Allow yourself to receive life as it unfolds in the deathless nature of your true being."

Stan called back two days later to say: "How fantastic to watch doubt dissolve in the vastness. To see that even that is not me. No wonder the mind is so full of self-pity; it is jumping in so many directions at once; it has learned to be so confused. There is no place to put my feet, nowhere to go, but this moment is enough—in fact, it is all there is and all there ever has been."

S: "And all there ever will be. Just this luminescent now in which all life floats, in which death does not exist. In which there is only being, only this present moment passing through the presence of being."

Over the next month, as Stan became weaker and found it increasingly difficult to speak, his wife Clarice would call every few days to tell us how things were going and to transmit any questions he might have. She said that he wanted to tell us, "I don't know who it is who is dying, but whoever it is, he's chock-full of love."

Clearly his closeness to the family had increased over the past six months, and now they found little that remained unsaid, now a soft touch of the hand or the contact of clear eyes seemed the language of the moment. Clarice said, "When Stan first received the diagnosis, he was so depressed and withdrawn and frustrated that it seemed like this was going to be a horror show for all of us. But that's not the way it's turning out. He used to be so involved with his business. He hardly had time for the family. But now his priorities have changed so. The children feel so cared for by him that they often mention how good it feels to go into his room even though they say it 'smells funny.' I have a feeling that we have finished something together, and as he says, 'I don't know anything that could have happened that would have brought this much love and this much feeling into the house. It's a miracle.' " She went on to say, "Sometimes I don't know what to feel. It was so hard for Stan at the beginning, but now it seems as though he has been doing this work his whole life. Maybe he has. Maybe we both have. We haven't been this close for so long. I will miss him awfully."

About a week later she called to read us part of a letter from a friend of theirs whom we had worked with who had lost two children in the last three years. She quoted: "The pit I was in already opened at the bottom and I really started getting down. We buried Michael and someone suggested we get in touch with Stephen and his wife Ondrea. They came to our house immediately and to say that they helped is an understatement. . . . 'Who dies?' Stephen asked over and over. Ondrea hugged and hugged us and absorbed all our tears. Stephen insisted we answer. 'Who dies?' Eventually we snapped and experienced the oceanic, edgeless feeling or state that the question 'Who dies?' leads to.

"You know," she said, "if I had read this a year ago, I wouldn't have known what they were talking about, but now it feels like whatever grace might be. And you know, I think that 'edgeless, oceanic feeling' that our friend spoke about in his letter is a regular experience for Stan in the last few weeks. There is a part of me that wants to thank you without limit for sharing this with him, but there is another part that knows how hard he worked to get through his pain, and so I thank him instead and I thank the universe for our ability to go beyond our doubt and fear."

A few days later Clarice called to say that Stan had died at sunset the evening before with his children sitting next to him on the bed and his wife gently stroking his brow. It had been difficult for Stan to speak in the last few days, and so on the afternoon of the day he had died, he had indicated that he wanted crayons and a piece of his five-year-old's drawing paper. In the next two hours, working on and off with the crayons, he had completed a picture of a family of four standing happily outside of a house, surrounded by trees and flowers, pets and other familiar objects. All four were holding hands and looking at the sun. On the bottom of the drawing in strong lines he had written a quote from Crazy Horse, the American Indian shaman, one of his favorites over the last six months, which said, "Today is a good day to die for all the things of my life are present."

Losing Life, Choosing Death

EVELYN

Evelyn first called about four years ago. Her physician, who had attended our workshops in the past, suggested she contact us. Evelyn's body was slowly deteriorating from ALS, also known as Lou Gehrig's disease, a neuromuscular degenerative disease that often consumes the body in discomfort and eventual paralysis and death. Her husband had died from cancer two years before, "As I stood next to the bed, his eyes receding into the darkness." Within a year after his death Evelyn had received a limited life prognosis as ALS became more evident in her body. Her hands and legs began to stiffen, losing their practiced agility. No longer able to work her ceramics or "play with the potting wheel," she was grieving the loss of her hands. In the first month of our work together, we investigated the possibility of her sending forgiveness to her body while gradually opening with some "don't know" to what the future might hold. The slow and often painful investigation of "the way I'm losing the world" seemed useful and our sharings continued for over two years until her death. What she laughingly referred to as her "almost sensual rasp" became instantly recognizable in the dozens of phone sharings we experienced together.

After having sat with our meditation group in Santa Cruz for nearly a year, Evelyn decided to "take the next step" and attend one of the Conscious Living/Conscious Dying workshops. On the second afternoon of the workshop, as we left the meditation hall walking down the hill toward the dining room, her foot slipped and she collapsed like a puppet whose strings had been cut. Walking a few feet behind her, I knelt and caught her in my arms, our eyes meeting in recognition of this "turning point." It was the first time her legs hadn't worked properly.

The fear of that moment was interrupted by an ironic laugh as she hoarsely said, "Act III," tears slowly forming in the corners of her eyes. Clearly the end game had begun.

Over the next year the increasing inability to control her body guided her into many "frightening and remarkable experiences." "But if only I could throw a pot, even one a month, it would make me feel so much better. But as this ALS eats my body, I find life less and less available."

At the second workshop that Evy attended, in the introductory circle a woman in her mid-fifties stood up wearing a Grateful Dead T-shirt that exposed her double mastectomy—flat-chested as a teenage boy—and said softly to the group, "Two years ago I was graced with cancer." Evy was instantly drawn to Barbara and they spent "good time together" over the following months. Eight months later, when Barbara died, Evy felt a yet deeper loss of her connection with life. As the paralysis affected her chest and lungs, her voice became thin and weak, broken by the sound of her gulping air in an attempt to maintain an even air pressure through her vocal cords. By now even speech had become a tedious, often painful undertaking.

Soon after Barbara's death I received a phone call from Evy, her voice shaky and broken by tears.

E: "I am experiencing total confusion and frustration. My mind is like a vise. All I experience is my illness. Sometimes I see the sun through the clouds, but usually it is just murky sickness. I feel like I am locked in a closet."

S: "As the life force is no longer so evident in the body, you are beginning to feel a kind of claustrophobia of being 'locked in' a deteriorating body. Now you can hammer and beat on the door of that closet and scream, which makes the experience hell, or you can sit quietly in the closet and begin to recognize it as only another room and that which sits within it as only experiencing 'a moment of darkness.' It's only a matter of time—something will open the closet door and eventually you will be let out. Now you can either kick down the door and run out frightened and trembling, wanting a place to hide, or you can sit with all the emotions that come up in the darkness of the unknown and begin to open to it and investigate the fear. Knowing that whatever work you do now locked in that closet will be the freedom which accompanies you when the light causes you to squint as you emerge from the darkness."

E: "I look everywhere but I find nothing but doubt and fear."

S: "If you are looking for peace of mind, you are, in a sense, going to be disappointed, because even under the best of circumstances the mind is movement and agitation. The only peace to be had right now may be the peace of the heart, the soft opening to the unknown, the allowing of the dark closet to convey its teachings.

"All you can do right now, Evy, is settle back into an investigation of what you are feeling. And when you ask yourself, 'Who is in such frustration and pain?' and come up with the answer 'I don't know,' don't be frustrated by that answer. *That 'don't know' is your freedom. It opens the mind to investigation of that which is beyond thought.*

"You can expect the mind at times to be very agitated and perhaps at other times to be somewhat more quiet. Just watch the ever changing process—don't be drawn in any more by the peaceful than by the fearful. Evy, this is the time to let go of your suffering. To start singing in the closet. It is your fearful projections of the future—which you have so often said moves toward you 'like an avalanche,' taking your body away, removing even your ability to stand or walk or move your bowels or speak clearly—that so darkens the closet. But we don't know what the future will bring. If this fearful anticipation can be seen as just another layer of mind that filters out the possibilities of the moment, this seeing can lead to an awareness that goes beyond fear and experiences the immense ocean of being that underlies it all."

E: "I feel like I am too inside it to get beneath it. This ALS is getting worse and worse. I have worked with so many physicians and healers and nothing seems to help. In fact, I met a couple of healers who felt real good to me and they worked with me a couple of times a week, but it didn't seem to get at it and finally I decided nothing would help. But then things kind of leveled out with the meditations and all and went along pretty alright for a while and then I broke my leg two months ago. And from that point on, it has just been one thing after another. The leg healed fine. The only thing that isn't healing is the ALS. I can't swim like I used to, so my range of motions has gone down.

My arms are almost useless and my leg that was broken—it weakened the muscles so and I guess the rest of it too. So my legs aren't all that good anymore and the trunk has totally gone west—literally. I have fantasies of eighteen feet of guts sticking out in front of me. So all the intercostal muscles seem to be gone and most of the support muscles in my abdomen. The only strong area in my body is in my shoulders and in my back. My lung capacity has gone to about fifty per cent of what it was. I am able to walk a little with a cane. My legs could probably get me around but they can't hold up the trunk."

I reminded Evy of the cancer patient we had worked with who, after a period of seven months remission, noticed a new tumor and called a healing circle of some of the most powerful healers in her area. The energy in the room was palpable. After an hour and a half all in the room said they felt the accumulated healing energy that had been generated. A week later the woman broke out in thirty new tumors and said: "Ahhh, the healing energy has worked. The next step has come about. Perhaps my healing will be beyond the body."

E: "I don't know if I'll ever get to that place. It is still such a struggle. In fact, I feel like I am in a last-ditch effort to keep my body. I am going to Los Angeles this weekend to be with a group of real strong healers, and I think part of what I feel is anticipation of what is going to happen when I am there. A part of me sits back and says, 'We will see for sure which way you are going to fly.' Maybe my dying *is* really the healing I am looking for."

We spoke of how to maintain healing meditations while it seemed that she was entering the final phases of ALS. How she might work with the falling away of the body and the falling away of all the ways she had been in the world as a deep healing of the heart. How the very nature of that holding was hell. "Because you can't hold onto how things have been in the past. They are not holdable. And all you are going to be left with is the rope burns from trying to grasp that which is being pulled beyond your grasp." To which she responded, "I understand but I just wish it were all over."

S: "Evy, although it seems like there are no alternatives, there is still one: the deep investigation of what is happening now. You have a chance to work with the falling away of things in a way that is seldom given. The yogi sitting in the cave has to go through it. It is in the biography of every saint and sage. The letting go of the world as the only reality. The moving through the pain of our suffering, our holding to things being any way at all. The yogi sits and has fantasies of food, of sex, of being home, of not having to work so hard—all the doubts of 'What the hell is this all for?' arise. They are the callings of the mind to distract one from the energies of the heart, from the pure openness of being that always awaits. What you are going through is very little different from a person who is in extreme and often isolated spiritual practice. The days when you lie there and cry because you don't know what is real and whether you are fooling yourself, whether there is such a thing as liberation—all that is the path of liberation. Don't expect your mind to die quietly. It fights yet harder than the body for its imagined existence. The full range of emotions will roll through again and again on the way to a deeper recognition of the deathless."
E: "I need to be reminded of that again and again. When I understand, I feel such peace. But then I will get caught up again in not being able to talk well or use my hands much and I think of what's yet to come and I hear the closet door slam behind me. The light is so short-lived."
S: "Evy, you know, it's ironic, but maybe you will have to be even weaker before you can let go. Maybe you have to lose even more facility before that thing inside you which holds on so frighteningly will at last see that it is impossible to maintain its grasp. And in that letting go—not the surrender of defeat, but the surrender of courage and a willingness to go beyond old ways of being—it may come that great freedom arises because you are directly in the present and less drawn out by the fear of the future. Then perhaps there won't be so much pushing away of what is happening, so much hell blocking your experience of the moment. No one is saying it's going to be easy, but it seems the only alternative to this fear and identification with the body.

"And whenever you do leave that body, whenever that may be, you may see that this whole situation was the reason you took birth in the first place. For this work is the work of understanding with trust and patience the process through which life passes. This is your marriage with yourself. As much as the death of your husband a few years ago, this is a deep exploration of your relationship to life—when you see all the ways of your doing peeled away and stunted in the world, you may discover the only satisfaction left is of pure being. Perhaps this is your teaching of trusting just being, of trusting this process. Indeed, look how much you have grown in the years we have known each other."

E: "God, yes. I have learned so much. I don't think I could have made it this far without the self-examination that I've done. I wish I had started earlier. It feels as though there is just not enough time left for me to get through it all. I sit here and look at the boats from my window and think, 'God, if there is anything in the world I would love to do before I die, it is to go sailing again.' "

After a moment's silence we both laughed because she knew what I was about to say.

S: "Well, my friend, you may be about to go sailing all right. But I don't think you are going to need a boat for it."
E: "That's called flying."
S: "Well, gliding actually. But you know, although it seems as if nothing is happening for you, Evy, it feels to me like a lot of work is being done. Living in this degenerating body is sort of like a mother forced to be always at home with her newborn. She is saying, 'Oh, this newborn is so much trouble, so much work. I just wish I could go out and go dancing. I want to go sailing, I want to work in my pottery studio, I want to go roller skating. But I can't.' The more that feeling of being deprived manifests itself, the less communion exists between that mother and her child. In a sense, my friend, you are in a process of giving birth to yourself right now. Your body is becoming more and more cocoonlike, less and less active. What is inside that chrysalis is going to break free, is going to go on and leave that

aching body behind. That body is your classroom. The illness is
your curriculum."
E: "You know, I believe this. That part I have no problem with.
But living is so beguiling and it hasn't been all pain. It has been
an enormous amount of pain, but it has been great joy too. And
it has all been worth it. It is just that sometimes I lose sight of
that. Sometimes I feel so cut off from the understanding that I
feel at other times."

Because Evy was having some trouble concentrating, we
spoke of using music as a means of quieting the mind and
opening the heart. "You can concentrate note to note on the
music, just as if each note were a breath, just moment to moment. Use guitar music or some individual instrument where
there is a single sound changing from moment to moment. Not
listening to the melody so much as going note to note. Each
note will dissolve behind you and each new note will arise in the
present. Music too is birth and death and it is a perfect analogy
for watching the mind."
We spoke some of the "reservoir of fear," the hidings and
posturings of a lifetime being focused in this moment, creating
the walls of "the closet." Her fear locking the door behind her
and closing her in with an ancient darkness that perhaps was
never so noticed or so acknowledged. "This fear is like a deep
well that is forced to the surface by the shifting pressures of an
earthquake. And as it is spilling across the ground you say, 'Oh,
my God! I've got more fear!' But it is not that there is more, it is
just that you are in touch with what has always been underneath. And though you may be dismayed by the amount of it, all
you can really do is be merciful with yourself. Send this fear
your forgiveness too. See that all this fear and doubt is natural as
the mind and body are confronted with their impermanence,
with a sense of their nonsolidity."

E: "You know, I think you are right, because it is not the ALS
that frightens me anymore, it is the unknown. Perhaps a little
anticipation and some resignation—sometimes it is even acceptance and sometimes I can't tell the difference. My mind goes
on like a steamboat and I wish I could just shut it off. But I
remember that magic word, 'soften,' and it helps me greatly to

just let things be as they are. Even the fear. Even the ALS. I keep trying to remember to open around my fear, to just let it float. I think you are right, it is like giving birth. I am just having the same kind of doubts about my death that I had about my children's birth. All the fantasies of malformation and stillbirth are there in my fear of giving birth to myself as well. I just need to take one breath at a time."

Two weeks later Evy called again.

E: "It is like being in a trough. You can turn over and over but you just can't get out. It is like being in the bottom of that dark closet. As long as I am lying flat in bed and not moving, I seem to be totally capable. I am all there. But the minute I get up and walk across the room or something, then the weakness hits and my legs give out and of course my hands don't work anyway and it's so kind of ambiguous, this whole thing, so there are no guidelines for what I can do, what I can't do. My grown children and everybody else who is helping seem confused about it all."
S: "It sounds like you are entering unexplored territory, and only you know the right path for your moving through. There are no maps and there is really no doing it right. We all just do the best we can. Just feeling our way along from instant to instant, discovering what the next teaching is, what the next need is, discovering the unknown from moment to moment. You must help those around you to know what you need. You can't even expect them to understand. All you can do is discover what is right for yourself and trust what you discover. And just notice how resistance creates hell. This is the time when you learn the deepest meaning of kindness. Kindness to yourself might be the most difficult path you will ever tread, because it is so unexplored and we have so little support for that kind of self mercy. But now you must be merciful with yourself and speak directly and honestly with those who are attempting to be of support to you. Tell them what you need. This is your time of learning to die by opening to each little death. The little death of not having control, of not having the world the way you want it to be. As we have shared so many times before, this whole situation clearly holds the teaching of how to open our hearts in hell."

Evy and I shared a long silence and then came the long, slow breath that preceded any attempt to speak.

E: "This is the most difficult learning. Daily I am confronted with my body unable to take care of itself. To even move when it wants to. It's that dark closet. Sometimes when it is worst, at two or three in the morning, and there is no one to help and I can't turn over without getting my arm caught under me and I just cry and am so frightened, sometimes at that moment something will happen when there is just no where to turn and all of a sudden there will be great peace. It may last till morning or even into the day but always it disappears. Always my fear of having a body like this overwhelms me, and no one seems to really understand what I am going through. Very few anyhow."

For the next fifteen minutes we shared ways in which Evy could use those moments of clarity while lying there to explore her situation. To watch closely when things seemed darkest how the quality of surrender, of just opening to the present, changed hell to heaven. We explored "the magic of opening even to the impossible and discovering what lies beyond." How even holding onto the peace that sometimes arose could cause pain. To allow her heart to be torn open to the impossibility of this moment. So that she could experience herself as something more than a body, than a dark closet. And always to be kind to herself, gently letting go of her suffering as she might without force or self-judgment.

E: "You know, this disease is like an entity of its own. It is an incredible thing. It is almost like a third person in the room that affects every relationship and every communication. Even with my married children it seems as though it is stirring up old pains. Sometimes we have fierce disagreements. Sometimes I can't tell if the disease is stirring up these resentments we have never worked through or is itself a reaction to so much life left incomplete."

When I asked Evy how she was resolving these difficulties with her children, she said, "I don't know. I just sit and listen and hope the kids can find some way to say all the things they need to say before I die."

S: "Are they speaking of anger from the past?"
E: "Yes. The disease and the unfinished business seem to be drawing each other out, if that is possible. It draws out my children's resentments and it draws out my resentments as well. It is like another presence in the room. And no one is protected from it."

We spoke of the contagion of fear. How if one holds to it instead of investigating it, it can solidify in the mind and be transmitted to all those about. How her children, in finding they can't protect her body from dying any more than they can protect their own, may feel considerable frustration from this lack of control and how it can cause emotional upheavals and great consternation, particularly on the part of those who care for her most. "But confusion too is just not knowing what to do when there is stress. They are stressed and their reaction to stress isn't a particularly useful one. As most people's aren't. They want to blame someone for your being sick and they can't find anyone to blame. So they just get stuck in the place of blame and it all comes spitting out."

E: "I was thinking that there are things I want to say to them, but I don't know."
S: "I would say whatever there is to say now while you still have the energy and ability to say it. But in a sense, that doesn't really finish business. What finishes business is when you let go of your holding to the old accounts, the end of relationships as 'business,' and just send love. I know it is very difficult now, but to whatever degree you want them to accept you, that is the degree to which you just won't allow yourself to be who you are, how you are. And now, as no other time in your life, is a time to just be there for yourself. Because under that resentment is frustration and under that frustration is more love than you can imagine. Don't try to bargain with their fears and resentments. Notice the hardness and mercilessness of the mind and send it forgiveness. Though the body seems recalcitrant and stiff and inoperable, you may find access to a place within your mind,

within your heart, that allows the deepest sort of completion to
come about, the deepest healing imaginable, allowing your
heart to come into its fullness as your body goes whichever way
it will."

E: "That is evident too in these sessions. My son has specifically
stated that he wants to resolve the relationship. I think the thing
that is so astonishing to me is how badly they think of me and
have for so long. I had some illusions about being a good parent
—at least for a while—but those are all shattered now."

S: "Well, now is as good a time as any to let go of the past. Trying
in retrospect to be a good parent will just make you crazy. It is
interesting how the mind reacts, because if they had said, 'Oh,
you're a great mother,' then you would think, 'Oh, what a good
mother I am.' But if they are feeling at some moment that you
were not what they would have wished, you think, 'Oh, what a
bad mother I am.' But whatever created the life you shared has
long since dissolved behind you in the past. Their calling it A or
B doesn't mean anything. Your mind is going to go for it, but it
doesn't have any meaning of its own. We are not a good this or a
bad that, we are all of it, constantly changing. You can see how
irrational this whole situation is. Now it all exists as only a dream
in the memory. Their momentary opinion of what happened is
not necessarily what happened. It is just their frustration in the
present. And when they are angry, it comes out, and later there
is remorse and guilt and then they are overly protective. By
now you are familiar with the old roller-coaster mind. Don't get
caught in it. Notice your feelings of guilt or remorse as they
arise and pass away but don't mistake those feelings for who you
really are. Your work is not to be a good mother to them right
now but to mother yourself for a while. Whatever resentment
you feel for yourself, whatever you imagine you have done in
the past, it is time to send all that forgiveness and to just allow
yourself to enter the moment as being."

E: "But you know, when I get up like this in the morning with
my gut all mixed up, I just don't know what to do. I seem to be
losing more feeling in my hands and body, and I just feel like I
need to touch the ground, which is odd for someone who can't
bend over, or hardly even open their hands."

S: "When your body is like that, if you fight against it, it is like
hammering against the door in the dark closet. When you are

hammering against the door, you don't have time to investigate the closet. Although it seems impossible to the mind, the heart, that aspect of being in which Jung said occurred 'the resolution of opposites,' will need to open to this one. Life has usually been driven with pleasure as a goal—psychological or physical pleasure. But that is not happening so much now. The only pleasure you may find is the satisfaction of the discovery of who you really are. Of your direct participation of what for lack of a better term we will call the 'spirit.' That is one of the few options left to you now. Isn't that remarkable? How this illness has left you alone with yourself to find what qualities arise in the mind to block the heart."

E: "Well, Stephen, as we speak I know that. But this morning where I was, any opening seemed impossible. At times it is unbearable. But now it has changed again. Will it ever stop?"

S: "The mind never stops. It always has something to say. But that in which it all floats seems to have no beginning, so where is there an end? If you live your life in the mind, it is often unbearable and you live in hell. But if you start to focus on the space out of which all of this melodrama is arising, you start to find some sense of the deathless, of the ongoing peace and edgelessness and invulnerability of just being. When you notice the darkness dispelling, just note it as change. When you notice the denseness returning, again just note it as, 'Ahhh, change.' In fact, if you could watch the mind as change itself, you would notice the changeless nature of the space in which all these mind moments arise and dissolve."

E: "I am so different at different times. When I am with certain people, I become animated and somehow I don't get stuck in these places. But with others I feel the darkness encroaching and it seems as if there was never any such thing as peace."

Not wanting to put any more models on Evy of how she "should" be, and sensing her difficulty in letting go, we finished the conversation in soft laughter and much "don't know." As she said good-bye, her voice was still fatigued by "the struggle" but softened some by a bit more caring for herself and those around her.

A few weeks later we received a call from one of Evy's hospice helpmates who said that Evy wanted to speak to us but that her voice had become so weak because of the suppression of her respiratory system and her gag reflex that she could hardly be understood. In the previous weeks her condition had deteriorated rapidly and her family was considering putting her in a nursing home, but Evy wanted most not to leave her home. Evy's hardly discernible voice reached out to us over the phone. "It is hard to talk. My breath is very short. I guess you could say I am fighting my environment."

S: "Which environment? Your body or the house you are living in?"

E: "Every environment. I just can't stand it. I don't know what to do, but I know if I am going to do something about this, I have to do something pretty soon, as I won't be able to move my hands or take care of myself in the least in not very long. If I am going to let myself off the hook, I better do it now. I must decide if I am going to help myself out of this mess while I still have the opportunity. Soon I will just be a vegetable and people will do with me whatever they want."

S: "What are you thinking about now?"

E: "You know, when I was a kid I had a dream that I was looking into a snake pit and I remembered it all my life. And today now I feel as though I am tumbling headlong into that pit, and I will do anything to stop that. I don't want to go into the noise and smells and no privacy and no control that would be my last months or even, God forbid, years in a snake pit like the convalescent homes I have seen. I feel as though my race may be run. It is true I have gained a lot from all this but enough is enough. And if I am going to have any control at all, now is my time to make that decision, before my life is completely taken out of my hands."

S: "Well, it is odd you should say that your life is being taken out of your hands, because it is when your hands first began to become disabled that you began to feel the despair that has been visiting you off and on in the past months. In a way, my friend, life is out of our hands. Our hands are the manifestation of our control, of our doing, of our being able to 'work' the world to our image and likeness. But for you all that is gone now. And you are left with only the mind's constant change and turmoil and the heart's longing to be free. Whatever you choose to do, do it with consciousness and compassion for yourself and those about you. The healing never ends. Even when we leave the body, it is the heartfulness and care for ourselves which seem to allow us to stay open to the next moment of experience. There is no act that cannot be done with God in your heart and with a sense of 'don't know' openness to the next unknown moment."

For the next five minutes there were occasional words and much sobbing as Evy allowed an ancient river of remorse and self-doubt to flow out of her. "It is just too much at times, and I fear that it will get worse and that there is nothing I will be able to do about it. I just want to die now."

We shared a guided meditation for the next twenty minutes in which Evy attempted to let all the objects of fear and remorse, of doubt and trepidation float in some greater spaciousness, after which she said, "If only I could be in that space all the time, but I guess I have been into my fear for so long that something still thinks it will protect me, and I am left feeling so damned dense, so claustrophobic, I just want out of this body. I just want to be free of pain."

Evy went on to say that the moments of peace were becoming fewer and that the fear was becoming more intense. "I don't know where the problem is. I feel as though I have cement in my head. The only way I can 'just let it be there' is to try to pray or work with some of the meditations we have shared. But my energy is so low and my mind so dull and scared that I have almost no peace at all, and the possibility of just becoming a bag of flesh lying in a convalescent home repulses and frightens me. I just can't get any space around it."

It felt at this point, after two years of our working together, that much which could be said had been shared. And that now our contract called for a letting go of all methods into a place of just love. That any further encouragement even to let go would just block our communication, which she obviously needed very much at this point. It seemed that any more "teaching" would just create more self-judgment to accompany her on her way. All we could do was encourage her to trust the process and open to the spacious essence within her. This being done with gentleness and without the least taint of a judgment of what she was considering doing. In a sense, the fear was debilitating her

even more than the ALS. Her inability to let go of control was
causing the walls of the dark closet to close in on her. She could
see no alternative except a quick death.

It felt as though Evy was beginning to bog down, to get stuck
in her fears. We had occasionally seen situations where a person
approaching death had remarkable periods of growth and insight only to fall back into old ways of holding, caught in unexamined fears or in a last-ditch effort at control. In these individuals' growth, as in any learning situation, there were
experienced peaks and plateaus. Often after peak experiences
of openheartedness and access to his natural wisdom, a patient
might slip back into identification with fears that just weeks
before were seen to be quite empty. We do not grow from A to
Z. We are a process constantly integrating its learning into itself.
And it takes time to move through the spirals of personal evolution. But some don't have the "time" to do it before they die.
Some approach death in a "learning trough," the downside
movement during the process of integrating new understand-
ings into a new relationship to the world and to life itself. And
always as this happens, as it seemed to be happening with Evy,
there is a moment when Ondrea and I look into each other's
eyes and silently acknowledge that there isn't a moment to
waste, that one cannot wait until tomorrow to begin the long,
subtle investigation of life.

Five days later Evy's son called to say that the night before,
the family had had a long discussion about Evy's consideration
of suicide and that although it had been a very difficult conversation for everyone, they had at last agreed that Evy's life was
her own to do with as she wished. He said that it had been an
incredible process for him, for he felt that in these hours late
into the morning of hope and tears and frustration that what
remained was a residue of love and acceptance of each other
that they had seldom known. He said that Evy was more peaceful this morning than he had seen her in some time and that she
wished to speak to us as well as she might. Evy's voice came
weakly over the phone, "Well, I made my decision. I am going
to take the Seconal barbiturates I have been saving up for the
last few weeks, and I just want to thank you for all we have done
together. I hope I am doing the right thing. I know you feel that
suicide is not so much 'wrong' as unskillful and that I may have

to do this one all over again because of my acting on so much aversion. But I will take that chance. I just don't see any other way out. I have given everything I have, and although I know I could probably give more, this feels all right to me."

S: "There is no judgment in any act and there is no act we cannot do in a sacred manner. If your decision is made, then just go about it with as much compassion and forgiveness for yourself and all others as is possible. No blame. No judgment. Just allow being to dissolve back into its true nature."

Evy said good-bye and handed the phone back to her son. "I really don't want my mother to do what she is considering. But I really can't say that she shouldn't do it or any of that stuff. I don't know what I would do in the same circumstances. I guess I can only wish her well, as hard as that may be. I only hope that she will give herself the time to do this thing with the same thoughtfulness she has used during these years of being sick. It has been suggested that if Mom is going to do this that she turn off the television and close the curtains and just meditate and be quiet for a few days so she can take the leap with some peace. But she seems so jumpy at times I am not sure she will give herself that much space. She said she doesn't need to meditate, she only needs to die."

We spoke for a while of the power of love to bring a sense of completion to these final days. That it was a time for everyone to let go and merge and continue on the path that seemed appropriate.

We received a phone call three days later from one of the hospice attendants telling us that Evy had met with a counselor who had encouraged her to quiet down for the last few days and to contemplate clearly what was being approached. To recognize whatever aversion to life death was being approached with so that she did not cultivate more resistance to accompany her into the unknown. He had even mentioned to her that perhaps the taking of Seconal might present a problem, in that her weakened throat muscles made it very difficult to swallow pills, so she planned to open the capsules and mix the bitter barbiturates with applesauce. He had suggested she test the mixture for taste first, just to be sure she could stomach the extremely alkaloid taste which might cause her to gag or even struggle at the time of her chosen death. But her eagerness to "get off the hook" had caused her to wave away the suggestion. He had also suggested she be quiet and meditative for the three days leading up to the taking of the applesauce and Seconal, greeting each day as though it were the last, sending love to those she had shared life with and sending thankfulness for all she had learned so that she might die openheartedly and with some sense of completion and peace.

Although it had been agreed that the taking of the mixture would be done alone so as not to involve anyone else in the possible legal ramifications, since in most states it is illegal to "aid suicides," one of her nurses who loved her greatly and wanted to see her released from her suffering, had agreed to come an hour after she had taken her potion and sit with her to guide her lovingly toward her goal of light. The nurse had said that because of her fundamentalist Christian background she could not aid Evy to die by her own hand and that even coming in afterward was against her moral fiber, but that she would go against her better knowing and at least be there later to help her in whatever way she could.

All the arrangements were made. Evy said she would be taking the barbiturate-laced applesauce at nine in the morning so when the nurse came in at ten she would already be in a deep coma if not already out of her body. But when the nurse hesitatingly entered the room at ten, Evy was sitting up in bed crying that she was scared and begged her to feed her the poisoned applesauce which sat there in a dish. The nurse was quite disturbed. In her mind it was a "sin" to commit suicide, and although directed by a sense of identification with and compassion for Evy, she said she could not allow herself to participate so directly in Evy's taking of her life. It was agreed, because of Evy's pleading, that the nurse would instead just go across the street from Evy's house and sit in the car for forty-five minutes until Evy had already taken her applesauce and then return to help in the final transition.

Ten minutes after the nurse had gone out to her car, her mind full of guilt and confusion, she looked across the street and pulling herself to the door, leaning against a chair as though it were a walker, in the doorway of her house stood Evy with vomit dripping from her chin, crying out, "Please help me! Please help me! Don't let me take just half of this and be trapped in a coma! Please don't let me go to the nursing home!" The nurse, much against her will, entered the house, cleaned up Evy and slowly, spoon by spoon, fed her the applesauce concoction, constantly soothing her, gently stroking her throat so that she would not gag and would be able to hold the mixture down. She sat next to Evy as she left her body.

A week later I was called by one of the hospice workers to say that the nurse who had helped was in a deep depression, feeling she had "lost her immortal soul" by aiding in a suicide. I was encouraged to speak to the nurse, whose name was Helen.

I called Helen to find out how she was feeling. She lamented the "terrible thing" she had done, and "what was worse, I felt a great sense of peace. Somehow I felt I was doing something right at the time, but now I feel that I have been misled by my pity for poor Evy." We spoke for some time about the emotions she felt sitting in the car when she saw Evy come stumbling to the door with applesauce and vomit dribbling from her chin. Of the feelings of love and compassion that arose in her heart. "But if I was a good nurse, I never would have done that. Jesus will curse me forever." After she stopped crying, we spoke for some time and began a speculative fantasy about what Jesus' response might have been to that moment with Evy. Of what the reaction of any merciful being may have been. I asked her, "What would you rather be, a good nurse or the mercy of Christ?"

Helen called back three days later to say that things felt a bit better and that although she would never do it again, there was some forgiveness for herself. Clearly, Helen's work was to forgive herself and to trust the "don't know" of the moment in which action had arisen from a sense of the appropriateness of the love and compassion felt. She was "working to forgive Evy her impatience" and forgive herself. It is a process that I suspect will be going on for Helen for some time.

At the memorial service Evy's children and many friends came to wish her farewell and safe passage. There was song and poetry and dance and great lightness for her being freed from her "dark closet." Afterward some of the more spiritually righteous said that Evy had "not gotten it," that her suicide was a sign of her not having "received the teachings," that she had backed out of life instead of merging with death. Their righteousness was their own suffering and pain manifested as judgment of another. It is my sense that Evy learned as much as she was willing under the circumstances and that perhaps considerable progress was made and would continue even after death, perhaps a learning about opening to life, to being itself, in whatever environment she found herself. As she had said, "My race is run." Her fear of pain, her self-doubt, her agitation, her moments of peace, her desire to be free, are a part of us all. There can be no judgment. Only a deeper recognition of how we hold to life and a sense that there is no better time to prepare than in this moment. We wish her well.

Coming Home to Die

ROBERT

Robert called late one evening: "My wife is dying. I brought her home from the hospital today and someone recommended I call you."

Robert's wife Kathleen had for some time been treated for stomach cancer, which had in the last few months metastasized (spread) to her liver, brain, and lungs. Robert said, "In the past four days or so she hasn't been talking very well. It takes a lot of effort to understand her. But she is losing control in a very dignified way and I am proud of her." I mentioned to him that she may not be "losing control" but "letting go of control"— that the self-composure, the "dignity," was perhaps a sign of her finished business. He told me that it was "her impetus to get out of bed and make the physical effort to go home." I asked him: "What are your feelings right now? I mean, if indeed Kathleen died while we were talking on the phone, how would you be with it?" Robert replied, "This was her choice to die at home and I am with her in this all the way. But I could use some feedback on how to make this a better experience for her. I want it to be all OK."

S: "For it to be all OK you will have to investigate where it is not OK. When you think of her dying can you feel that place in your chest where it hurts? Can you feel the place of loss inside of you where you may be holding back from her death?"
R: "There is a part of me that says I want to keep her alive, and I am very much in touch with that. And there is a part of me that says I want to be with her as she dies, and that is OK too. I have really been following her lead. She is a very strong woman. Her biggest problem right now is breathing. The tumors in her lungs

have made it difficult for her to breathe. She has had a lot of wheezing and had to fight for every breath in the hospital the last few days. Even with bronchial dilators only temporary relief was given, and finally the dilators weren't doing that much. She has for the past twenty-four hours had minor heart changes, so I expect her not to live for long and I want to be there for her in any way I can."

S: "Breath anxiety is as primal as any fear that arises. Not being able to catch your breath, not being able to breathe deeply can be very scary. There is an old resistance that comes up to meet the fear, the breath anxiety, and tightens around it and intensifies it—the emergency bell goes off, the survival light flashes—which may cause one to contract and greatly magnify the discomfort. What you can do is help her to soften. The term 'soften' cannot be underrated in its power to aid in letting go and allowing fear and tension to float in something bigger. It is much like a woman giving birth. Kathleen is in a process of giving birth to herself. Sometimes, as with a person who has done some preparatory work to give birth, from the outside it seems like the person's predominant experience is pain, but if you ask them their experience from the inside, indeed there is discomfort but there is much more to it than that. There is also great wonderment at the process, an enormous strength and willingness to stay with it—and the greatest painful push is followed by the greatest joy and release and sense of wholeness. Don't second-guess her experience. If you want to know what she is feeling, ask her."

Robert replied that he felt this was so and she too had said that she was not in a lot of pain and that he might be projecting more pain into her experience than she was actually feeling. And that he understood that the word "softening" would be useful for himself as well.

R: "Since I brought her home, she has been sleeping very well. Breathing on the heavy side but with much greater ease, it seems."

He added that since she had been home she had been using much less medication. She had asked him to let the process go as it was and not to remove the secretions from her lungs.

R: "That is the part that is hard for me, particularly since I have been trained as a respiratory therapist. To have her here breathing through her secretions as they mount up and knowing that I am not going to suction her. That I am not going to do any heroic measures just as we have agreed upon."

I mentioned to Robert that this moment that he and Kathleen were sharing was perhaps the most intimate of their lifetime. To which he said, "This whole day has been incredibly intimate, and I wouldn't have it any other way even though I am very tired. I haven't slept much and I have come through a huge thing with this process today. I was feeling overwhelmed with grief for the last couple of days, but I've come through something very beautiful for me and I am feeling just very clear and very happy that we got home. I thought she might not make it. Her effort to get out of the bed and into the cab was so strenuous I thought it might be too much for her. But I know that Kathleen is very aware of what is going on, and I just feel so good that I can do what she wanted to have done."

Robert mentioned that sometimes it seemed as though she were almost in a light coma. And I suggested to him that he keep talking to and with her, whether she responded or not, just to keep that gentle contact going as seemed appropriate, as that might be very helpful and of considerable support. Not to be too rational because she can't respond, thinking that she is "out of it" when really she is "just getting into it."

R: "We have been hugging a good deal tonight and it has really been wonderful. And I will continue to find ways to talk to her also."

I suggested that Robert might also read to her from writings that she likes and just speak to her of his love and his willingness to let her die her own death.

R: "I like to read aloud anyway, so that will be great. She has been very much in tune with nature. She is religious but not in a standard way. Actually, she is more spiritual than religious. She loves good poetry. She is a writer, so I could relate to her in that way if I could find some good poetry."

When I suggested Thoreau, he responded that he thought that would be "right on for her." The enthusiasm of his response caused me to add: "But there is a catch with that. There is an attachment to the aesthetic beauty of the planet, and I wouldn't intensify that at a time when she is about to leave it. The more 'light oriented' the things you read to her, the better. Just so as not to reinforce any strong attachment at a time when it sounds like she is in a rather balanced condition."

R: "Yes. I feel in some ways that things couldn't be better."
S: "I suggest just reading to her as a good-bye to this beautiful plane of existence. She sounds like she will do fine in moving through what she needs to move through. Just trust the process with as much intuitive connectedness with her as possible. Let it all come out of your heart.

"And if she should possibly go into that comalike space, just stay with her. Just encourage her to notice that she isn't this body and even the fact she can hear you in coma means there may be more to her than she ever imagined. That who she really is is much more than this dying body or the mind's fantasies."

Robert said he had wanted to talk to her more in these comalike spaces but hadn't trusted his intuitive sense.

S: "It is incredible grace for her to be at home. You couldn't have helped her more."
R: "I just feel so good about that. I cry and I laugh. I feel very solid about it. It has been like a birth today in a very special way. I have never experienced anything like it."
S: "Good. And now she is doing the last thing that she needs to do. I think it is going to be very extraordinary for both of you. And in a sense, your only work now is to open and to soften and to just let it move through both of you. Do you have any other questions?"
R: "Well, it is a little odd not giving her these medicines. There is something in me, my old therapist conditioning I guess, that is propelled toward 'treating her.' "
S: "I would let her be the guide on that. And you can suggest to her that she may pay attention to what she needs in painkillers so that she can judge for herself. She might find that she needs

less than she is taking, or more—whatever. But that she needn't rely on anything but her own intuition at this time. It is a time for both of you to trust yourselves in the deepest way."
R: "Another thing that I need to mention is that I have a tendency to want to feed her."
S: "But she probably doesn't have any appetite."
R: "She doesn't and hasn't for quite a while."
S: "I have been with people who haven't eaten for weeks, who have only taken fluids. Your tendency to feed her is indicative of many things. Perhaps you really have to let go of her at yet a deeper level. Don't wait for her to be dying to let go of her. Now. Which is very hard. To the degree you can open to this process and let it be as it is for her, you will be able to go through it with her in the most profound way. You will be able to share her experience in as deep a manner as you ever have in the past, perhaps deeper. She has to be allowed to do what she senses is necessary."
R: "I got some hints from her tonight. Just kind of mumblings like 'not necessary.'"
S: "Everything is OK for her. She just needs now to go through this process, which may take hours or days, there is no way of knowing. Offer her fluids, of course, but if she does not want food or suctioning, let it be as she wishes. Just notice your need to take care of her in any other manner than she wishes, as a way of holding on to her in a time when you both need so to let go and melt into the next moment."

Robert added that although it seemed as though everything was all right in Kathleen's mind and she was "ready to give birth to herself," as it were, still there seemed at times a kind of restlessness that he had difficulty in understanding. I suggested to him that, as we have seen with many people who appeared very open to the process of dying yet still seemed a bit fidgety, sometimes, "the body sort of grasps back at its own existence" at a level beyond the usual holding—there may not even be much mental grasping behind it. At one level it seems to be that the discomfiture in the body tends to create a little restlessness in the mind. At yet a deeper level it is perhaps one of the survival mechanisms that curls back on itself in a strange way even though the mind/body is not resisting much. That this seeming restlessness is sometimes misinterpreted as confusion or doubt in the process but is actually something primal to existence in the body. I have even heard people who were quite spacious with their dying say, "It is like the body hugging itself good-bye." And that there is nothing he couldn't speak to her about if he wished.

Robert also mentioned that there was a difficulty in that Kathleen's mother was insisting on visiting, while Kathleen said she really did not want to see her. Their relationship had always been very difficult. Kathleen felt more comfortable dying with just Robert by her side. But Kathleen's mother was insistent that she be there whether Kathleen wanted it or not.

R: "My tendency is to think that I am generally going to keep people away from her room as she wishes. I have arranged for her mother to be in a nearby motel, and that is the way it is going to be. I have made it very clear what Kathleen's wishes are. It has been hard for me to do that, because I like her mother; but I have had to be very strong, because she understandably has a mother's tendency to want to come in and see her daughter before she dies. Kathleen does not want that. She says that they have talked it all out in the past few months and more is not needed. She said it would spoil things if I let that happen. So I am in quite a quandary."

S: "How about them talking on the phone?"

R: "Kathleen wouldn't be able to talk on the phone."

S: "That might be OK too. Maybe it is just time for her mom to finish business with her, and perhaps there is nothing Kathleen need say. Ask Kathleen how she would feel about a nonresponding phone call where her mother called and the phone was just put up to her ear. She will hear it however she hears it, but it may allow her mom to finish up too. If Kathleen can do it lightly from her heart, if it feels OK to her, it might be skillful. She doesn't have to respond, and her mother may be able to say some things that she wants to. Perhaps Kathleen will get a lot of loving-kindness from it without having to be anyone else but herself in this most precious time."

R: "That is a good idea and we may try that."

S: "But just remember that this whole scenario is up to Kathleen. If she wants to speak to her mom, fine. If she doesn't, fine. No judgment and no blame. In fact, her mother might be helped by just encouraging her to 'write it all down' in a note for Kathleen to read when she wished."

R: "Well, they have had many months of going through this illness to communicate what they need to. Perhaps this is all her mom needs to do to say good-bye."

S: "Just trust Kathleen's sense of it and it will work out fine, and you will do it together whatever it is. Kathleen's experience is OK, and she knows what is disruptive and what she needs to trust in herself now. This is essentially just another moment in her life where she has to trust and call on the powers of her clarity and openheartedness. Indeed, not only is she finishing business with you and her mother at this time, it is a time of finishing business with herself. I don't know what her psychological state is, although I would say that the best she might do for herself is what she has already done, to surround herself with loving-kindness, the beings she loves most, especially you. And you can gently encourage her to practice whatever loving-kindness and forgiveness might be useful in her bidding herself adieu. If there is any place where there is a little holding, without getting into some neurotic searching procedure that would just be more discomforting, encourage her to open deeply. The more she can die now into her heart and say 'I love you' to herself, even using her own name, even saying to herself, 'Kathleen, I love you,' the more she will enter into the process, surrendering the past, letting go of any blockages to a clear passage—the more beneficial for whatever follows. And speaking of being kind to oneself, Robert, what are you doing about sleep?"

R: "I am tired but I am not ready to sleep."

S: "Are you going to sit up with her tonight?"

R: "Yes. In fact, I think I might sleep with her. I have been dying to sleep with her for all the time she was in the hospital, which has been quite a while, so it has been really nice to have her home. Her blood counts came up higher, and it has been nice to give up that quarantine thing and get back in touch and hug and do all that."

S: "Now is the time to give up all the quarantines, including birth's quarantine within the body. Her being home is the most wonderful thing that could have happened to her right now."

R: "I knew it was good, and I had the good fortune to follow her lead and also to come through my own process of finding that I

need to take initiative for this now, to do it and to feel that accomplishment, and it feels just right."
S: "Well, you have done something for her that no one else in the world could have done, and there is nothing more skillful that you could have done. Rest well, friend."

The next morning Robert called to say that Kathleen had died at 4:15 A.M. as he lay next to her in bed, with a soft breath out of the body that was not followed by another. "She really died beautifully. She decided it was time to let go and she sort of shut down in stages. She died very quietly, peacefully, relaxed, and I am just incredibly impressed by it. It was just incredible. At one point about an hour and a half before she died, she looked up at me and told me good-bye, then she sort of, very lightly, started to count down from ten. And when she got to zero, she sort of giggled and said, 'Ohh,' and started to count back up again. When I asked her if she felt like she was dying, she said, 'Yes,' in a very light way. It was almost as though I had asked her if she wanted to go to the movies or something. Just this very soft yes, and I played our favorite cantata, and her breath became completely clear, not the least struggle like before, just clear as a bell, just softer and softer, and the last time I sat her up with the pillows, I felt her body to be at least twice as heavy as before. And I knew she was already beginning to leave, and I quoted to her from Hamlet, her favorite—'Good night sweet princess, may bands of angels sing thee to thy rest'—and she was very quiet and then just seemed to melt away."
His joy and sense of wholeness, he said, was greater than at any time in his life. It was the perfect consummation of their long relationship.
Though it may seem to some that the joy Robert was experiencing at the death of his wife was somehow "inappropriate," it is not uncommon in our experience for a husband or wife, after tending to a mate through the protracted difficulties of a long illness, to feel great relief at the release of their loved one from that pain. But for some there seems to be more to it than that. Some, though they have little language to articulate it, have what amounts to a transcendent experience. A glimpse of the mystery which leaves them in a somewhat bewildering state of near ecstasy for weeks afterward. As this "high" diminishes, the loss of the beloved partner cries out in the mind and the work of

opening to grief commences. It seems that for those who have worked so hard for so many months or years attending to a loved one and sharing in their death at levels beyond description find the grief somewhat more accessible, even somewhat "easier," if I can use that word in the midst of such pain. Perhaps this is because the mind never quite obscures the depth of the heart connection shared. For these beings, the grief in time more readily sinks back into the heart, where the departed is experienced in his or her essential connectedness and love. Their joy is the joy of completion. Their grief is their loss and their opening to what lies ahead.

The Light Reflected in Three Faces

A DAY IN THE HOSPITAL

Occasionally, a hospital will invite us "in." One such hospital on the West Coast we'll call St. Elmo's. Having worked with a few patients who were hospitalized there, we gradually met the staff and were asked if we might offer a training for hospital personnel. What had been planned as five weekly talks for the staff, when it was opened to the community, became instead a meeting of about a hundred and forty people every Tuesday and Thursday for ten weeks. Many health care workers from the area participated with the nurses, doctors, and technicians that attended each session. During these months, the hospital became quite open to our techniques, and we were invited to have "the run of the hospital," to join grand rounds (staff meetings about courses of treatment for specific patients), and even to take a few of the students we were working with into autopsies. A technique we have found effective with other training groups, so that they might more deeply contemplate death and the emptiness of the body; a practice many have found quite useful in connecting with their fear of death and identification with the body. As one student put it, "This is so valuable, because as I stand next to the empty corpse, I experience that what is absent from that dead body is precisely that which is watching, just consciousness itself. That is who we really are, and when that leaves, what remains behind is just old food, the body, disintegrating into refuse."

Ondrea and I were offered pastoral counseling badges, which

gave us an "acceptable identity" to the patients we were asked to visit.

Several days a week we would take turns going to the hospital, where we would don our badges and go first to the pastoral counseling office where our friend Arnold, who helped minister to the more than three hundred patients in the hospital, would tell us who had arrived in the few days since we had last visited and whom he sensed it might be useful for us to spend time with that day. Most of those we were asked to work with were dying or in considerable pain, individuals who might find some softness and release working with the pain techniques we had developed over the years.

On one particular day Arnold suggested that I see "these three beauties, if time allows." The first was Miguel, a Spanish-American fellow dying from cirrhosis of the liver "whose condition seems quite grave and who is in an awful way."

The second patient was Madeline, a sixty-seven-year-old woman "on the edge with lupus disease" who had twenty years before worked as a maintenance person at the hospital and who had spent most of her life alone in a trailer outside of town. The staff's inability to relieve her distress had left Madeline quite isolated and without visitors. The nurses on her floor, feeling "unable to help," seldom allowed themselves the vulnerability to just sit quietly with this being agonized by her physical condition. An overworked, understaffed floor left several patients in need of some additional attention. Only an occasional visit from a local hospice volunteer punctuated the long stillness of Madeline's room.

The third patient was Mary, a nurse who had once worked in the hospital and was presently being treated for metastasized breast cancer. "She seems very confused about her cancer and keeps asking the same questions over and over even though she knows the answers, having worked with cancer patients herself in the past."

Heading up to the second floor, I had a feeling this was going to be quite a day.

As I entered Miguel's room, standing around his bed were four members of his family. At the foot of his bed sat his seventy-four-year-old mother with her head in her hands. To the right of his bed was his wife Maria, who looked quite drained by this highly charged, emotional environment. On the other side of the bed stood two of Miguel's cousins, both in their thirties, as was Miguel, old drinking buddies there to witness their friend's great illness from the enormous amount of alcohol he had consumed. Miguel's liver was so swollen from the cirrhosis that he looked as though he were six months pregnant, his belly greatly distended from the swollen tissue of his nearly nonfunctional liver. Miguel's eyes were butterscotch yellow. The brown-golden tint of his skin had gone brown-gray; his face was drawn and wearied by a long, painful life and a long, slow dying. When I mentioned to Maria that Pastoral Care had suggested I come up and see if I could be of any assistance to Miguel in his physical discomfort, at first disappointed that I was not a priest, she nodded tearfully and said, "Anything that can help." She turned to Miguel's mother and cousins and in Spanish explained that I had come to take Miguel's pain away. But instantly I sensed that the tools I had considered were not the tools for the job. The language barrier made it difficult to communicate, and the guided meditations which had been of use to so many were out of the question. All my "doing" had to be completely dropped; only the sharing of being was appropriate.

Miguel's first language was Spanish and although I had lived in Mexico some years before, my Spanish is quite poor. Also the pain and fear had caused Miguel naturally to withdraw into the familiar. He was not speaking any English at all. All my words were useless. All the remarkable techniques for relieving pain were untransmittable. I had to speak hesitatingly in the simplest of terms—it forced the mind to dissolve into the heart's greatest simplicity. In pidgin Spanish I said to him: "In your heart there is a pain. It is the pain of old life. Let old life go. Open to new life. Remember your sacred heart (pointing to a picture of Jesus next to his bed). Have faith and move toward him." There seemed little I could do for Miguel, but the connection I felt was clear and strong.

Though there was little I could transmit in words, because my presence seemed helpful to the family, allowing them to sit and rest a while, I stood next to the bed and put my hand on the top of Miguel's head, gently stroking his brow, saying nothing. Standing at first and then sitting beside the bed, just touching him lightly, I began speaking to him silently through my heart of the need now to ever so gently let go of the suffering of this life. "Miguel, this life of pain comes closed now behind you. Let it go. That which you responded to with suffering, all that caused you to reach for painkilling alcohol, is now closing behind you, my friend. The fear and holding that surrounds your heart is like a barbed-wire fence—let it melt and change—let it become the circle of thorns about the sacred heart of Jesus. Let it be His great teaching of compassion to you. Your work of this lifetime is done. Just try to let go lightly of this worn, damaged old body. Let go lightly of this suffering that has always shrouded your life." His mother, forgetting that I was not a priest, asked me in Spanish to pray for Miguel's soul. The six of us in the room spent the next fifteen minutes in silence as I sat with Miguel singing songs of Jesus to him silently in my heart while the others came together quietly in the corner and whispered quietly among themselves. I felt that there was little I could do but just silently share the love I felt for him. It felt appropriate to just *be* there. His loved ones' deepest wish was that I could make death go away, but all I could say to Miguel in my pidgin Spanish was to soften and trust the process and to those about the bed, "Just take him into your heart and surround him with love and prayer for his well-being." The cousins' muscular, tattooed arms hung helplessly by their sides. They were fighters and drinkers. They had nowhere to turn. They were beaten by death.

Miguel and I did not say a dozen words to each other in the forty-five minutes we were together. Then, since the room seemed a bit more relaxed and I felt there was little more I could do, I decided to go visit one of the other patients and to come back later. Leaving the room, I stood for a moment in the hall, feeling my heart and contemplating the next visitation just down the hall, when Maria came out into the hallway and asked that I return to the room because "Miguel said he would like you there." I came back into the room and again sat next to Miguel's bed, stroking his brow, singing silently to him in my heart, and every once in a while saying, "Soften," or "Have faith and move toward God."

After perhaps another forty-five minutes of quiet heart meditation, as I was about to leave the room, the family came up and thanked me and asked if there was anything else they could do.

I asked Maria what Miguel's relationship was to his Catholic upbringing, to which she said: "Miguel has had a very hard life but he is a good Catholic. He loves Jesus. Sometimes he would come home so drunk he could hardly walk, knocking over chairs, and would fall down on the bed and begin to cry and would say, 'Maria, Maria, pray to Jesus for me. I am too drunk to pray. Help me.'" I suggested she might pray that mercy surround Miguel and allow a smooth passage into "the mansions of God." At that point Miguel painfully sat up and said that he was very thirsty. I went out to the nursing station and requested that some fluids be brought to him, and just as I returned to the room, the nurse entered with a glass of orange juice. With some help Miguel's hands brought the cup to his lips and he took a sip, but his tongue was so deeply cracked and split from the disintegration of his body, the ravages of a liver no longer able to filter the toxins from his system, that as the orange juice touched his tongue, he let out a shriek from the burning sensation it caused. The nurse sheepishly left the room, realizing that she had made a considerable error by giving an acid-based beverage to a patient whose tongue was so badly fissured. After getting a glass of water for Miguel to rinse his mouth with and spending some time quieting his family's anger that the hospital seemed "not to give a damn because he's just a drunk dying and a Spanish drunk at that," I left the room once again. While I stood in the hall taking a few breaths before visiting the next patient, once again Maria appeared and requested that I come back because Miguel had said, "Ask him to stand near me again. Ask him to be close." I returned to the room. Obviously, although there was little said, the power of the heart's connection was somehow felt through all the pain and confusion that Miguel was experiencing. As I stroked his brow, he lay very quiet and still. His mother sobbing in the corner, his cousins pacing, his wife wan and exhausted, standing on the other side of the bed holding his hand. Speaking silently through my heart to Miguel, I encouraged him to "trust in your faith in Jesus. This painful life is now left behind, sweet friend. Your only work now is to merge in the sacred heart of Jesus." All of a sudden, he sat straight up in bed and said, *"La luz! La luz!* [The light! The light!]" I put my hand behind Miguel's shoulders to support him as he sat, and I said, *"Esta la luz de sagrada corrazon de Jesus.* [That is the light of the sacred heart of Jesus.]" At hearing this, Miguel sighed deeply, his whole body seemed to soften, and he lay back gently onto the pillow murmuring in Spanish something I could not understand. Soon he was sleeping peacefully, and I gave his wife our phone number at home and offered to come back again tomorrow, but just in case, she could call us during the night if Miguel's condition seemed to be slipping.

As I was leaving the room, his wife asked, "What was the light that Miguel saw?" To which I replied, "It is the light of his true nature; it is the light of Christ in his heart and mind, the light of his approaching death, a sign of peace and wholeness that awaits him." She nodded sadly and turned to the others in the room to translate what I had said. As I left the room, even the cousins, who had been keeping a very stiff upper lip, were crying the soft cry of those who love and lose a dear one.

Five minutes later I walked down the hall and entered Madeline's room. Madeline had lived much of her life in isolation and now found herself dying in that same manner. Her children living some miles away had not come to visit. And as the difficulties with her disease had become more acute and fewer nurses and doctors felt they could be of any direct help to her, few spent any meaningful time with her. She was dying alone and in considerable pain. A wire cage arched over her legs, because even the weight of the blanket would add considerable discomfort to her already pain-wracked body. Entering the room, considering some pain meditations with her, I approached the bed as Madeline turned her head slowly to look up at me. As our eyes met, I knew beyond knowing that Madeline might be able to touch a place of deep peace within her. Her eyes were like deep, shattered ice, a glacier blue-green that had the crystalline hue of one who has experienced long periods of pain. But within them there seemed a great stillness just behind the pain, just behind the isolation and fear. I only had a chance to say, "Hello, my name is Stephen; perhaps I can be of some help to you," before our eyes merged in a powerfully magnetic joining of our beings. Nothing needed to be said. Our eyes met in such a manner that it was clear that our work together was the work of letting go of everything that eluded pain or joy, fear or grace. I sensed that somehow Madeline could touch some deeper part of herself at that moment and I said: "Madeline, don't push the pain away. Even the lupus. Just let it be there. Don't try to change any of the fear or pain. But can you feel that somehow, beyond this pain, beyond this fear, beyond this isolation, without trying to change them even a little, that somehow, miraculously beyond all these things, somewhere, there is a place of peace, of even OK-ness with all that is happening. Can you feel that? Can you sense that vastness just behind all this incredible confusion and seeming emergency of pain and the possibility of dying? Can you see that? Can you let yourself, without pushing any of the other pain or fear away, just melt into that place of peace, that somehow, beyond reason, beyond anything we have ever been told, that somehow what is happening is OK. That somehow, beyond all this, there is just being, just spacious peace?"

Her throat made a sound of affirmation. A kind of grunting as we moved deeper and deeper into a wordless participation in each other's being. Beyond who I thought I was, beyond who she imagined herself to be, we met in just being. The power of the moment was evident as our minds melted away like fog before the sun to expose the immensity of the love that connects all that lives and breathes. It felt as though the whole world was composed of love, of a singular luminescence that lit each mind, that burned in every heart. For nearly an hour, with both hands held tightly, our eyes locked into a space of vast love and caring, we joined beyond language in the power of shared being. Slowly, that face that had been drawn in such pain, etching lines of distress and hellish resistance, melted into a smooth roundness lit by the melting ice in her eyes, the hard line of the chin, the gritting of her teeth, slowly dissolving into a gentle smile: "Yes, it is OK. Somehow it's all OK."

Feeling ourselves coming back into the hospital moment, I asked Madeline, "How is it now?"

"Very different," she said.

S: "How is your pain?"
M: "It is still there, but very different."
S: "How is your dying?"
M: "If death is the peace we just shared, then I am ready."
S: "There is so much more to you, Madeline, than this lupus. Even this aloneness. If you just trust it."

M: "I know. I feel so much better now. I think it would be OK if I died right now. I don't feel so alone. Somehow I feel protected."

S: "Just know that you always have access to that place of peace within you beyond the sick body, beyond the confused mind; behind it all there is just the peace of being, just the sense of wholeness that nothing can disturb, that nothing can destroy. We are all in this together. If there is any way I can help, let me know."

We sat together for another ten minutes speaking of her son in California, whom she asked me to call, and of the beauty of some of the nurses who had felt so confused and frightened by her pain. The compassion for the nurses, for her children, for herself filled the room like a golden light. I felt my heart fill with the immensity of her love as she let go of her pain and experienced herself as something so much greater than her body.

As I left the room, promising to return on the next day, she smiled a crinkly-eyed wink and said, "Yes, it is all OK and so much love."

Madeline died two days later with her son by her side and three of her favorite nurses surrounding the bed. There was a peace that room had not known for the two months she had inhabited it. And on the morning she died, she looked up at me as I entered the room and winked and said, "Yep. It's OK."

But not to get ahead of the story, as it were. After leaving Madeline's room, I took a break for lunch before visiting with Mary, a nurse who had been admitted to the hospital for tests and treatment for advanced metastasized breast cancer which had begun to affect many of the major organs in her body. Mary was quite angry. "I staffed in this hospital for years and now I've been sick nearly a year. When I was first admitted, the nurses would look in and ask how I was doing, but as I got sicker and the chemotherapy didn't seem to be working much, they stopped coming by, until if my door was open, they turned their head the other way when they passed. I'll be damned if I ever come back to this place again!"

Breathing her anger into my heart on each in-breath and breathing it out again as warmth and patience, I sat with her and listened to her story of having been divorced fifteen years before and "never dating since." She spoke of her nineteen-year-old daughter, chomping at the bit to get into the world. Mary and I talked for a bit more than an hour about her predicament and the ways we had found many could work with discomfort in the body. Then just as I was about to leave, though I wasn't sure how deep she wanted to take it, I asked almost as an aside if she might like to attempt a guided meditation to open around her pain. She vaguely agreed. More, I suspect, for the company of another warm heart in the room than from any confidence in the process I was offering.

A few minutes into the meditation, encouraging her to soften and open around her pain, to allow it just to float, a noticeable release of tension shuddered across her body with a great sigh as she settled yet deeper into the bed and for the first time seemed somewhat relaxed. After another few minutes of investigating what the nature of this discomfort in her body was, she slowly opened her eyes to reveal a sparkle I had not noticed before. She looked up and with a wry laugh said, "God, that anger is too much. I feel better now, lighter. You know, as we got into the pain, I could feel it as anger and fear. I'm so tight in my back and chest and shoulders."

S: "And how does your heart feel?"
M: "Sore as hell."
S: "All that grieving you are doing, Mary. All that anger and fear make the heart feel as though it had a manhole cover laying on it. Yes?"
M: "All this pain in my chest and around my heart. Maybe it is grief. I am so damn mad at this cancer. But these last months have really shown me something. For years I did special one-on-one duty with patients dying from cancer, and with all those patients over all those years, I can see how I never really wanted to be with them. I stayed so distant and stiff and now I understand," she said, beginning to sob heavily. "I have so much to learn and so little time to do it."

Apparently Mary and I had some work to do together, and because she wished soon to return home, I suggested we get together in a few days at her house and continue with whatever it might turn out to be. As I left the room, she smiled and said,

"Who was that masked man, after all?" (As it turned out, Mary worked with Ondrea and me over the next nine months until she died. Her story follows.)

Leaving the hospital and returning home to eat, we had just sat down to supper when the phone rang. It was the head nurse on the second floor. Miguel's wife had asked that I come to the hospital as soon as possible, as Miguel seemed to be dying. Twenty minutes later I was standing by Miguel's bedside, my hand on his brow, my other hand lightly touching his chest just above his heart center, telling him in pidgin Spanish to trust the light. *"Esta la luz de sagrada corrazon de Jesus,"* I repeated slowly, his mother and wife crying in the corner, comforted by an extremely compassionate male nurse. At times Miguel seemed to be fighting to hold on, his breath held tight, gasping, struggling. His struggle causing his family to tense and become yet more frightened. But it seemed that everything was going "according to schedule." "Just let Jesus breathe for you. Let each breath go into his heart," I repeated over and over in a Spanish I can't even recall right now, caressing his brow as he began to quiet, eventually becoming very still until at last he breathed out one last, soft breath and melted quietly out of his tormented body. His letting go felt like that of a little child who had tired of their circus balloon and let it go lightly to watch it float up to the clouds. There was a sense of the pure child within him leading him by the hand to the "good shepherd" of his true nature.

As he dissolved out of this lifetime of pain and withdrawal, out of this life of alcoholism and confusion, I continued to encourage him, "Go to God. Trust the mercy that awaits you." And I reminded him of the light. "It is simply the light of your heart, of your sacred nature." As I stroked Miguel's brow, after his final breath, I repeated in Spanish, "Merge with the heart of Jesus now, let go now, go into the light, go into the light of your sacred nature."

For the next two hours I stayed with Maria as the body was taken to the morgue. She spoke of all the times in Miguel's life that he had so wished for peace, but how he had grasped for alcohol to dull the constant pain in his heart. "He always said that he knew Jesus and that Jesus understood his pain. But he said that he could never look Jesus in the eye because he was so drunk, but when he said, *'La luz! La luz!*, I think that maybe he did see the Lord's eyes. I think he died as he had always wished he would have lived. I will go home now and tell the children that their father died speaking of the light."

It had been an interesting day and one which I felt might be worth making some notes about when I returned home later that evening. It demonstrated to me once again that we don't have to spend weeks or months with patients in order to be of service, but that all that needs to be done is to open to the precious moment, beyond our knowing, in the heart of the matter.

A Confusing Grace

MARY

Mary was a fifty-year-old registered nurse who had moved to
town eighteen months before to work in the hospital in which
she now resided as a patient. A breast biopsy had confirmed
carcinoma of the breast some months before. For the past five
months she had been in and out of the hospital for chemotherapy and radiation. When we first met in the hospital, she was
quite frightened and feeling a sense of considerable isolation.
"When they (her former coworkers) thought I might get better,
they all came to visit. But as this cancer thing gets me, I must be
some kind of a failure or something to them, because they can't
face me. I guess I am kind of scary to them."

S: "What do you think frightens them?"
M: "Maybe they are afraid to be me. I am a nurse just like them
and I've worked with cancer patients too. And I know that
many of them die. And I've turned away too. But you know, I
am very different than I was then. In fact, having this cancer has
made me see how separate I felt, how I put them away maybe
just like these nurses are kind of putting me away, pretending I
don't exist. I think I could have done a better job."

Mary had a lot of resentment toward life. Having been divorced fifteen years before, she had "not gone out on a date
since. It's better that way." While she was in the hospital, her
teenage daughter visited infrequently and was quite hesitant to
enter the room, seeing her mother's condition deteriorating
from visit to visit. In a shaky voice Mary said, "I just want to get
out of here, but I've got no place to go—there is really no way I

can go home. My daughter lives away from home and has her job to look after, so there is no one to take care of me."

We offered to set up a support team that could be with her when needed. Speaking of Mary's predicament at the weekly hospital lecture, we asked for volunteers to set up a home care team. A dozen people signed up to help. When we told Mary of the considerable response, she couldn't believe it. She kept shaking her head and saying, "A dozen people?!" The next day the local visiting nurses association and a local hospicelike group who often volunteered to attend those in need joined the team.

It took a few days to organize a schedule of support. Grocery shopping, laundry to be done, meals to be cooked, house to be cleaned, medications to be administered, doctor visits to be scheduled, etc. When the team was set up, Mary signed out of the hospital and was brought home and greeted by many warm smiles and much loving support by her neighbors and new support team. As she entered her living room, she turned to us with great gratitude and some sense of unworthiness and said, "Why are these people being so nice to me? Do I deserve all this kindness?"

Though speaking to her by phone daily, twice a week we would stay with her for several hours at a time, occasionally staying overnight as the need arose. Often she would ask that we read to her from the Bible, saying, "I was never much of a Christian back in Iowa. Maybe I should have prayed more. But maybe a miracle can still happen. Yes? Maybe I will still get well."

We spoke for a while of what it meant to experience "a miracle." And I asked her: "Even if your body doesn't get better, is it possible that you still have experienced a miracle? You said you were so much different before you received the diagnosis. You were afraid of everything, of life itself. You never thought of yourself as heart or spirit as you often seem to now. Maybe you have gotten what you prayed for."

M: "Maybe. I have never had so many friends or so many people care. And I have never felt so much kindness. I never knew how important just simple kindness could be. I have never felt so comfortable around loving people."

Clearly there was a miracle in her life. The miracle of her heart beginning to open, of the mind attending to life with a bit less fear and some greater willingness to experience what might come next. Her life had been a struggle from day to day, but now the days melted together in a new camaraderie with life, the deep hum of being, a bit more noticeably resonating in her heart.

Two weeks after returning home Mary discovered decreased sensation in her hand and began to have some difficulty speaking. Considerable fatigue often made it impossible for her to be "up and about" much. Her steps began to falter and she needed a walker to support her. It was diagnosed that the cancer had spread to her brain. She had increasing problems with speech and coordination and was admitted to the hospital once again, where a left frontal craniotomy with needle drainage of metastatic tumors was performed. Soon after, she began having seizures. Though there was on occasion inordinate temperature spiking, she said, "If there is nothing they can do for me here, I want to go back home. I don't need to be here. I need to be with my old furniture and new friends."

Her daughter did not come to visit her in the hospital, and when she returned home it looked as though the house had been ransacked. Apparently her daughter was sending a message of her increasing difficulty of being around her dying mother. Soon her daughter's fear and confusion became more evident. Acting out in various ways to display both her disdain for her "mother's weakness" and a rage at "not getting out from under her thumb." Repeatedly her daughter dipped into her pocketbook and stole money and food stamps. At other times, various objects disappeared from the house.

On a few occasions when members of the team approached her daughter to sit down "for a little talk," they were met by a cold hostility that turned them away. When asked by one of the nurses if she would pick up some medicine for her mother, she said, "I just wish my mother would die and get it over with," storming out of the house, leaving the prescription behind. Mary continued to make excuses for her daughter with the same frightened blindness that many had recognized as denial when she had first confronted her cancer. Indeed, she never mentioned the missing money, food stamps, or furniture and would on occasion spin a fantasy of "our closeness," referring to conversations with her daughter of years before, of a contact long since broken. She never mentioned her nineteen-year-old daughter's fifty-year-old boyfriend who sat outside in his silver Cadillac and waited for her to return from a flash visit to the house. The daughter's silk blouses and expensive fashions were overlooked by her mother, who thought she was working at McDonald's.

The unfinished business between Mary and her daughter was a teaching in helplessness for us all. All we could do was remain available. It was an opportunity for each of us to let go of any judgment we might notice arising in the mind that the daughter, the relationship, or even Mary herself, be different in any way.

One day we brought Mary a large picture of Jesus to put on her mantel since she said she would like "something of that sort to refer to." When calling one morning three days later, as she began to speak it became instantly apparent that her speech difficulties and hesitancy were absent. "I had the most remarkable thing happen last night. I was coming back from the bathroom, using my walker very slowly, and for some reason, I don't know why, I've never done anything like that before, I went up and kissed the picture of Jesus and all of a sudden I felt so wonderful, I felt like I could have jumped up and clicked my heels. And now, today, things feel so different. I have never felt so peaceful. I don't know—mmmm—am I crazy?"

We told her we didn't know what it was, but "we wouldn't mind having two of those on toast for breakfast every morning." We encouraged her to trust her experience as it was and allow it to be. To accept grace in whatever form it presented itself.

For the next two and a half days she was without symptoms. Her speech was normal. All traces of aphasia (scrambled phrases and words) were absent, as was her need for any support when walking. Within a few days, however, once again fatigue arose, and the difficulty in maintaining clarity and unaffected speech returned. For some days thereafter a certain happiness seemed to remain in her heart though the grace of a moment before was no longer reflected in her body. There was an openness and a great, soft smile greeted everyone who came. "I don't know what happened last week but it sure was something! I feel different—mmmm—I am not so afraid for some reason or other."

During the next week she had two seizures. The seizures frightened her greatly. Her lack of control had never been so evident. Because she had some sense of warning just before the onset of each seizure, and since she said she wanted to be able to "handle these alone," we created a comfortable place in the corner of her room where she could lie down on well-arranged pillows, "just in case no one was there," and put a tongue suppressor, which we spent a very laugh-filled afternoon practicing with, in her mouth. When the "seizure palace" was finished, she apparently felt quite satisfied and said that now she could go through her seizures without "bothering anyone." Much encouragement was given her not to resist the seizures.

S: "Let them move through you like a wave through water. Your resistance makes you feel like you will shatter. Perhaps there is some other way you can work with the seizures, some openness, some softness you can bring as the first tension and fear meets your recognition that you are about to go into that space."

Her work with her seizures paralleled her work with her healing/dying—to let go and open to what she kiddingly referred to as the "great softness," which, though it sounded like something out of a Peanuts cartoon, seemed to allow her a little more room for her fear and acceptance.

About a week later Mary had one of the volunteers dial our number: "You know, mmmm, another funny thing happened last night. I woke up and I thought I had left the light on in the room, because it was so bright around the mantel. And I looked up and there was light pouring out of that picture of Jesus. Mmmm, does that sound crazy? But the glow was so bright that I could read the titles of the books on the shelves nearby. There was no other light in the room, just this shining from his face."

From whatever level, for whatever "reason," Mary obviously had a strong connection with Jesus. Thus it was suggested that she might explore the use of the Jesus prayer, the mantra used so exquisitely by the Eastern Orthodox Church—"Lord Jesus Christ have mercy on me"—which we have found useful with many patients. It seemed appropriate for her to start repeating the prayer silently over and over again in her heart. In times of stress, in times when she thought a seizure might be approaching, in times of frustration when communication became difficult. When the mouth could not form words but the heart was yet attentive, she could repeat that mantra over and over to remind her of the light of her true nature and the quality of mercy and forgiveness for which Jesus is the perfect metaphor. After repeating the prayer aloud with her for some time, we reminded her that it wasn't even really a prayer. "Prayer is usually thought of as an asking for something, but remember the deepest prayer is the deepest listening. You are not so much asking Jesus to have mercy on you, even to hear you, or change you, so much as you are listening, opening, to the merciful quality of the universe. It is for some at one level an asking to see as God sees, to feel the compassion for all sentient beings that is represented by the sacred heart of Jesus, to feel the heart of Jesus beating in your chest."

M: "I can't even believe it happened but I know it did. That light was so bright in the room. In a way it is sort of like this cancer. I can't believe this happened either but it has."

Her words would falter now and again as she attempted to make this impossible grace communicable to others even though she did not completely believe it herself.

As the support group around her grew over the next weeks, two opposing polarities became evident, each vying for Mary's attention. A few of the volunteers and nurses were fundamentalists who insisted she could get well if only she "believed." On the other hand were two or three people who had attended a few of the Conscious Living/Conscious Dying seminars and had worked with a few patients before, who wanted her "to die consciously." As each of these factions began to present themselves, at times they seemed almost like the cartoon characters of an angel sitting on one shoulder and a devil on the other, each giving conflicting advice as to what she *must* do to be whole. Never had we seen such a distinct conflict between philosophies confusing the patient and undercutting her trust in herself, each side competing for her "soul" as a means of bargaining with their own feelings of unworthiness. Those saying, "She must believe," were manifesting a considerable lack of faith and in a sense were using her to bargain with their own confusion about their relationship with God.

On the other end of this tug-of-war were those few who maintained that she *must* "die into the light." These too lacked a certain awareness and confidence in the natural process of dissolution and spiritual evolution. In vying for her attention, they "fire and brimstoned an unconscious death," reciting poorly interpreted quotes from the *Tibetan Book of the Dead* and personalized "Buddhaisms" to make their point. As one of the team who was not involved in the war commented, "They are 'Sething' her to death." Instead of encouraging her to open to the moment, these unconscious "conscious diers" were filling her mind with their spiritual confusions, defining imperatives of what she should be doing and how she should be dying. Because they were not investigating their own motivations, they were not encouraging her to investigate her heart and mind but instead calcified her natural momentum with a lot of rules and expectations which only caused her more insecurity and self-doubt. "You must soften. Try harder to let go. If you don't stay clear, this is going to be terrible for you." They displayed little compassion for her while insisting she "die the right way."

She had become for each team in this tug-of-war an object of their doing rather than the subject of their love. She was being assaulted by aura-balancers, Bach flower remedists, charismatic healers, traditional medical personnel, ministers, priests, and confused do-gooders of every dimension, each with their own ax to grind, each with "something to sell."

We spoke individually to the competing clans but to little avail. Each clique thinking we were supporting "those others." Each of the five or six helpers threatening to quit the support group and leave Mary without the ability to remain at home. Under other circumstances we might have offered the healing meditations, but as things were developing we sensed it might be better not to feed any more "directions" into what was becoming an increasingly confusing situation for Mary. When the confusion was most evident we would simply try to reinforce her faith in herself and the opening of her heart so she might trust her own way through.

Gradually, as urgent advice was transmitted by each faction

that she was "doing it wrong" by following the others, her trust
in the grace that had lit her for so many weeks began to be
dimmed by the old holdings that in the past had been her
normal modality of existence. When she would lament the confusion caused by these different perspectives, we would encourage her to trust her heart, that what she was seeking in
others resided deeply within herself.

One evening, returning home from a healing gathering with
a number of charismatic healers, she said that they seemed a
little peeved with her because when they asked if she felt anything after the hour-and-a-half healing session, she honestly
admitted "nothing in particular." At which she felt them withdraw. She said: "They are all uptight about the Holy Ghost.
They are in such a hurry. I thought it might take a while, but
they acted as though if I wasn't going to say I was healed right
then, they might take their cure back." When I asked why she
didn't stay the weekend as she thought she might, she said,
"They didn't want me to stay overnight. They were afraid I
might die there." We both laughed at the fear these healers
were bringing to what was supposed to be the openhearted
quality of healing. To which she said stutteringly, "Hmmmmm
—I thought it was me they couldn't heal, but maybe there is
more to it than that, eh?"

She went on to say that on the way home when she mentioned to her healer friend who had told her that this was her
"only way out" that she had a pain in her leg, her friend became
quite angry and said: "You mustn't say that you have a pain in
your leg, you must trust this healing. How can you be in pain if
you are going to be healed? You lack faith." Mary was very
confused by all this, and it took several minutes of sharing to
approach the recognition that the confusion lay all about her
and need not be her responsibility. "But I do have pain and if I
say I don't, then I am not telling the truth. Is that what I am
supposed to do?"

The beauty that shone from her when she just allowed all the
confusion around her to float free was quite incredible. Much of
our work together was just to accept the symptoms as they arose
—the faltering speech, the inability to walk easily—to demag-
netize some of the heaviness that a few of her "helpers" were at
times projecting onto her situation. Humor was one of the most

powerful tools employed to cut through the confusion and to allow some insight into the various imbalances of her predicament.

One day on the way to a matinee with my children, I stopped off for a moment to leave a book that she had said she was interested in. Though we had been with her the night before, she asked if I was going to stay a while, to which I replied I had the kids in the car and that we were off on our Sunday adventures. Hesitatingly, she said, "Well, have the p-p-p-pigs come in. Oh no, no. I didn't mean 'p-pigs,' I meant 'k-kids.' " We laughed so hard there were tears in our eyes. As always when the words got scrambled, we just came back to that place where "there is really nothing to say anyhow, it is all shared in the moment our eyes meet." On another occasion, when she had some sense that she might not be getting well and might actually be dying soon, when I asked her how she knew, she said, "I have a b-b-but feeling," then blushing, she said, "Oh no, I didn't mean 'but,' I mean 'g-gut' feeling." We shared deep laughter in these moments when it all became less of an emergency and the humor that had so often been lacking in her life became the medium of exchange.

Enter those who imagine themselves "conscious diers," who, when they saw she was not being healed, could be heard just offstage sharpening their harangues and holy books for the final assault on her mind. One of the fellows who was very busy being someone who could help others die consciously began fighting assiduously for her soul, reading her holy books and quoting her many things of which he himself had little understanding. Indeed, it turned out that at times he would call us, and when I would question his motivations and would explain the power of just encouraging her to let go with love instead of holding onto some idea about death, he would on the next day, sitting beside her as though in trance, recite some of what we had just said to him as though it were words from on high that she must conform to if she were to be a "spiritual person, a good one." He just made "letting go" something else to hang onto.

Much of Mary's confusion arose from her inability to understand, as her heart opened, why those she had known longest— her brother, daughter, family—seemed so "standoffish." Sometimes she would say to her daughter, "Oh, I am so sorry, honey, that things are like this," for which she would receive a frown and hunched shoulders which stalked angrily out of the room. Mary's heart seemed to be broken from the lack of response from her loved ones as her mind seemed broken by the intense response she got from those few "healers" that stood on either side of her bed, vying for her attention, each turning her into a trophy.

At times, she seemed almost to comprehend the holy war going on around her, though we never attempted to "overcome" the combatants with any negative references to their "stuckness" but just encourage her to trust her own heart, to remember: "You are the path. All those we meet are just a mirror for the mind, for our holding and fear—a reminder to let go and trust the heart of the matter." Often during the foot massages she enjoyed so much, to give some perspective, we would investigate how her "helpers" each differed. Some seemed to bring great energy and love to her, while others, those who thought of themselves as healers or conscious diers, were taking energy rather than giving it. With her foot in my hand I would laugh and say, "Well, I guess I've gone beyond them all, because now I've got your soul/sole right in my hands." To which she would reply, "Oh, Stephen, sometimes you are so c-c-c-corny."

About six weeks before she died, speaking over breakfast of the travail of the last year and a half, Mary said: "You know, in a way it has all been worth it. The loss of my job, the loss of my hair from the chemotherapy, the loss of my mobility—it has really been worth it, because I used to be a nurse and I see how I wasn't open to other people as I might have been. I feel like I have been taught what I have always needed to learn."

There were moments when she could touch that spacious understanding, but because her fear had met with so little investigation up until that time, and because her doubt and anger had always been her confidants, she could still very easily "lose it," contract, and close off because of the confusion surrounding her, which was a perfect projection of her own inner conflicts and doubts.

One evening after what turned out to be her last meeting with the "healing people," she called in tears to say that she thought Jesus was abandoning her because she couldn't heal.

"At least that is what they have told me and maybe it is true."
And she said that she had hoped to receive a baptism from the
group, but they felt it wasn't appropriate, and what could she
do? But instead of getting lost in the fear and doubt which had
so often been her way, we started a creative spiral upward,
playing with the idea that it might be time for her to have a
baptism–pizza–good-bye party for those who had served her
and loved her over the last six months at home. She became
very excited about the idea and for the week preceding the
baptism-pizza party would ask daily, often forgetting what had
been said, about when the party was to be held.

On Sunday evening twenty of her closest friends and "helpers" came to form a circle about her as she lay quietly in the
center, singing "Amazing Grace" and other songs of the heart,
sharing the "Holy Pizza of Infinite Compassion," holding hands
for a slow circle dance, ending with "a farewell song" as each
person went into the center of the circle to hug her good-bye
and wish her safe passage, dipping their fingers into the holy
water that had been brought from a nearby monastery, sprin-
kling it lightly on her forehead, saying adieu as she clasped the
picture of Jesus to her heart. It was for her a time of spiritual
healing, a moment of love and quiet. The peace that filled the
room was for many the peace that surpasses understanding. For
others, however, confusion raged in their eyes that she should
have "the nerve to give up, to say good-bye, when she could still
heal herself." The makings of every holy war that ever existed
were present in that room in that moment. Righteousness.

As the last pieces of the "Holy Pizza of Infinite Compassion"
were passed around to the tune of "Happy Birthday to You,"
tears flowed from Mary's eyes as each person about to leave
came up again to kiss and hug her good-bye. Some surrendering
into her, their bodies disappearing with each embrace, others
stiff and needy, meeting her death with fear rather than love.
Their own morality only too clear. Their lack of faith like ripples
in an otherwise still pond.

We stayed for some time after everyone departed, laughing
and singing with Mary about the joy that even death could be
met with when one's heart was open.

Within a week Mary's seizures had become so intense that she
felt a need to return to the hospital. In talking with her about

the difficulty she was having in surrendering to these seizures, aside from the obvious lack of control, she said: "Well, I keep a picture of Jesus near me, and I look into his eyes as I lay down and put the tongue suppressor between my teeth and feel that strangeness coming over me, and looking into his eyes helps, but somehow I just clench down. I just can't surrender, something is holding me back." As we talked further, it became clear that it was not, as she would say in her typical innocence, some "spiritual problem," but rather the fear that she would become incontinent and "defecate in my clothes during a seizure." This very deeply conditioned taboo was even more frightening than the shaking of her body or any drooling that might occur. Once we saw together what was happening, we began to explore this profound taboo and began again and again to melt into gales of laughter, at which point she said, "W-w-w-well, I guess I'll have to figure out which is stronger, my love for Jesus or my fear of poops."

A few days later we visited Mary in the hospital. As we entered the room, we noticed that the wig she always wore to disguise her baldness had slipped off a bit. Hearing the door open, she opened one eye and weakly reached to recover the wig laying beside the pillow and put it back on her head. I laughed and said, "Mary, if you think you are your hair, what are you going to do when you drop your body." To which she shyly, almost coyly bowed an acknowledgment with a shrug to her body's weakness and its approach toward death. A long conversation ensued about letting go of identification with the body and beginning to focus more on each sensation, seeing the body as something rented on which the lease had expired. I encouraged her to go deeper, to remember the light pouring out of Jesus' picture, the light of her own true nature. "But," she said, "I can't even remember the Jesus prayer at times, I can't remember how it goes, and all I can do is say over and over, 'Jesus, Jesus, oh, sweet Jesus.' "

S: "That sounds just right. It isn't the words, the mind of it, it's the heart that cuts through the holding and fear and opens us to the mystery and invulnerability of just being. You have Jesus in your heart and the words don't matter anymore. Just sweet Jesus moving through your heart. Let him absorb your body.

Give your body up to the light of Jesus that you know exists when you trust yourself, when you trust your deep nature."

Over the next three weeks as she approached death, we visited almost daily and noticed that fewer visitors had preceded us each day. The healers fell away "because she was not doing it the right way," and the conscious diers sought to escape because they said: "She doesn't want to die consciously, what do I have to hang around for? It is just awful to see. I didn't think it was going to be like this." Soon only those few who had stuck by her "as is," who had loved her for herself, remained by her bedside. They would sit quietly by her in prayer or meditation or just reading to themselves, just there for her as she might need. And though at times it appeared she was in a light coma, as we sat speaking silently to her in our hearts, she would occasionally open her eyes and turn her head to look and say, "You know, I love you," and then close her eyes and return to the mezzanine.

In the last ten days she complained bitterly that the nurses were not answering her bell and had told her she was "getting to be too much trouble." The nurses had in fact put her in a restraint so that she couldn't "keep bothering us." We brought this up in general rounds and were told a "seven-point plan of greater nursing attention and counseling was in the works"— but it never came to pass. A halfhearted attempt was made to deal with her problems but seemed to diminish in direct proportion to the degeneration of her body.

It felt as though the staff had emotionally given up on Mary. When we brought this to their attention, there was an angry denial and much less eye contact, which, after three or four other such cases of giving up on a patient, eventually caused us to withdraw from the hospital and move on to another institution which had requested a training for their personnel. Her leg muscles contracted and drew her legs up under her in a stiff embryonic position because she was so seldom moved or massaged. Bedsores began to develop. We gave her what aid we could, massaging and washing her, but our daily visit was not enough. Her tongue, because no oral care had been maintained, became fissured, and her gums bled and increased her distress considerably. She refused to come home with us, because her fear of dying and her old conditioning made her feel "the hospital is the only safe place." Again and again, our work with her was simply to encourage her to soften and open to how things were as we continually attempted to get better care for her from the staff but were met with a kind of indignant resistance that said, "She is all right, she is dying anyhow."

Three days before she died, she looked up and said, "Isn't there something that can be done? Some operation or something?" Her tears flowed. The denial that so many had reinforced found root within that part of her that was already too willing to withdraw from life and death.

Although our names were in the records, to be called when it seemed that she might be approaching death, it was because of a sense of the moment on awakening that we called one morning and were told that she seemed "to be dying right now." We arrived at the hospital half an hour later, perhaps three minutes after her last breath. Despite this embryolike corpse lying beside us which looked as though it had died in considerable distress, there was nonetheless an extraordinary feeling in the room of incredible expansion. There was the unmistakable presence of peace. It felt as though she were at dance in fields of light. In fact, one could almost hear her saying, "This is just too good to be true." We encouraged her to trust the light and move toward her real nature. To let go of the body, the painful life just left behind, and remember the connection with her Jesus, to merge with the sweet, sweet Jesus she had called on thousands of times in her heart.

Because Mary had signed her body over to us, we called the funeral home and made arrangements for the cemetery to prepare her plot. Returning home, we called those she had designated to be present at the funeral and told them it would take place later that afternoon. The arrangements had been made weeks before at the cemetery and mortuary; however, three hours later when we called the hospital to make sure everything had been taken care of, we were told that the mortuary still had not picked up the body. The funeral was less than an hour away and it seemed that Mary's life-style of many confusions and long hesitancy had not stopped with her dying. It made us laugh remembering that sometimes when it would take her ten minutes to go from the bathroom to the bed with her walker, she would laughingly bemoan her "slowness" and say, "Mmmmm, g-g-g-golly, if I'm not c-c-c-careful, I'll be late for my own funeral."

Several phone calls later it seemed that the hospital and mortuary were coordinated in their efforts and that arrangements for a funeral could continue once again. An hour later we turned off the freeway toward the cemetery expecting to find her friends and her at graveside, but instead we noticed that her hearse was indeed behind us and had followed us off the freeway. We shared one of our last deep laughs with her, "Ahh, Mary! Again, eh?!" And you could almost hear her slow, giddy, laughing reply: "Mmmmm—what's the rush?"

It was a gentle ceremony attended by many of the people who had already said good-bye to her at her baptism-pizza party. Only the healers and those who insisted she die their death for them were absent. Her neighbors and many of her support group were present with soft tears and songs of love.

About a year later, passing by the cemetery, we decided to stop by and see how Mary's plot looked. But when we went to where she had been buried, beneath the piñon trees, the bewilderment and helplessness of a lifetime were still in evidence. Her headstone was fifteen feet away from where she had been buried.

Ondrea, kneeling next to the unmarked identation beneath the piñons, put her cheek to the ground and said, "It's OK, Mary, some days nothing goes right."

A Deeper Pain than Dying

KATHY

Several years ago, about a year after setting up the Dying Project, we received a note on the back of a Xerox copy of our most recent newsletter: "I am a nun from a convent in Alaska visiting the west coast on sabbatical. Someone gave me your newsletter and I was much impressed that the work you are doing is the work of God. I so much appreciate your service in the world. Also I must admit my interest is somewhat personal in that I am presently in the process of dying of leukemia." It was signed "Sister Katherine," followed by an address and a phone number.

We called Sister Katherine that afternoon. Her voice was childlike as she told us quietly of the course of her illness over the past two years. As we spoke, she melted into tears, displaying her anger at the mother superior of the convent in which she had lived for the past five years. "Being the youngest nun, it was my job to take care of all the older nuns when they became ill. Until the doctor told me I had leukemia. Then they said I had to leave. I took care of all of them, but when I got sick, I was told I had to leave the convent because it was not set up to care for someone who was dying."

Because there was soon to be a five-day intensive retreat about fifty miles from where she was staying, it was suggested that she come as our guest.

I met Katherine about an hour before the workshop started. Her pale, moon-round face and green eyes emanated a certain spiritual urgency as well as an open warmth. Many who met her during the next five days commented on her softness and her seeming openness to life.

During the first day of the retreat, she spoke of her feelings of betrayal by the Church and the nuns with whom she had been cloistered for so long. A wave of resentment could be felt moving through the sixty-five participants in the meeting room. Indeed, on one occasion it became appropriate to investigate with the group how their hearts were closing in anger to the mother superior as they listened to Katherine describe her difficulties. Clearly, her story affected most who heard it, triggering that place of impotent rage at injustice. As Katherine talked about the doctor she had been referred to in San Francisco, her tone changed considerably, speaking of how much she appreciated the care and attention and respect she received from Dr. Millston.

On the third day of the retreat, at seven in the morning just as the group was going to meditate, I was called down to Katherine's room by her roommate, who said that Katherine seemed to be very ill. I asked Katherine if she would like me to call Dr. Millston, but she said, "No, this might be my time, and if it is all right with all of you, I would like to be able to die here in this place of peace and loving." We quickly established a support group of volunteers drawn from nurses and hospice workers among the workshop participants. They agreed to stay with her in twos for two hours at a time. And although I had to be with the workshop most of the day, when I had an hour or two during meals and through most of the night, I stayed with her, working with guided meditations, massage, and quiet sittings together. Sometimes we sang, sometimes there were hours of silence, my hand resting gently on her arm as she tried fitfully to sleep. By the second day of this, the concern of the group was so strong that, with permission, every half hour as she felt up to it, another individual would come and sit with her and share these final moments. At the end of two days she seemed to be coming out of her considerable discomfort. Her hemorrhaging, she said, had stopped, and the bruising that often accompanies the phenomenon of leukemia seemed to be no longer increasing. A couple of members of the retreat volunteered to take her home to San Francisco where she could rest yet more easily, in that she was too weak to attend the rest of the workshop.

When I returned home, a phone call from Sister Katherine awaited me. I called to find out that her physician had increased her dosage of morphine to counteract some of the pain that she said was "like the marrow in my bones had turned to molten lava; my whole skeleton felt like it was on fire."

Over the next six months Sister Katherine became Kathy to many of those who were working in support of dying patients in her area. Many came to love her, spending a great deal of time with her in her periods of distress, at other times taking her out to eat or going to a movie with her because she knew so few people, her life having been cloistered up until that time. Her only other friends were a few brothers in a nearby Christian order and a few other patients.

I remember one night in particular when someone had lent her their apartment while they went on a pilgrimage to Mount Athos in Greece. All about the apartment were pictures of Christian saints and in a predominant position a picture of Thomas Merton. We spoke of Merton for hours, and she told me of her wish "to live again in cloisters." She said that much of her life had been dedicated to the service of Christ and that even her death she wished to use in such a manner. But as we talked, it became evident that there was a kind of unexplored "dead spot," as she called it, that "lacks the great faith that I need to surrender into God." Surrender was still an idea in the mind that blocked the willingness of the heart.

Over the next weeks it became clear that the reinforcement of her faith was the perfect preparation for her death as she spoke more often of periods of hemorrhaging and difficulty with pain.

On one occasion while visiting her, her pain became so intense that, because she had run out of her pain medication the day before, we called a physician friend in a nearby emergency ward. He prescribed enough potent pain medicine to take her through the next couple of days until she could once again see Dr. Millston. The medicine seemed to help some, and we sat up through the night talking, as she dozed off and on, able at some moments to let go of her pain, while at others frightened of the approaching unknown.

Around four in the morning Kathy turned to me and said, "I have been so sick so long I almost don't know any other way of being. But the help that you all have given me has reinforced my faith. In a way, I feel I am more in sanctuary now than I ever was in the convent. All I ask of you all is that you be here with

me in my times of need. I hope I am not being too much of a
problem, too much trouble. It is just that this is so hard for me to
go through alone."

Having worked together for about nine months, it seemed
that it might be appropriate for Kathy to participate in a considerably larger, longer Conscious Living/Conscious Dying intensive that was coming up. She arrived at the workshop with an
open smile and a bright smock, greeted by many she knew and
by others who had heard of her plight. On the second day of the
retreat she felt too weak to attend the sessions that were going
on in the main meeting hall, but because she had become so
much a part of the collective heart of the group, periodically
various teachers and participants came to visit her as she lay in
bed. She was never without a few loving faces and kind hands to
support her as she went through her process. Once again her
hemorrhaging increased and the black-and-blue discoloration
on her legs intensified. "My body is on fire. All I have is the
loving hearts and hands of those about me to keep me cool." On
the second day her pain was so intense that we took her to a
local hospital, where, after a few questions, the physician gave
her a strong shot of morphine and a prescription for more to be
taken orally to alleviate her discomfort. Gently, we took her
back to her bed and in turns sat with her much of the night. For
the next few days several people carried her into the workshop
where she would participate as she wished. Mostly, she lay
quietly, occasionally a sound of discomfort arising from her
when she tried to find a comfortable position.

Over the next five days Kathy consumed a considerable
amount of morphine in order to help her cope with the immense discomfort she was experiencing. Nothing seemed to
help much, so the minstrels and storytellers came to try and
lighten her spirits as the meditators sat quietly in the room
sending her loving energy. Her room became like a sanctuary.
Those who were agitated found peace upon entering. Those
whose intellects were most active found their minds speaking
less and their hearts a bit more able to hear. Clearly, the process
of serving her was deepening all who had come to the workshop. After being driven back to San Francisco from the workshop, she was greeted by many of those in the religious community in San Francisco who had heard of her predicament and

were more than ready to help. As she left the workshop, the
more than one hundred participants sang to her, wishing her a
sweet farewell, each thinking they would never see her again.

In San Francisco, it was obvious that she needed more care
than living alone would allow. A roommate who cared greatly
and a temporary home were found for her. About five days later
I received a call: "I am dying. Could you come up and be with
me?" Within an hour and a half I was sitting by Kathy's bedside
looking at her pale, round face thinking that this was perhaps
the last farewell after these ten intense months of working
together. But somehow the pain passed and we encouraged her
to rest easy.

Once again the shadow of death had passed across her and
she was, as she put it, "given another moment of reprieve,
another moment to find myself before I meet my Maker." Because the house she was living in did not offer the kind of round-
the-clock support she seemed to need, arrangements were
made with a local Christian brotherhood whom she had spent
some time visiting with who willingly offered to take her in and
care for her in her final days, weeks, or months. "Whatever is
necessary to serve her," they said. It was planned that she
would move to the care of the brothers the following week.

Three days later I received a phone call from one of the
brothers who knew of our work with Sister Katherine. "Something is wrong," said the brother. "Having heard her mention
Dr. Millston, we called to see how we might better serve her
but were told that Katherine was not his patient. Checking his
records, he found that she had visited only once some months
before, but after she had made appointments for subsequent
blood tests and other workups, she had never returned. Apparently, each time someone dropped her off at the doctor's office,
she just sat in the crowded waiting room until they left and then
departed herself. Apparently, she is faking it. She is not sick
with leukemia. What do you make of it?" For some time there
had been a sense in Ondrea and I that something was amiss. But
because each time we would open that subject to Kathy, asking
her if there was something else we needed to investigate in
order to allow her some completion, that dead spot she referred
to, an unwillingness to wholly surface appeared. Indeed, to my
surprise, when he said she wasn't sick, I wasn't even surprised

and found instead ironic laughter welling up in the heart. Obviously, she was in more pain than any of us suspected. After hearing a bit more of the uncovering of Kathy's painful history from the brother, I promised to get back to him the next day. I called Kathy to share with her the phone call I had just received and asked her what indeed was going on. At first, she said, "They must be crazy, Dr. Millston couldn't have said that." But something didn't ring true in her tonality, and I said to her: "Kathy, now is the time to confront the truth, whatever it may be. We have usually been talking about living, not dying, anyhow. And I would ask you in all honesty, 'What is happening in your life right now?'" There was a long silence and a deep sigh. "I don't know why they would say anything like that, I don't know what they are trying to do to me. Those brothers always were weird. They are just like the nuns in the convent, they just won't really stand behind you when the going gets tough." When I told her that the brothers had, upon speaking with Dr. Millston, called the convent in Alaska only to find out that she had been expelled for faking illness and excessive drug use, there was another long silence. "Kathy, now is the time for you to die out of whoever you have been and to become who you really are. Don't hold onto this suffering even a moment longer. You know, it doesn't matter whether we are talking about the pain of leukemia or the pain of the mind. Our hearts still touch. But the honesty of the moment must really be honored. Now is the time for you to let go of all masks, even the leukemia mask. Now tell me, what is the truth of this moment?" There was a muffled shriek and then she responded: "I have been doing this since I was five years old. I just don't know how else to be. This is the third time I have gotten into this number. Each time I have pretended to be real sick I have promised myself never to do it again. I hate myself for doing it but I just can't seem to stop."

We spoke for about an hour and a half about how she felt "being uncovered" and who was really under all the pretense and fear, that posturing at life. It turned out that at various times in her life Kathy had become addicted to morphine through these pretenses that often even physicians did not recognize. It was true that she had been in a convent in Alaska, not for five years but for eight months, and had been expelled because of an inability to respond to the environment with any sense of surrender or serenity. A call to Alaska clarified that the mother superior had been very deeply concerned for Katherine and was completely taken in by her until a local pharmacist called the convent to say that Katherine had tried to pass a falsified prescription. The mother superior had begged Katherine to seek psychological help. Katherine had left promising she would. Two months later she had written to us to draw out the attention and love she was unable to give herself.

But for us the response is always the same: to let go of attachment to results, to work with others to soften around their pain, to let go of the mind and open into the vastness of our original nature.

When I met Katherine in San Francisco about a month later for lunch, she told me how isolated she felt, how most of the support group was judging her and had pulled away. She said she felt "real put down" but that she intended to stick it out and "once and for all break this thing."

We spoke to her over the next weeks as she found an apartment and sought a job, no longer taking medications. Of the symptoms of leukemia, she said, "the blotching and even the hemorrhaging took a few days to go away even after I admitted that it was a ruse."

Some called her illness "hysteric conversion," a Freudian term for the mind becoming lost in itself, manifesting its imbalance in the body as an "imagined condition," which is on the one hand very real while at the same time false and illusory. But before the judgment became too thick on the part of those who had been counseling Kathy, it was pointed out to them that in a sense for most perhaps the very taking on of a body, the very desire-driven leap into incarnation itself, might be humorously seen as a type of "hysteric conversion" of the spirit into matter. "And can we even ask if an illness is 'real' before we ourselves fully understand the nature of the relationship of the mind to the body? Much less until we understand the nature of form itself? If illness is indeed as it seems, an imbalance of the mind and heart manifest in the body, what is it in us that gives preferential treatment to one who is ill from cancer over one who is sick with fear and confusion? Indeed, there are some who insist that cancer is a manifestation of such imbalance. Why should our heart open any more to an imbalance in the body than it might to that same distress in the mind?"

Clearly, our work with Kathy had changed very little: to prepare for the unknown of each day, of each hour, of each moment, opening to the present millisecond in which life was unfolding. Learning to let go of fear and merge with the underlying sense of being that connects us all. Kathy seemed to be working hard to correct her "miscreancy" of the past. Letters of apology were sent out to many, and many felt she was "really beginning to heal."

A few weeks later Katherine called to say that she was returning to her parents' home in North Carolina. "My mother understands that I have been troubled on and off and has welcomed me home." A week later Kathy called from North Carolina to say that things were going well and that she was enrolled in school and "who knows, some day I may take on robes again." I smiled when she mentioned that and said, "Well, it will be a different 'habit' than the one you donned last year." We both laughed. I wished her well and suggested she stay in touch as seemed appropriate.

A few months later I received a call from a very tired voice that identified itself as "me, Katherine. Stephen, I am in New York. I have been doing it again and I have been busted by the police for attempting to acquire narcotics under false pretenses. What can I do?" It was suggested that she reinstate her therapy in North Carolina and yet deepen her healing by investigating her relationship with God, to pray. "But I have no faith." "Then pray for faith. Prayer is not telling God what you want, prayer is listening to God. Indeed, in this society if you speak to God it is called prayer but if he speaks to you it is labeled schizophrenia. But you are already ahead of the game since so many think you are schizophrenic already. There is nothing happening now that won't dissolve in your surrender and prayer. The healing never ends." We finished the conversation with a line from Thomas Merton: "True love and prayer are learned at the moment when the heart has turned to stone and prayer has become impossible."

We told her that we were open to working with her to the degree she was willing to begin to let go of her suffering. We said that most of what we could share with her had been said and would only be useful to her to the degree she was willing to work on herself. She was in our prayers and in our hearts but she must remember that "you are the path and must tread yourself honestly and lightly with kindness and compassion." We shared that this healing she was going through might be a slow and tedious one and that indeed at times she might wish for cancer rather than the fierce fire of a mind so drawn out of itself. We encouraged her to seek deep psychological reflection and said that if she wished, she could call back at any time for whatever feedback might arise at the moment.

We have since heard a rumor that Katherine had been arrested again and sent to prison. This, however, remains unconfirmed. But as a friend said when we heard the rumor, "Well, it looks like she got her monastery after all." We have not heard from her in years.

Although Katherine was the first patient we had worked with who was, as some put it, "faking an illness," she has not been the last. Of the thousands of people we have spoken to and worked with over the last seven years, perhaps a half dozen called because they had nowhere else to turn for the attention they so desperately longed to receive. One such situation occurred about two years ago when a woman from California called nightly between two and three o'clock each morning for about ten days. The woman's story somehow seemed amiss, but since facts and details can often be confused by one who is under heavy medication, we just shared with her as seemed fitting and sat back to watch what would unfold. After a few such early morning calls it was asked if indeed there might not be something else the matter. It was asked whether we might not indeed investigate her feelings of abandonment and confusion to discover some deeper meaning in these calls, to which we received an angry response: "I didn't want to say this, I didn't want to play on your sympathies, but I am having my cancerous right arm amputated in surgery this weekend." We didn't receive another call from her until three weeks later, at which time she lamented how little support she was given and how little her loved ones cared. When we suggested she meet a counselor we knew in her area and perhaps join the healing group there, she was enthusiastic that she had "somewhere else to turn." Calling on our counselor friend, we outlined the circumstances of the woman caller's situation, her lack of support, her recent amputation, her need for love. The following week we received a call from the counselor saying that the woman caller had shown up "in a silk dress and both arms." When the counselor had asked her about her supposed recent amputation, the woman had become very angry and accused her of "not being there for her" and had stormed out of the office, never to be heard from again.

Clearly, our work with Katherine as with all such beings is work on ourselves. Another teaching in helplessness, another opportunity to let go of ourselves, to be no one special, to gently watch the constant changes of the mind—going beyond hope and doubt until at last fear dissolves in the sense of endless being, in the connectedness that joins us all. Katherine's mind is no different from the minds of any of us. It was just that she held in fiery pain to her suffering. We can only wish mercy for such beings and for those parts of ourselves too that scream out for attention and in confusion rail against the way of things. Her suffering is as real as anyone's we have worked with. We wish her Godspeed.

The Intense Work
of Healing

GERRI

In early 1979 Gerri wrote us a long letter outlining her condition and wondering if we might act as a "sounding board for the changes I'm going through." Living in an isolated area of Minnesota, she said there were few people she could turn to who could understand her predicament. A few months before, while giving birth to twins in a cesarean operation, an unsuspected cancer was discovered. It had already become quite massive, though little indication of it had been recognized before. Rather than having the joy of two new baby girls, she had instead the confusion and agony of cancer and the distinct possibility that she would not live to see those children enter school. We spoke on several occasions and often wrote back and forth, long letters of sharing and introspection. What follows are excerpts from letters over a two-year period.

In one of her early letters she said: "I think you have begun a worthwhile venture. It seems there is a need for us to be aware of the emotions involved in the process of dying. Our society deals with death about as validly as it deals with life. Most people's awareness is incredibly egocentric and if you try to deal with death on that level—well, it must be quite overwhelming.

"The diseases I have contracted taught me many lessons. Shortly after the operation which revealed the tumor, I became extremely weak, to the point where I could not function on my own. I was unable to walk and barely able to feed myself. I spent the summer in a hospital room. I finally got things arranged at home—my husband was caring for our three-year-old daughter and our then three-month-old newborn twin girls. We obtained a hospital bed and I came home. My mother flew in from Dallas to spend time helping me with physical therapy and other needs. Progress was slow. Tiny movements increased my abilities daily.

"About the time I was beginning to get out of bed by myself, the muscles that allow one to swallow began to weaken, so after three weeks I returned to the hospital for another couple of months. It was the low point of my experience. After inserting a nasal feeding tube, they decided to switch to a tracheostomy and a gastro-tube. I was unable to speak or eat for about eight weeks. At the time I had no idea if the muscles would regain their ability to function, and I was quite miserable. I finally decided that I could not hope for any assistance from doctors and medicine and therefore put my energy to work on recovering.

"Today I am practically back to my full strength and ability. I feel I have gained much from my experiences. I seem to require this sort of thing as my life seems to continually test me in various ways. As far as the cancer goes, it is making me a better person and is therefore worthwhile. I suppose I chose it inasfar as we all create our own reality on some level. It has created in me a mysticism—a feeling of connectedness with nature, a closeness with the environment. I mean, we all realize the environment is getting messed up, but when it happens to us as a part of that environment, we feel that we are a direct extension of it.

"I have gained a lot from our work together, reading the book you sent and working with the meditations you recommended during the time I was confined to bed in the hospital. It helped me keep things in perspective. You know, anything can make you go crazy or not make you go crazy depending on your viewpoint. I view the cancer as serious and frightening, yes, but I also view it as a vehicle to learning and growing. I am more able to stand away from my emotions and let them flow by me. I am not as easily entangled in the physical realm. You would think the possibility of an early death would make one more involved in clinging to the physical world. Perhaps the separation I was forced into—from my newborn babies and my husband and daughter—helped me to adjust to that idea mentally. I don't know. I feel more challenged by the disease than threatened. I feel I can overcome it. There is reason to believe I will and I focus my energy to that purpose. The tendency we all have to look to the past or future as a better time is gone too. I can't relate to my past any longer and the future holds as many potential horrors as it does bliss—so I am pleasantly focused in the now. That is a nice feeling for me, for I used to tend to see my past or the future as somehow better than what I was going through at the time. I am currently enjoying myself, so there are benefits to the disease, believe it or not!"

Gerri and I continued to investigate through conversations and letters the deepening of her sense of participation "even in this melodrama." Her willingness to understand, to investigate the present moment into which she found herself catapulted, deepened our communications as well as her sense of "just being."

Some weeks later she wrote: "During my hospital stays I have begun to meditate and read, and my impression would be that I should chalk everything up to experience and not be attached to any of it. That is a difficult task for a mother of three! Our work together makes it clear that not being attached doesn't have to mean not feeling caring or responsibility toward others. I find myself catching myself in things now—in anger or frustration or even in love.

"I notice how deeply involved in this particular dance I am and I wonder how I will be able to detach—I mean, it is so hard to let go. Not only am I dealing with the illness and all its extensions into my life—like the radiation causing me to experience early menopause, and the hormonal/emotional trip that brings—but I have a mother-in-law just out of the hospital with cancer, a sister-in-law going in next week with an abdominal mass, and my only sister-sibling, who is mentally ill, to deal with. And I am beginning to laugh as I write all this down! It is getting to the point of overload—maybe I am trying to 'squeeze myself out.'

"I suppose one thing that troubles me is that with all I have experienced I don't seem to have had any 'peak experiences'— no visits from Christ, no melting into the One—I mean, I feel cheated at times! (More laughter.) I was discussing this with my husband Bob and he laughed and said, 'A gradual awakening, remember?' I suppose I am too Americanized—everything has got to be instant—which puts me in mind of fast foods—they are instant all right but look at the quality.

"My state of mind lately has been tumultuous—as I said, the hormonal thing has me on the verge of rage without cause sometimes, and general summer business, plus my cousin who has lived here with us since I got out of the hospital last September has returned to Philadelphia. It is a big change."

At times, Gerri was able to experience deeper and deeper levels of herself and at other times meditation seemed almost impossible, but always her honesty guided her on "the path with a heart."

"My attempts to meditate are a fiasco—I still have continual pain to disturb me, although it is much improved. I have a wild mind—I mean it really seems out of control, flitting from one thought to another—but sometimes I can catch a glimpse of what it is doing as part of a process and that inspires me with a bit of hope.

"I still feel edgy when it comes to true spiritual reality. I mean, I have been blocking it out for years due to disillusionment with Catholicism—Western culture—the white-male-guy-on-the-throne routine. It seemed much more sensible to be an atheist or at least agnostic. But I always felt there must be something more than this too. I want to find that ability to blend and let go because that is far more real and greater than the sticky fingers of the ego—but it is hard! And I appreciate your help."

Often we spoke of the "roller coaster mind"—the ups and downs of attempting to open to a mind that has been guarded for a lifetime, "that has so seldom allowed itself a vulnerability to the truth." Continually, I was impressed with her honesty. She seemed, unlike many people who regard themselves as "spiritual," not to be so attached to nonattachment. Always she seemed ready to face the truth and willing to discuss the places she was holding rather than exaggerating the places she was not.

After working together for a year, as her practice deepened, she wrote: "I am finding the path to be rather rugged right now. At times, that is. I am still having trouble with my physical being and have a great deal of pain due to a back injury. The mental stress of coping with the pain, and the drugs used to deal with the pain, have me a bit fumbled. I sometimes catch myself involved in bitterness and negativity—feelings that life is meaningless and that suffering is too. But then I will go out to the garden or out to feed the goats and feel at one with it all and know that is real. We are all part of the physical/spiritual world, and if we allow ourselves to blend and flow with it, we'll find peace. It is just difficult to let go of the mundane. The meditations are very helpful but oh, does the momentum of the past have power!

"Often I feel a great loneliness, like I am the only one in the world with this sort of trip to deal with. I have met others in the oncology wards that I have visited. They are strong, hopeful people. There is a fellowship that instantly exists between us that is nice—sort of like being a hippie in the sixties—instant rapport. We exchange our stories like hobos sitting around a campfire.

"Just took the three daughters out for a walk. Spring is here and today is exactly a year since I was operated on. It is the time of year I enjoy the most. I have been working outside in the greenhouse and a lot of my seedlings are up. I planted peas last week. It has been two years since I have been in the garden. It felt wonderful.

"My mother-in-law just discovered that she has cancer of the uterus. She has been having radiation therapy and will be operated on some time this summer. It was hard for me to accept. I felt that my having cancer would exempt anyone else, at least in my family, from having it. I have some strange ideas at times, don't I?"

As Gerri allowed herself more and more to "die into life," it was her involvement with friends that seemed to cause the greatest tug and confusion at times.

"My involvement with people is intense and I don't like to let go, but I know I have to. This is one of the lessons I am learning. There is no permanence. Everything is constantly moving and changing. Eastern thought seems more able to grasp that concept. My husband Bob is more Eastern in his philosophy than I. He sees things in a much different light than I do and finds much of my mental meandering comical, which delights me and keeps me from getting bogged down in too much bullshit.

"I guess what is happening is a kind of split in my personality. One part sits back and says, 'Look man—what will be will be. Relax and enjoy it.' The other part is a freaky soap opera character who runs around trying to be normal and occasionally cracks up. Somewhere in between and hopefully leaning toward the first is me."

We spoke occasionally of the "me that was lonely" and the occasional "parting of the clouds in the mind" and a going beyond loneliness to an "aloneness with God." An "at-one-ment."

"Still at times I do feel lonely though. I hear through my nurse sister-in-law of other young people who have the disease, and I want to run to the hospital and talk to them. I forget that the initial days after the discovery are pretty earth-shattering and that reaching out doesn't come until later. I am trying to discover, though, some small way, since I am relatively busy now, how I can help. I feel like I want to give support to someone who has discovered they have cancer, because I was given support by so many wonderful beings and it helps. I am afraid I am still into 'causes' sometimes, which I realize is ridiculous but still can't help but say 'Why me?' at times and try to find answers. But as I already mentioned, these times pass too. It is so wonderful to be open even to 'the darkness' without having to feel a need to escape or be anywhere else. It is not easy but it is so worthwhile!"

A little bit more than eighteen months into our work together, Gerri wrote: "I am doing well physically and mentally. Much has happened to improve things for me since I last spoke to you.

"The meditations you suggested, and particularly the pain meditations, are very helpful. The pain meditation is incredible —when I could quiet myself and relax around the pain, soften, it truly helped. I am happy to say that the back discomfort is greatly improved and I am getting off the codeine almost completely now.

"And as if this circus didn't have enough sideshows, I went to Atlanta a few days ago to see my sister-in-law, who had to have a hysterectomy due to an infection. She was pretty upset, because they have no children, etc. It was good for me to be with her and to try to help her through the initial rough period. I shared with her some of the meditations, knowing they will help her.

"Since I have returned, Bob and I have really begun to work on our problems. We have just been going through so much together, and now that things are relatively normal again, we have some adjustments to make. He was still treating me like the invalid I had been and my responses were all screwed up. Soap opera-ish at one moment—'You'll regret this when I am gone!'—not giving a damn the next moment. Expecting him to cure the situation, as though I was the only one who had been through an ordeal. We had begun to talk again in a deeper way. It was easy not to talk when we had my cousin living with us. She and I talked quite a bit.

"And as I come back into life, in some ways I feel more alive than ever. And that 'lifeness' makes me want to help others who are going through what I am. My sister-in-law who works in the oncology ward at the hospital told me about a twenty-year-old guy who just found out he has acute leukemia. I called him to let him know he wasn't alone. I think it was one of my biggest difficulties, the feeling of isolation. If you can feel like you are not the only one this has happened to, it helps somehow. I am hoping this fellow will call me back to talk. Perhaps some sort of gathering will evolve. I would like that very much. I feel better being able to help others somehow. This society doesn't offer many ways for us to help each other—we are all so closed up—unless a disaster strikes—anyway, maybe this fellow will be giving you a call one of these days.

"I have been working with *Who Dies?* quite a bit and it helps. Often I don't see any improvement, and then a situation will come along that I haven't experienced in a while and I will notice how effortlessly I respond to it. Not at all the confusion and darkness of the past. The light dawns so gradually you can hardly notice it and then along comes another scare—a fluky pap scare, a biopsy—but I did better with this one. When I had the liver biopsy this winter, it really upset me, but it turned out all right and I decided at the time not to become so snared in the mental/emotional hassles of the next one. But when this one came, it didn't seem to need a decision. There was just a bit more space. These events have become a way of life to me."

As Gerri's healing continued, she felt "more and more in touch with others who have gone through the same things I have in the last two years."

"Guess what? I have written an article. I hope to have it published. I could use the money. But also and more importantly, it seems like a nice way to help. I really hope 'my story' can be of use to others. I recall reading an article about a woman who had struggled to regain herself after being completely paralyzed in a car accident. It really encouraged me to keep trying.

"It is difficult to write a story much less finish a letter around here. My baby-sitters all went back to school and I am making the mental readjustment to full time mothering! This is the first time since my illness that I have had the three children without any help, except my husband's, of course.

"The full moon and eclipse took their toll on me. I felt uneasy, restless—this healing process brings a new kind of energy I haven't known so much in the past. Sometimes I feel almost as though Don Juanian figures are stalking me with hidden teachings. Oh, isn't it true, 'The mind goes first!' (More laughter, yes?) The ups and downs of this situation are wearing. They are so drastic, so dualistic—life/death, black/white. It is interesting but taxing. I have real trouble gearing down. I seem to have so much energy. I try to meditate for a while each afternoon. It is a busy time putting things in order for this coming winter."

As the healing deepened, the qualities that Gerri found had "blocked my life in the past" were becoming more evident. "This healing is a tremendous responsibility. I have re-entered life at a different level. I see and feel so much more than I did in the past. Not that it is any easier. But there is more of a feeling of being connected with life than I have ever had before, and it sustains me. In some ways this connectedness is the richest nutrient of the day.

"I am going to Philadelphia this weekend. A cousin is getting married there. My four-year-old is coming with me. I have an uncle there who has nephritis and is on a kidney machine three times a week. He has had it for ten years and has progressively weakened. Everyone says he wants to die. I can't really help but feel I can relate to his situation somewhat. I didn't want to live when I was feeling lousy all the time and was only alive because

of the tubes I had in my throat and stomach. I really didn't feel I
could accept *that* as life. And if the progress hadn't kept up in a
positive but slow way I was pretty sure I would have died. My
cousin asked me to see if I could cheer him up . . . I can relate
to it too well. Why go on suffering? I mean, I don't think he will
stop his medication or anything, but I think he will make a
decision to die and I can only support that. Not try to talk him
out of it. It is a big topic in my mind—if I have a recurrence,
what will I do? When do I decide that I have had enough? Just
the idea that I might have to face those treatments again terri-
fies me at times. I don't know if I could do it. And yet I never
thought I could do that one in the first place. I know it is
ridiculous to project like this, but it is like I said, a topic. I
suppose I am fiercely clinging to being well, but I notice that
any clinging causes some pain, and the idea of being unwell is
still frightening to the mind. Well, you really can't take that one
too far, because the mind has everything to say about everything so I will just let it be for a while."

As Gerri's health continued to improve, her joy became evident. "The weather has been incredible. Fall is an amazing time
of year. That hospital didn't have any means for enabling sick
people to be out and I missed being outside so much. I really
needed to be outside. That really helps to keep things in perspective, to sort of feel your insignificance/significance.

"Just saw my surgeon and he didn't recognize me. A real
thrill for me. Since I stopped the drugs I look like myself again—
not the bloated red beet I was! I feel, oftentimes, like a mirror
that has been shattered and then pieced together again so you
can clearly see the cracks but you know it wouldn't take much
to shatter the whole works. Sometimes my mind particularly
feels that way—fear, doubt—and sometimes it all comes apart,
floats, and reassembles. I try to keep aware, to keep tuned in for
the messages that come in. I always felt the ability during my
illness to pick up on these perceptions bouncing around. It
seemed to signify 'a greater me'—perhaps it has been the tuning into the One that has allowed me this connection. I still have
trouble with my atheistic tendencies at times, but clearly the
mind is what it is and I don't need to believe in anything to see
the underlying truth. As I see how wrapped up I was in Eastern
thought and basic Christian beliefs, I see how merciless I have

been with myself and how much healing there is to go, mentally even more than physically.

"It has been almost three years now and in some ways I feel better than I have in my whole life. Not that the fear has gone away or even some of the anger, but there is more room for my life. I have never been so alive."

After a few months we heard from Gerri very seldom and knew that the healing had come about on many levels. That in some ways by taking herself into her heart, she had healed at a more profound level than she had ever imagined. Cancer had been "a great teaching for me" and it seems she was up to the task.

Just the other day, rereading these letters some years after the fact, it occurred to me that I did not know how she was doing—whether she was dead or alive. But what was evident was that the work she had to do had been approached with honesty and courage and with a great deal of heart, and in many ways she had healed beyond dying by opening to herself, by becoming one with life.

Listening to the Heart of the Matter

WORKING WITH COMATOSE PATIENTS

During a weekend Conscious Living/Conscious Dying work-shop, at the lunch break, Don, a biochemist from the University of Washington, approached us through the group of well-wish-ers. The expression of bewilderment and chagrin on his face drew our attention. Don came up and said, "This may sound crazy, but if you have a moment now during lunch, I would like you to come visit my wife. She is in a coma in a hospital not a mile away from here." On the way to the hospital Don told us that a year ago, "coming home from a friend's house, Loretta had a seizure." For the past year she had existed in the shadow realms of coma resulting from that stroke, her every need at-tended to by Ann, her private duty nurse, who had come to the workshop and accompanied us on the journey to visit Don's wife.

Don had approached us because earlier that morning we had been talking about the patients in coma whom we had worked with over the past few years. We had mentioned that "a coma is like being on the mezzanine: You are not on the second floor yet but you have a whole different perspective of the first floor." We had said that coma was "like being between floors" and that it seemed, in our experience, to hold an extraordinary opportu-nity for communication and loving guidance. Don's attitude was quite agitated. Clearly, he was going against his religion, "science." This was all a bit irrational for his taste, but he had come to the end of his tether, unable to make peace "with her living death." "Maybe this is just silly, maybe we shouldn't be

going. I don't know what we can do anyhow. I hope this isn't
taking too much of your time."

When we entered Loretta's hospital room, we were met with
a wave of what felt like intense anger. "You had to wade
through it the closer you came to the bed," as Ondrea put it
later. Although when one is in a coma, one is supposed to be, or
is thought to be, "out of contact," we have found this not to be
so. As we stood on either side of her bed, eyes closed, Ondrea
placed her hand on Loretta's heart and we began to meditate,
sending loving-kindness to this form before us. Speaking silently to her in our heart, we shared something like, "Loretta,
wherever you are, if you can hear us, obviously you are not who
you may have thought you were. You are not this body lying
here like an old bundle of rags. If you are frustrated or angry,
that is natural under the circumstances. Be ever so kind to
yourself. You don't need to hold to this pale body even a moment longer. You can let go into your real nature. What are you
holding to?" Although no words passed between us, there was a
distinct "felt rather than heard communication" which responded with something akin to, "But I can't die. I am not
worthy to go to Jesus. I can't go to heaven. I am not a good
enough Catholic." To which we responded in our hearts, "You
are the very essence of purity. Your true nature is light itself.
Just let go of your feelings of unworthiness and fear. That is all
that keeps you from merging with your beloved Jesus. Allow
yourself the forgiveness of his great teachings. Experience yourself as Jesus must experience you—in great mercy. Let yourself
flow into the next perfect moment. There is no reason to hold
on. You can finish your business in a moment of forgiveness and
love. Try to see yourself as God sees you." As we meditated with
her, her breathing pattern changed and she settled down a bit.
Yet still there seemed to be a kind of psychic twitching, a ner-
vousness just beneath this seemingly immobile exterior, a
mental agitation and confusion that persisted through it all, a
sense of anger and immense frustration. We had never experienced such a degree of anger in a coma patient. It was our
sense, even beyond the frustration of not being able to move,
that "something else was up for her."

Driving back to the workshop forty-five minutes later, we
asked Don and Ann what could be the matter. "Is there any

reason you can think of that might have made your wife feel this kind of frustration and anger?" We went on to tell them of our sensed reception of her feeling of unworthiness and not being a good enough Catholic to die. Don blanched. "I never told you she was a Catholic. How did you know that?" Since this process of working with people in coma is such an intuitive one, going beyond the rational to just receive what seems to be available, we emphasized to Don that there was no magic in this, that this was available to anyone who would quiet down enough to listen beyond the more obvious voices of the mind. To hear the whispers in the heart we all share, being itself. "But, Don, let's not get too far astray thinking this is all something special. Let's get back to our original question of our sense of 'something being the matter' for Loretta, something blocking her heart. Is there anything you can think of that would make her feel such anger and frustration beyond the obvious difficulties of her condition?" As we pulled into the workshop parking area, Don put his hands on our shoulders and said, "Can you wait a minute? Can we speak a moment more?"

Don looked into Ann's eyes for a moment as if for permission to go farther and then turned to us and said, "Well, I don't know how to say this, but maybe this is the problem. Ann had been working with Loretta in a wonderfully loving way. Almost acting as a second mother to the children, being very supportive and perceptive of their needs. And although neither of us were looking for it or even thinking about it, all of a sudden one day we looked at each other in a different way. We fell in love after about nine months. We didn't want this to happen, but we have been lovers for the past few months. But there is no way that Loretta could know about this, is there? That isn't possible, is it?" When we asked Don and Ann if they had ever spoken of their affection or shown affection around Loretta while taking care of her, they looked at each other once again, rather sheepishly, and turned to us, Ann saying, "Well, we have such feeling for each other, we are often quite demonstrative when no one else is around." Ann's beauty shone like a light. Clearly, her extraordinary care and kindness had been the medium in which this love had grown. Obviously, their love was a powerful energy in their lives.

S: "But there was someone around. Just because Loretta's body is not moving, it doesn't necessarily mean that her presence is diminished. She is right there even though she can't communicate to you what she is feeling or thinking. Perhaps it is time for you three to have a little talk."

We explored with them their intention to do nothing to harm Loretta and how they were continually buying into the intense guilt that both were manifesting. "It might be more skillful to just recognize the purity of what you are feeling for each other and your original motivation to just serve Loretta. Your intention was pure. Any judgment that follows is just old mind looking for trouble, as is its wont. Rather than make guilt the coin of the realm, why not start investigating these feelings and allow your hearts to meet the confused mind with a little more understanding and forgiveness?"

We suggested that Don first go into the room alone and talk quietly with Loretta, letting go of his intense rational/scientific conditioning, and just speak softly to her from his heart, honestly and openly, about his relationship with Ann, which we sensed Loretta already knew about. Then perhaps a day or so later they could go in together and speak more fully to her, without any need to get into "confessional details" which might just create more confusion in their overcompensation for the mind's old guilt tape. To tell her of the feelings that had inadvertently developed between them. Not with fear but with compassion for themselves and for Loretta as well. On this second visit, more unasked questions might be answered, as they sensed was appropriate. And lastly, it was our suggestion that perhaps Ann could go in a day or two later and just speak "woman to woman" to Loretta. For the last six weeks another private duty nurse had been hired to take care of Loretta, for Don and Ann's guilt had become too much for Ann to "be there with Loretta in the way I would like to be. It is like my relationship with Don has come between Loretta and me. I feel so two-faced being around her."

Returning to the workshop for the few hours remaining, occasionally I would look over at Don and Ann sitting next to each other and have the sense that they were hardly present, their minds spinning with reruns of our earlier conversation.

At the end of the workshop they came up and thanked us for
our "time and energy." They seemed dazed as they walked
away with heads bent, hardly speaking to each other.

Three days later Don called. "Well, I went in there as you
suggested and I sat with Loretta . . . it was incredibly difficult.
I didn't know what to say. I felt like such a fool, but I didn't
know what else to do, so after a few moments I just said to her,
'Darling, I hope you won't hate me, but Ann and I, after all
these months of working together to help you, found that we
were falling in love." He went on to tell us the twenty-minute
conversation he had with his wife, "trying to explain how this
thing happened and how we both felt about her and each
other." As he spoke, he was very agitated, but he said that he
"felt better for being honest with her." Clearly, his rational
mind kept getting in his way, but something deeper, something
felt, was beginning to make its voice heard in his heart.

Three days later we received a call from Ann, her sweet, soft
voice choked with tears, her heart torn wide open. "It was
awful. But what a relief. We went in there and maybe for the
first time ever, with each other even, we were real straight
about what our relationship was and tried to explain it to
Loretta, just as though she were sitting listening to every word
—and by the way, I had an uncanny feeling she was.

"We told her how it had happened and how we had resisted it
for so long and how after months of confusion we had gone into
each other's arms and how badly we felt. We told her how we
would take care of the children and how even if she came out of
the coma, we could work it all out somehow. But for her to
know how much we loved her and how much we wanted her to
be well wherever she was. We cried and laughed and cried
again. What a relief at last to bring it all out. I love Loretta and it
just kills me to cause her pain. But it felt so good to be so straight
with her.

"Even now there is such a pain in my chest. In fact, ever since
we spoke yesterday this pain has been here. I feel as though my
heart is being ripped. It is almost like what I have heard you say
about the grief process. I guess I am grieving. I am grieving the
loss of Loretta's family for Loretta, I am grieving the loss of her
life for her, but I am also grieving for the way we have not been

honest with the world, with her family, and with her. It feels better now."

Don came on the phone: "I can't remember ever being so frightened as when we went in there to speak to her. But I don't love her any less than I ever have, and I only hope that somehow this can resolve something for her if that is at all possible."

When Ann called two days later to tell us of her "woman to woman" talk, her voice was much more steady. "I almost want to say, 'We talked for an hour this afternoon,' but she didn't say a word, although somehow, maybe because of what you said, I trusted something, and it almost seemed as though I could feel some of her responses. We would like you to come visit her again when you can."

About ten days after our first meeting with Loretta, she was moved to a convalescent hospital, for the doctors had long since said that there was no seeming chance of her "improvement" and that there was no reason for her to remain in the hospital, as treatment would be to no avail. When we visited Loretta in her new room at the nursing home, we both noticed how much more softness was felt. Standing on either side of the bed, meditating, we both sensed that she had let go of something that had been holding her back. There was still some feeling of tension, of frustration in her, but nowhere near the amplitude of our first meeting. Speaking to her in our heart, acknowledging the three conversations she had with Don and Ann, we encouraged her to recognize once again that she was not the body and that she could finish up business with herself with forgiveness and a deep letting go, to see her being as connected with, as a part of, the being of Jesus, to follow her path home as Christ. After our silent meditation, Ondrea and I sang softly to her, a song of great grace written by our friend Jai Gopal: "Lord, keep me shining for thee. In a world full of night make me pure, make me light. Lord keep me shining for thee." As we sang, Don's and Ann's voices rose gently in love and a deep communication of their care and hope for Loretta's well-being.

In the next two weeks we spoke to Don and Ann perhaps five times. As their contact with Loretta deepened, they put aside an evening and had a "sit-down with the boys," Don and Loretta's children, telling them much of what they had shared with Loretta. The older child was angry and agitated; the younger acted confused and resentful. Clearly Don and Ann's path was not going to be an easy one. But the honesty they had brought to it was opening the way for deeper communication and a possibility of "a long working through." When asked by the children if their mother was dying, they answered honestly that they did not know. When asked, "Couldn't Mommy wake up one of these days?" they answered again that it was beyond their knowing but that the doctors felt she could die at any time, that her condition seemed not to be improving in any way. And they added, "We are all in this together. We will just have to play it by ear and be very honest with each other, not pull any punches or overprotect each other." This truthful sharing had the potential of healing the fractured sense of family that had been experienced for the last year.

On our third visit with Loretta, about a month after we had first met her, the feeling in the room was one of stillness rather than agitation. Of some peace rather than the anger and sense of unworthiness we had experienced when we originally met. We stood on either side of the bed speaking gently to her. "You need do nothing now, Loretta, but melt into the sacred heart. Why hold on even a moment longer to this old body? Trust the light of your own great nature."

Upon leaving the room and being introduced to the head nurse, it was obvious that in the nursing home there was considerable judgment of the relationship that Don and Ann were exploring "behind his wife's back." The nurse told Don that it seemed that Loretta was building up some fluids in her lungs and that there may be the possibility of some pneumonia and that antibiotics would be required. After staying up most of the night, Don and Ann, "trying to get some perspective," decided that antibiotics should not be administered. When they told the nurse, they were met with a scowl and waves of disgust and disapproval. In the parking lot Don shook his head and said: "What are we to do? In a way, we are even more alone in this than Loretta. So many people think we are doing something wrong and sometimes I do too. It is so confusing, wanting Loretta to be free and happy yet wanting us to be free and happy too. But she does somehow seem more peaceful than she did a month ago. I don't know what this is all about, but somehow it seems to be working."

A week later Don called to say, "Well, they gave me such a hassle that I approved the antibiotics anyhow. People are so damn sure they are right. They gave her the antibiotics and the lung condition seemed to clear up almost immediately. But somehow there seemed to be something else going on. It almost seemed as though Loretta was 'finished,' as you would say. I don't know. It's all so weird when I hear myself say it. I don't even trust what I feel. It was OK with us that her lungs had cleared. We had long since committed ourselves to be with her as she needed, but something felt different. Well, the whole family went over that evening to sing Christmas carols to her, because it was Christmas Eve and we all just wanted her to know how much she is still a part of the family. But Ann and I really felt something had changed.

"After we sang to her, we just sat around real quiet. It may have been the first time that the five of us had any comfort together. The children seemed less frightened by it all. It was a beautiful moment, all of us just hanging out together. And three hours after we left she died." Don cried softly. "She really let go. We told her how you had said that Christmas was a time of birth and to allow herself to be born out of the body into the heart of Jesus. Normally, those words couldn't even come out of my mouth, they would have felt so odd, so unreal, but somehow as we were saying it, they weren't your words, they were our words. They were our hearts speaking and it felt like something was completing itself."

Don and Ann were married six months later—"after waiting for the children to accept our relationship a bit more." And they added, "Sometimes we look at each other and speak through our hearts of our love for the other. And send energy to Loretta for her well-being."

Again I would mention that there is nothing mystical about communicating with or sensing communication from those in coma. They seem to be on the mezzanine, apparently viewing all that is happening from a new perspective. It is a rich opportunity for encouraging them to see they are not the body and to recognize that their real nature is beyond harm.

Such was the situation with a fellow we had been working with for about six months as he went through the process of treatment for liver cancer. Near the end of his process, Carl was in and out of what one nurse called "a light coma." In the week preceding his death he laid very still and seemed "completely out of it," only twice answering a question and then only with a word or two, otherwise volunteering nothing. One evening four of us sat down around Carl's bed to meditate and wish him well with what he was going through. After about forty minutes the other three people went into the kitchen, but I sensed some deeper contact with Carl and began opening the mind to the place where it was just an allowing space, recognizing all the contents that passed through, noticing each thought as a fragile bubble, each feeling as a vague shimmering cloud passing through the vastness of our true nature. As this state of being opened, I suggested silently to Carl in my heart: "Brother, this space is available to you whenever you are ready to open into it. This is the open space of your real nature. Even your body is just another idea floating in this vastness of being. No thought, no fear that passes through, has anything to do with your original vastness. Only if you identify with these passing forms will they block your reception of your natural spaciousness. Let go, brother. Open to the luminescent spaciousness of being." The meditation continued for about another hour, allowing mind to let go of all that arose so that a glimpse of the peace of our underlying edgelessness could be shared.

During the meditation, even though the rational mind occasionally interjected that all this was "a bit showy" and questioned its efficacy, that too was just more content floating through the vastness, nothing that needed to be held to or reinforced. Just trusting the "don't know" open space of mind that clings nowhere and has room for everything. The meditation was shared with no particular attachment to results. Just another experiment in truth. Just a moment of awareness and love amidst the life-support machinery that hummed in the room.

A distinctly different sense of Carl's presence was acknowledged by the other three care givers when they re-entered the room after the meditation. Carl seemed now to be in a complete coma; spoken to, he would not reply. Even the loud sounds in the room, which had earlier caused him occasionally to stir, were now of no seeming effect.

The following morning while giving Carl a bath, I looked at

his emaciated body, perhaps half its former weight, and said: "Carl, how can you hold onto this old body even a moment longer? How can you imagine this is who you are? You are the light. Allow yourself to merge, to melt into your true being. Let your heart join with the deathless." Just as I had spoken the last word of encouragement, from the corner of his eye a single tear rolled down his cheek and he took one last soft breath and left the world behind. And I stood again in the midst of the unknown, trusting the intuitive mind to sense the next appropriate moment.

There are many stories of people we have worked with in coma. We have also heard many stories in workshops when we bring up the subject, from nurses and loved ones who say they too have "felt something" in their communication with those in coma. One nurse told about being with an eight-year-old boy who had "gone into full arrest on the operating table and never fully recovered." He had been in a coma for six months, but it seemed that no treatment could change his state, so after much deliberation the doctors and his parents decided to disconnect him from his support system and allow him to die. But he had not died when disconnected and for a month had remained an inert bundle of flesh which continued to dwindle to about twenty-five pounds. His appearance was so distracting that his parents had nearly stopped visiting, only coming by every few days to see how he was but spending little time with him. No one could understand why Mark was unable to die.

But one day, as the nurse told us, "I spent some very special time with Mark, massaging him and speaking to him and playing music and receiving a sense, almost a 'communication,' that what was keeping him from being able to let go was his concern for his parents' well-being. After work I called his parents and told them of what my experience had been that day and how I sensed that Mark was holding on because 'he didn't want to hurt his parents by dying.' " She related to Mark's parents the quality in children's minds whereby, though it is not always evident, they have a great sense of protectiveness for their loved ones and their parents in particular. She suggested to Mark's parents that they visit and, although they had said it was all right for him to die and had followed all the textbook recipes to help him let go, that it wasn't only his needing to hear that he would be OK, but that he also might need to hear from them that *they* would be all right too if he died.

Later in the evening the nurse said she received a phone call from Mark's tearful mother saying: "We went up to the room and played some of his favorite music on the tape recorder you left by the bed and told him that he would be OK if he died and so would we. And the nurse put his thin, thin, body in my arms, and I was just rocking him back and forth, loving him and telling him we would be OK, when all of a sudden there was a stillness in the room and Mark just let go and died in my arms."

Many doctors and nurses have related stories of working with patients in coma, speaking to them, reading and playing music, and generally relating to them "just as if they were there," and some of the remarkable experiences that ensued.

At one of our workshops, a woman who was in our long-established meditation group told a story about her eight-year-old daughter. Four years earlier her daughter had contracted a severe case of meningitis which after a few days the doctor had said was "too serious to cure." It was presumed she would die before the week was out. But the week passed and she remained in a coma, at which point the doctors suspected partial brain damage and said that she would never be mobile again, never again able to walk or see or speak for the rest of whatever life remained to her. Her mother, however, sensed some deeper possibilities and decided to spend as much time as possible sitting by her daughter's bedside, communicating with her and telling her, "I know you can hear me. I know you are in there. Trust me. We will bring you through this." And every once in a while, in long hours of looking into her child's eyes, she would get a "sense that she was passing by for a moment, that somehow she was there." And she would speak to her daughter, would "call her out" and tell her to "look out through your eyes now just as you are passing by, look out through your eyes, see through your eyes, let the light in through your eyes."

It worked. Within a month her daughter "was again present at times." There were moments "when our eyes met in bright contact." Within six months her daughter was on her way to being completely well. Within a year she had returned to school.

About a month later, in the front row of another workshop,

there sat beside her mother this same soft-eyed girl, now twelve years old, the light shining from her face. After the workshop, when I asked her if she had understood all that had been said during the course of the day, the language being so different from what she might have been used to, she replied: "Well, I didn't listen to everything, but everything feels real nice in here. In fact, this is the most peaceful group of adults I have ever seen and I would come back again just to be around all this love." A week later she sent us a picture of a mariposa lily under which was written, "Thanks for letting me join the workshop, it was gnarly."

No One Can Die
Your Death for You

MAGGIE

Part of the early process of working on one's self while serving those in crisis is that occasionally a patient will come along who for some reason tugs at us in a manner beyond our recognition and instead of being "connected" we become "attached." Somehow we lose our perspective and don't see them as spirit or process in transition. Instead, to the degree we too are caught, identified solely with our mind and body, there is the tendency to get lost in the melodrama, to meet suffering with fear and personal need rather than the openness of compassion. We "take it personally" in the same way that one might take frustration or anger, doubt or displeasure, personally—we think we are it rather than seeing it as just more of the clinging mind's old road show passing by.

Indeed, it is this potential for "getting stuck" that underlines the value of this work as a mirror for the mind, for our holdings and forgetfulness that no matter how many people there are in the room, there is still just a singularity of being shared by all. To the degree we think we are our body (as all seem to some extent) or the mind (as most do most often), we have the capacity for forgetting that the patient we are working with is not only an individual but also being in process.

Unfortunately, we did not record those early years of our work with the seriously ill, so it is not possible to share the moment-to-moment process of our holdings and insights with patients who we became identified with and held to in some subtle manner, though there were a few. However, as I write this, I recall the old Jewish woman, Sarah, with her crochet work next to her bed in the oncology ward. For weeks she had not wished to talk about her condition as we sat together for a half hour each day sharing the sunlight as it slanted through the hospital windows, talking about nothing in particular. These pleasant talks were like chats with my mother, whom she reminded me of greatly. It was a pleasant way to begin the day on the cancer ward. It seemed that Sarah and I were just together to share these pleasantries. It was not her temperament to talk about her cancer or the possibility of her death. Until the day I had to leave for two weeks to go to a meditation retreat. As I was leaving, she asked what such an experience was like, and we shared a few deeply loving moments about the heart work of understanding our true nature. When she said good-bye in a particularly meaningful way, though something intuited that this was the final good-bye, because I felt such love for her and a certain degree of attachment to my mother within her, something in me denied the finality of her good-bye and I missed the opportunity to share with her a moment of truth. It was the moment we had been working toward together all those weeks of just meeting each other in the sunlight, a moment when I might have shared some of the insights of other patients I had known as they entered transition, but instead I said, "See you in two weeks; be well." Three days later in meditation it was evident that I had missed the moment we had been there to share. It reminded me of the Sufi saying "If one offers words of the spirit to one who does not ask for them, you waste the words; but if one asks for words of the spirit and you do not offer them, you waste the person." I knew a week before I returned that she had died, and I sent Sarah my love and apologies.

These patients we get lost into as objects in our mind instead of the subject of our heart define our holdings, our forgetfulness of our true nature. They mirror those places we still hold to life as an emergency, as a struggle rather than as a teaching.

An example of this kind of "getting lost in a patient," of identifying with their separateness rather than merging with their moment as it unfolds, occurred for a counselor we worked with for almost two years. She was a dying counselor from the Midwest who for years had helped many people approach an "easier death." For a year and a half Maggie had been working

with Darlene, a woman in her early sixties diagnosed with terminal cancer, whose extraordinary vitality and interest in meditative practices had drawn Maggie closer. Indeed, there was a
way Maggie began to struggle to "clear Darlene," even to the
point that on occasion she would call and beseech us: "Please
call Darlene. I know she would like to talk to you." On several
occasions such requests had been passed on to us, and though
we seldom call anyone who has not directly asked for our ser-
vices, under these circumstances, trusting Maggie's insight into
Darlene, we would call. Most of our conversations with
Darlene, however, were not about her "spiritual needs" but
rather about her difficulty in communicating with her nine
children. Because she was so robust and active at times, they
had difficulty relating to her as someone who was dying of a
cancer of the blood. On more than one occasion Darlene had
said to us: "Because I go out dancing some evenings when I feel
up to it during these times of something like a remission, the
children will not acknowledge that I need more help around
the house at times and need more to 'complete' our relationship. When my energy feels up, I want to go out and dance and
have a hell of a good time, but still so often I am tired and I need
that help around the house. Most of the children are grown
now. And few of them seem to be willing to give me the support
I need. They are angry with me for having an affair when I am
supposed to be dying, and I am angry with them for treating my
dying as too light an affair."

It seemed to us that Darlene's work was to open to life by
letting go of resentments, to allow the healing of the heart by a
greater trust and straightforwardness with her loved ones, "to
stop buying love by being so damned nice." To which she would
reply, "Well, I don't want to get them mad at me, but on the
other hand, sometimes I am angry as hell at them!" Often when
we would speak to Maggie it seemed that she was interpreting
Darlene's actions in a much more spiritual context than we
sensed was fitting. The attachment in Maggie for her patient
and friend Darlene could be heard in what seemed a certain
misperception of both the depth and goals of Darlene's life. It
seemed as though in a sense Maggie was hoping Darlene would
die the death that Maggie would have chosen for herself rather
than allowing Darlene her own natural way.

After having worked so closely with Darlene, Maggie called in tears one day to say that Darlene had died the night before. Maggie seemed quite confused and in considerable pain.

M: "It is so hard for me to think that she is really dead, that I won't go back and see her on Monday. I've been feeling a lot of good memories and then regrets. Why didn't I say 'this' on the last day? I mean, no one thought she was going to die. Not at all. She was still being treated, so I have kind of mixed feelings and I am kind of worried about the kids."

We spoke of how it was not the depth of the involvement that was causing the confusion, it was the degree of attachment— "wanting to help her, protect her"—and how that may have caused her to forget that Darlene too was on her own spiritual journey and too was not her body or her mind but indeed another momentum in the universe heading toward completion. But one could hear the resistance, the holding to Darlene as "someone special."

S: "Doesn't your thinking of her as something special get in the way of your helping her? Mightn't it increase her fear of death by reinforcing the idea of something to be lost?"
M: "No, no, I don't think so. I just wanted to be with her when she died, and none of us sensed that the end was so close."
S: "You know, Maggie, everyone in this work, at one time or another, seems to experience some person they identify with. It might not be as obvious as 'she reminds me of my mother,' but there is a feeling that you are going to *lose* them when they die and, in a way, it is not OK for them to leave. So you become a dying counselor to someone you are trying to hold back from death, and the confusion ever so subtly undermines the foundation of the communication and the relationship."
M: "I guess my feeling was that it was OK for me that she died, but I feel really bad that I didn't sense her impending death and to call her daughters and get her children there."
S: "Her children had ample opportunity to finish their business with her. In fact, that was her biggest contention, it seemed. For almost a year there was such partial communication between her and her children that I doubt your last-moment, urgent

pulling of them into her deathbed would have helped much. In fact, she may have chosen to die alone, not surrounded by all the clingings of her family and counselors. It is not uncommon for people who have been surrounded by loved ones for months to choose a moment when they are alone with their own peace and spacious nature to allow themselves to dissolve out of that which everyone else is clinging to. That which everyone else is calling mother, father, daughter, patient. That which everyone else is thinking is in need of such help. It may be a moment of great compassion for that individual to just allow themselves to die out of being anything for anyone and to melt perhaps a bit more deeply into their original nature, the deathless."

M: "But they never worked it out together. I just wanted them to be able to say good-bye to each other without all the hassles of a lifetime coming between them."

S: "But we die the way we live. If we have been quarreling and living in a partial relationship for thirty or forty years, why should one day of just more hassling straighten it out. There was a place where she was quite unwilling to open to the children. She had quite a bit of pride, and I think that kept her thinking that somehow she was right, even something 'special.' Perhaps she felt she should have been accorded more respect than she was receiving from her children. She would often say to me that she had worked so 'damn hard bringing up those kids' and now they weren't 'coming through' in the way she thought they should."

M: "Well, you know, that may be true, because I said to her about a week ago, 'Do you think it's a good time—are you really feeling like you would like to talk to Stephen right now?' And she said, 'No, not unless I am feeling more sure of myself,' or something like that. 'Right now I am so into my worries that I will sound like I am self-pitying.' "

S: "I think you gave her everything she needed and then some and that when you asked us to speak to her it was only out of your own feeling of not being enough. You wanted us to talk to her because somewhere in your mind you wanted her to be more spiritual or something. But I don't think she wanted that. I never felt she was a particularly 'deep being' on a certain level. She was a lovely person who had worked quite a bit with her dying on some levels, and your help had allowed her to go deeper and experience more love in herself than she might have otherwise. I could hear the admiration that you had for her. I mean, she really had done a lot of work in her life considering where she may well have started from. And like all of us at the beginning of the search, much of that work was done out of feelings of unworthiness or that she ought to be more. Perhaps your idea of her as someone special intensified those feelings. No blame. No judgment. Just the intense learning that we receive from those patients we get locked into. I mean the kind of identification where you 'need' that person for some reason. I have had it happen and so has everyone I know who has worked with the dying. Rather than thinking of oneself as a failure with those patients, I think it more skillful to see them as a teaching in 'don't know,' to allow us to be yet more skillful with the next patient, to learn to love without holding, without a need for someone to love us back or even be 'worthy' of our love."

M: "Well, I think she was deeper than most people thought. She would meditate sometimes a few hours in the day while she was in the hospital. I never worked with anyone like her."

S: "Exactly. And you thought perhaps she was going to be that 'perfect patient' who was going to die consciously and disprove in some manner the suffering of death. That she was going to make it all right for all the other patients you worked with who couldn't get beyond the idea that they were the body. I suspect her meditations were of considerable help to her, but I very much doubt they approach the depth of your own sittings or introspection. My sense is that you projected a lot onto her.

"We both know people who meditate but yet who do not go particularly deeply into their true nature, because somehow they are still busy 'being someone meditating.' There is still a lot of self doing self. They are in the early stages of trading off being a carpenter or a mother or a potter for 'being a meditator.' Just more something to be. In a sense, they are just picking up more models of themselves rather than letting go and allowing the truth to arise as it will. There is a cultivated grasping in their meditation, an attempt to be someone or something other than the moment displays. There is never really the depth of 'Who is meditating? What is thought? What is desire? Who is dying?' And of course, there is nothing to judge in that. But when we have a model of someone, models themselves cause judgment, cause expectation, and therefore result in suffering. Our models put people out of our hearts, turn them into something with edges and an identity. Which is just more illusion, more investing the superficial with a reality which it does not inherently contain. Just more suffering."

M: "You know, as you speak, Stephen, I can feel the place inside of myself that was trying to rescue her. And perhaps that wasn't too useful. But I just loved her so much. I wanted so much for her. When she felt poorly, she was embarrassed to call you and when she felt good, she would say, 'I am feeling good now so I don't need to bother.' I guess there was just a place I didn't hear her. I think I may have been chagrined by her pride, because that didn't fit who I wanted her to be. So in a certain way I just denied it."

S: "Well, I think in a sense you may have been meeting her pain with fear and therefore were pitying her instead of really opening to her in compassion, instead of meeting her pain with your love and allowing her to be just who she was without any need for her to satisfy any idea that you may have had of how people should die.

"I always felt there was a place where you were having Darlene die your death for you. And that was something that wasn't so skillful, because it kept her looking outside of herself for help, looking to you, looking to me. Of course, I wasn't so close to her that I know what was going on. But it seemed that she was looking a lot outside of herself for the answer and as soon as she felt OK, not so vulnerable, she didn't look any further. And that somehow there may have been between you a subtle conspiracy to 'feel better' instead of experiencing the moment as it presented itself."

M: "My confusion was and probably is to some degree some unworthiness feeling like, 'Was I helpful? Can I help her to go deeper?' And I thought maybe you would help her to go deeper, push her to see beyond her clinging."

S: "But she never really asked to be pushed, never signed the contract, so to speak. When you first called and told us about Darlene, you told me you 'had a woman you were working with' who sounded a lot like some of the most remarkable patients we have met. In a sense, I could hear you saying, 'Now I have my conscious dier.' But when we had our first contact with her, that was not my sense of her at all. But it was difficult for you to hear what we were saying to you about that. And I sensed at the time that you both were learning together the art of dying."

M: "I think that is very true. When I first met her, I said to myself, 'Oh, far out! Somebody who responds to meditation.' "

S: "The places she clung to life, as we all cling in our stuck places, was making it all the more difficult for her. It wasn't like she decided just to meditate and 'delve the cosmic.' She wanted to live in the world a little more, to enjoy life, because she felt she had sacrificed so much bringing up those nine children and that the children didn't understand. She was angry as hell at them. I don't know if after our conversations she even used the techniques we offered her. My sense is that she just wanted to talk to another kind voice."

We spoke about how if you want someone to be any different than they are, less angry, more spiritual, anything at all, then in a sense you put them out of your heart. How if you want anything from someone, you won't be able to accept them, to love them fully. When you want anything from your children, your parents, your patients, you can see how that want creates a gulf between you. "If you want anything from anyone, you cannot love them fully, because they are still being weighed in the balance and found wanting. She didn't need to be more spiritual. She just needed to be kinder to herself. And I think at many levels she did exactly what she needed to do for her own dignity and her own self-acceptance."

M: "As you speak, I can feel the guilt. And it would be all too easy for me to say that it is something new. But actually I can see how this guilt is always there to some degree, and her dying is just focusing in on it. That feeling of not being there enough for patients when I want so much for them to be at peace. But I know better. I know you can't force peace. And I also know how to open to my guilt and my feelings of unworthiness and just to explore them in my mind and body. I guess I knew all along that she wasn't who I wanted her to be, but something in me, maybe some bargaining with all the people I have been with who died, wanted this one to be OK."

S: "And the others were OK too. They just died in their own

nature. In their own life. Not having to be different. Allowed
their own dignity and self-respect. If you want to take people's
pain away, you are in the wrong business, because this is the
business of opening to pain, of letting pain float free, not reinforcing a lifetime's aversions to the unpleasant. This is the work
of a willingness to love those who may be in pain, and may even
be unloving at the time.

"In a sense, we are not preparing people to die. We are learning to die ourselves. And the more profoundly we can die into
the moment, letting go of all that we think we are, of all the
mind's confusion and tumultuous changes, the more we can be
that silent space into which another can let go of their suffering.
But until we have come fully into our true being we too have
something to lose, to protect. And that is why this is such fierce
work on ourselves."

I shared with Maggie how I often will sit with a patient and
just meditate silently next to the bed and allow the mind to
come into the place of oneness where no idea of that being's
body or my body any longer reinforces the case of mistaken
identity that we so often suffer from when we think that another is separate from ourselves. And how in that place of oneness I experience the deathless and therefore do not reinforce
that place within them where they think death is anything
other than a further opening into their true nature, a deeper
uncovering of their not being their body or mind. Rather a
sense of light is shared, a sense of who we really are. And how in
that space of deathlessness there is nothing to be afraid of and
no one to protect.

S: "So much can be said without words. So much can be done in
silence. I think you gave her every impetus to do that deeper
searching. And I know that your meditations were touching on
a whole new space for her, because she acknowledged that in
our conversations. I think that was of interest to her, but it
wasn't the main interest in her life. She felt unlived and needed
perhaps a different sense of completion than you or I might."
M: "Well, this has been a tough one. I have known and felt the
struggle but somehow have not acknowledged it. I appreciate
your straightforwardness in sharing with me the places where

you see me holding. I think it is truly my lack of faith, my lack of trust in this process, that causes me to push people who have not asked and try and make them 'spiritual.' "

We shared how sometimes when you are talking with someone you often find you cannot go any deeper than their ability to hear. And you may say to yourself, "How come with some people I am so clear and with others it just seems so muddy all the time?" How it may have to do with *their* ability to understand. That indeed it may be another person's attachment to who they think they are that at times limits our intuition's ability to contact them at a deeper level. We cannot touch them in any deeper place than they are willing to go. So it isn't so surprising to notice that with one patient we will find ourselves deeply in that place of love, sharing it effortlessly from the very first contact, while with another it seems like a knot of intellectual folderol, just the same old tennis game going back and forth, just ideas being shared, never really touching the heart of the matter. That perhaps it is because it is not "our clarity." That we are just open channels to share whatever is appropriate in the moment.

As we were speaking, I remembered an experience the other day when a friend called and said he wanted to read me a couple of paragraphs someone had written about dying. It was really incredible stuff, and when I asked who had written it, my friend laughed and said, "You did! We transcribed it from a taped talk." I was impressed. Because we know so much more than we think.

I never know when I sit down to talk with someone what is going to come out, and I hear it and often learn myself from the moment's shared wisdom. Because The Great Teacher is our true nature, which is revealed when we let go of everything that blocks it: our identification with the mind, our holding to our suffering. I told Maggie how some of the beings we have worked with have so opened that we each came to a place where there was nothing to say, because what we shared had nothing to do with the mind. The silence entering into the heart of that moment.

S: "Our work seems to be only on ourselves. To learn to die into each being we meet with love. To allow our insecurity and fear to float in our experience of the boundaryless nature of being. To die into the shared moment. Without any expectation. Without any need for the mind to be different. But just to let it be."

M: "Thank you for being so honest with me. It is painful to hear these things, but I know that the pain is just my own grasping, my confusion. My imagining that I am separate from anyone that I work with. God, this is the most incredible work I could do."

S: "Letting go of our suffering is the most difficult work we ever do and the most fruitful. And in a sense, it is what makes it difficult that makes it so rich."

M: "It definitely speeds up the process of my evolution. Maybe in my next lifetime I will just take it easy and be a pastry chef or something. And my love to you."

Maggie's work with the dying is respected by many. Her work with Darlene some years ago gave rise to many insights which subsequently allowed her to be "present without need." Her teaching has allowed many hospice workers and hospital personnel to learn to "die into their hearts." What she has learned has been shared by hundreds. The effect of her work on herself has been to allow many a glimpse of what lies beyond their fear and self-doubt. She has become an angel of mercy as she has learned to be more merciful with herself.

Surrendering the Heart

RENA

There are of course many levels at which we work with patients. With some patients our work is just "to be there," an open space. But obviously, because our work on ourselves is still ongoing, this "open space" varies in density from day to day, much less moment to moment. Thus we continue to let go of what blocks the natural spaciousness of the heart as a part of "the path of service." But in these periods when "the heart just is," there is no "service"—for in those moments there are not two but just the one unnameable singleness of being, the manifestation of which is called "unconditional love" by some. Into this "open space" another may let go of suffering and investigate the nature of being as they wish. This is often a somewhat passive openness, a deep listening, with but a few suggestions as to methods or techniques.

For other patients, however, this shared spaciousness has given rise to a certain agreed commitment, as mentioned before, that we call "a contract." A requested agreement to actively "do whatever it takes to bring me through." There are several instances of this contract evident in various parts of this book. When a contract exists between two people, it is an agreement in honesty and truthfulness and is on the part of both players a willingness to investigate the truth without limitation. Again, it is not that we know "the truth" but only that we will share our experience and willingness to let go of its obstructions. It is with a relatively small percentage that the contract is ever asked for or sincerely committed to. Most understandably, only want to finish their business and die with some ease. Few desire to burn away a life's attachments, to let go of being "someone dying," and just dissolve into the next realms of awareness.

I met Rena some years ago while I was teaching with Elisabeth Kübler-Ross in the mid-seventies. At the time we met, Rena had already "gone through one battle with cancer" and had gone into remission for some months before discovering "new tumors." At first, our work together was to recognize suppressed emotional material and allow it to surface so that it could be seen for what it was: not some tragic miscreancy which she must correct but rather a natural flow of the conditioned mind. During this process Rena had at times a tendency to become almost ecstatic when she "uncovered another lump of shit in the mind" and then become attached to these previously unexamined emotions and feelings as being who she really was. On several occasions, as our contract grew, I had to remind her to "not gold-plate her shit" and that "shit" was just another way of looking at fertilizer, in the same way that one moment the mind might see "weeds" when at another it may recognize flowers.

When we first met, she mostly thought of herself as a body dying. Cancer was her whole life. She had been "quite intellectual" as her husband put it, most of her life, and as she started to discover a new depth and power to her ability to reason and "understand," she seemed to become caught in the idea "I am the mind, I am my thoughts, I am what I think," and she was tossed about from ecstasy to depression almost daily. Death was still a threat to the mind that thought itself dependent on the body for its existence. In time, as she discovered deeper feelings, long suppressed, and, surrounded by fear and self-doubt, she began to think, "I am these emotions, I am my feelings, I am what I feel, my emotions depend on what I think, and my thoughts depend upon having a body." But death was no less a feared presence in her life. Clearly, each level of self-discovery had its own trap: to think that any level of mind is all we are, to identify with the body, thoughts, feelings as one's true nature. But it is the allowing of thought, the recognition of the body, and the opening to feelings that allow us to go deeper, that allow us to go beyond our holding to any of these things as being all we are.

I would ask her, "When you let go of the idea 'I am the body, I am the mind, I am these feelings,' what remains?" so that we might investigate together without denying the body or mind or the feelings but recognizing just their impermanence, that each is constantly in a state of change that is endless and incessant. "Where is that which goes beyond change? Where is the deathless?"

Over the four years we worked together, Rena and I found ourselves again and again confronting her ongoing cycles of holding and release. Our work together led her into the use of meditation "as a tool for letting go." Not simply the letting go of the body in the face of death but a more profound letting go: a letting be of things as they are so we don't focus shallowly and can see beyond our accumulated resistance to life. A letting go of attachment to the contents of the mind as being all she was, which held the possibility of opening into the "don't know" mystery of the deathless. But this process of growth, of dying into our real nature, is yet much more difficult than the process of simply dying out of our body. And as with each it is not a straight line from A to Z. We go through many peaks and plateaus, many levels of learning and forgetting, many moments of insight and self-doubt, instant upon instant of ecstasy and remorse.

During periods when she felt well, we would hear from Rena every couple of months letting us know "how strong" her meditation was and how her meditation was "getting on top of it just fine." But beneath it all, as was pointed out to her, there seemed to be a way she was mistaking letting go for a subtle kind of repressive control. When I would ask her what she would do if things got worse, how she would feel if she couldn't "get on top of it"—that perhaps she might need to become less "someone meditating" and let go beyond her penchant for control—there was almost an audible shrug as though she just wasn't ready to deal with that one yet.

About eighteen months after we began this process together, she called to say that "things are going from bad to worse. I've been getting bugged a lot by my lungs again and the bones in my right shoulder. A little while ago I got real concerned and thought I was going to have to get into a whole new treatment thing again. But I kind of settled down and meditated through it

and decided that I was just panicking and that I had better slow
down. I don't know what I am going to do next. Things have
looked better."

S: "What do you think is happening?"
R: "What I have in my lungs and what I had before is called
lymphogenic spread. It is kind of a diffuse spread that makes
breathing difficult, and I get so tired so fast. I had some tumors
in my lower spine which seem cleared up now. I used the active
imagery visualization that I used to do and a very small dosage
of radiation, and it did the trick. But now, with the spread of the
cancer, I have a little energy for a while and then I am out cold.
I try to meditate regularly but it is more like three or four times
a week. But it is the only thing that keeps me sane. In the
beginning, I started sitting (meditating) because I thought I
should. But now when I sit, it's because I really want to, need to.
That is a real difference for me."
S: "How is the active imagery visualization going for you?"
R: "It felt like I was eating my body up out of fear and that I was
kind of gearing up my aggression. I really rejected the kind of
attack imagery that it encouraged to marshal the immune system. And it was all so involved with winning and losing. I was
sort of competing with myself. But now I am doing a lot of
nurturing, accepting kind of imagery.

"Not long ago I discovered how important the image I chose
to imagine as the immune system is. When I try to visualize it as
white alligators eating up lumps of rotten hamburger, there was
something in me that wanted to protect the hamburger, that
felt I was being preyed upon. And besides, it didn't seem to
work too well. Sometimes I would get into it as white knights
attacking a black dragon, but that didn't work so well either—
the dragon often won. Though ultimately the knights got him
down, the battle was exhausting. And then as I was searching
for some image that would be right for me, I began getting a lot
of messages that I need to let go more, just as you have been
saying. The whole letting-go thing is the message. But it is still
something I haven't done."

We spoke at some length about the letting go of control meditation (see *Who Dies?*), and I suggested she just close her eyes

and bring the attention to the breath and allow the breath to breathe itself. Just noticing from moment to moment even the least desire to hold or shape the breath, the least little bit of an attempt at controlling the breathing. To allow the sensations that accompany each breath to just float in the vastness of awareness. To just let the body breathe all by itself with no one breathing to control the process. Trust in the natural tides of the breath. And then to allow other sensations arising from the body to be received too in the open spaciousness of mind. To let the feelings feel themselves. And as this process deepened, to begin to receive each emotion, each state of mind, in that edgeless spaciousness. Allowing thoughts to pass without the least attempt at control. Each thought seen as a bubble passing through the vast openness of awareness, clinging nowhere. Seeing all this mind which she took so personally as just passing show. Moment to moment change in endless space. A moment of seeing, a moment of hearing, a moment of feeling, a moment of planning, a moment of judgment, another moment of sensation—one dissolving into the other, moment to moment. Letting thoughts think themselves, feelings feel themselves in the edgelessness of awareness. Nowhere to go, no one to be, nothing to do. Just being. Experiencing a constant flow of sensations, thoughts, emotions as they constantly arise and dissolve in boundaryless consciousness. Letting go of even the slightest tendency to change or alter the contents of the mind and allowing it all to just float in the vastness of being.

She agreed, after a moment's silence following the meditation, that she would work with this deep encouragement to let go, and would call us back in a few days.

Three days later Rena called to say that her visit with the doctor was "not so much a surprise as a disappointment."

R: "The cancer seems to be spreading. I guess it never really went away. And I am not sure I can hold on much longer. I can only do that for so long, and then some of this cancer seems to sneak through and then I grab at getting it under control some more and then I get tired, and when I get tired it only comes faster. But goddamnit, I am going to beat this cancer!"
S: "Even if it kills you, huh? All this resistance, all this fighting is such suffering and leaves you so little room for life. Did it ever

occur to you that you might be on the wrong side? that you aren't on the same side as your healing? All the ways you have tried before don't seem to be working for you very well. Maybe your fighting with your cancer, your rejecting it, is keeping your healing away as well. Maybe you have to let your cancer in to let your healing in. Maybe you have to let go of your battle with your dying as a way of continuing to live. Healing may occur when you go beyond this needing to control. It is just like working with pain: When it is walled off by our resistance, the various alternative means of dealing with that pain can't get through. Perhaps your healing will occur only when you fully open to that which goes beyond death.

"It feels to me that in a way you are all too willing to die because you just can't 'get it all under control.' Surrender doesn't mean defeat. Surrender means opening to whatever harmonic may be the next step. It's just another name for that deep letting go into the present which, oddly enough, is the perfect balance for healing as well as dying, a direct participation in the moment that is not clouded by the mind's fears and desires."

R: "That is something that I keep thinking, but I am not quite able to figure it out so I think about it some more."

S: "If thinking got us free we would all have become enlightened long ago. Is it that you are afraid if you surrender, if you let go of your edges, that you will die?"

R: "Yes. And I am also afraid that I won't. To have no power, no control, is so scary. If letting go just meant that I would die and be gone, that would be easy. *But I've always been in control.*"

S: "How painful! . . . I know this is probably the scariest time yet for you, but this frightful scrambling for control only seems to be making things worse. What if you could just soften around the cancer and direct more of the immune system along the channels of love. Do you think that might be more effective for you? It sure would decrease the conflict that you seem to be experiencing."

R: "There is a place in me that has so little trust in life that I don't know why I hang on, but I do. I don't even know if I can 'let go.' I am working on my dissertation now, and what I am creating is a definition of the healing process as one of integration and inner peace. But I keep finding myself equating progress with dramatic improvement even though I know that is a really dangerous one. I have seen it in myself and others in my cancer group. Every time we have a backslip it reactivates the old 'Oh, I am not doing it right.' And we are as scared as ever. I am trying hard to work more directly with those insecurities and fears so they don't limit my healing or get me stuck in it being any other way than it is."

S: "But you are meeting it all with your mind instead of your heart. Even as you say these words, they sound so much like what I have said to you in the past that I wonder how deep their meaning is in the place from which healing arises.

"We are told to hate our illness, to push it away, to beat it under any circumstances, that survival is the most precious thing of all. But just to bring love, to bring care to such a place of imbalance and illness is a radically different way of approaching it. It seems to open the affected area of illness into a place of acceptance. It becomes part of the whole body, no longer rejected as unnatural or even as a victimization."

We shared with Rena the process of sending love into her cancer—that when her lungs were in distress or her shoulder burning, instead of withdrawing and pushing it away, meeting it in fear and a "need" to cure it, that she might begin to bring love to that area. To allow healing access to it. No longer walling it off with loaded terms like "cancer," or "tumor," or "pain." No longer experiencing the sickness as just more frightened mind but instead meeting it with love, sending wishes for its well-being deeply into it. We told her what others had said about the process as that connection between the illness and the heart was established. How one might see light flooding the area, or a color, or notice impurities emitted from the tumor as dark waves that were dissolved in the light of this love. And how some said these "dark mists" were washed away by waves of light penetrating the darkness that exuded from the unhealthy area until all they could see was pink, healthy flesh, vibrant and alive. "They seemed to be drawing out poisons, not attempting to 'kill the devil.' It is not a holy war but rather a healing peace."

R: "Sometimes there seems to be something that fights the healing, that refuses it. We are dying like the way a river is dying. Constantly flowing from its source, constantly dissolving into a greater ocean. At times, I can even see the river going from one level to another, a constant replenishment at the source, a constant outflowing at the greater reservoir of past flowings. The source is like the future, constantly feeding into the river. The ocean at the other end of the river is like the repository of the past."

S: "Well, that is a nice image and the mind really loves that sort of thing, but as long as there is a 'river' there is going to be flooding. Perhaps it is time to stop drowning and float free. There is no 'river.' There is only movement. 'River' is like the 'I,' just a name for a process, a moment of identification and definition. Healing may come from beyond definitions of who we are. Perhaps it is this constant defining of yourself that keeps you from trusting the healing techniques that you so often seek but seldom apply. Just as Gandhi titled his autobiography *The Story of My Experiments with Truth,* there is a way you may not be using your healing as an experiment in truth, as a way of expanding beyond yourself. It is almost as though the little self, the one you are always defining and thinking about and fighting with, just doesn't have the juice to heal itself, but it is still strong enough to defend against a going beyond it."

R: "Sometimes I can almost feel myself not 'a river' but just flow with nowhere to stop and nothing to be but substance acted on by gravity. Sometimes when I know I am just flow, when I have gone beyond that little self-defining self, the cancer is not a threat. But at other times I can't imagine how I could have been so clear previously, I can't touch it at all."

S: "That is all to be expected. Sometimes we are thinking about it to no avail. And at other times we just *are* it and there is no 'thinker' and no resistance to the process. It is so interesting when we relate to all these changing states just as flow. Even our fear. You know Rena, you don't have to be any different than you are. All you need to do is let yourself be. To meet yourself in love instead of rejection."

Over the next months it became evident that the practice of sending love to her illness which Anthony and others had found so useful was not a method that she was able to employ, because her mind kept insisting that she had to "beat it, force it out of my body." So as the spread of cancer became more evident, and she said that she felt she was "beginning to die," we worked together yet more deeply with the pain meditations (see *Who Dies?*), as they too encouraged the acceptance of "the unwanted" while deepening an openness to the changing phenomenon within "the unpleasant" as a way of letting go and healing.

In early February she wrote a long letter: "Much has been going on with me, both inward and outward, including another surgery and beginning chemotherapy again. The pain meditation has helped me a great deal to just breathe in and out during the surgery. My oncologist was so impressed with my response that he asked me how I was doing it, and I told him about the pain meditation. He is an exceptionally fine doctor. He said he is interested because he is going through 'all sorts of pain' with some of his sickest patients.

"My surgery was the long-avoided sacrifice of laying my ovaries and uterus on the altar of at-one-ment. It is giving up my dream of a daughter and knowing that my fertility now will be solely of the spirit. It is fitting that I began my long-overdue book the night before my operation. The timing was exactly perfect. So many things had to come together before that step was taken. I feel like an angel knowing well how to fly but just beginning to learn how to walk.

"I sat up and meditated almost the whole night before surgery, and it was an incredible high for me, as was most of the hospital stay. It was the first time I was the 'stillpoint' around which all dreams are danced. I hung out for several days in that fine, familiar place. How I long for it sometimes when I am slogging through the mundane mud of this world with only fragments of the memory of all paradoxes resolved and I am detached, but not separate, totally one with all, but unique. My dream remnants left me with . . . 'This is the place where *everything* is all right!' And, 'This is the place where all love is and nothing is lost.' And, 'This is the place where all striving ends.' For a while I made the trip home to rest."

After reading the letter, I called and we spoke about the experience in the hospital.

S: "But that moment too has passed. When it was happening, it was bliss, but to hold to it now is just more hell. You cannot control the light, you can only be it."

R: "I know. My trying to get it back makes me feel so bad. If I could sleep through the whole thing, I would. If I could knock myself out with drugs or books or TV, for that matter, I would. I get restless and agitated when I try to lose myself in my usual methods of distraction. So I have to keep coming back to just being here, and it is so very hard!

"It is difficult to explain, but there is something very foul and loathsome about how the body feels inside after chemotherapy. There is such contradiction to contend with! Willfully participating in poisoning my own cells is a tough one to deal with. That is, I keep trying to get away from myself and it doesn't work. Then all I can think of is your saying, 'Can you keep your heart open even in hell?' and I understand that the cancer is the practice offered to me. I am a most reluctant learner whose oversoul knows enough to choose a curriculum sufficiently demanding to get me through. It really kind of blows my mind that I can hate it so much and still see how damn perfect it is!"

S: "Do you hear the contradiction in all this? It is one of the top forty that I hear your mind repeat again and again, and I think we both know that it isn't caused by your cancer or even the possibility of your dying. It is that old tune of 'Yes, I want it, no I don't.' On the one hand, you are saying that 'I would do anything to get out of this,' while on the other, the mind is sending, 'Oh, how wonderful to have such an opportunity to see!' The mind is full of such conflicts. At one moment it says, 'Have an ice-cream cone,' and a moment later, just as you have swallowed the last sweet morsel, it whispers, 'I wouldn't have done that if I were you.' No wonder we are all so crazy. The friction between these opposing desire systems, the heat they produce passing in opposite directions, is guilt and a feeling of unworthiness and weakness. Some even say that it is this kind of conflict which allows disease to establish itself, because in some way it weakens the straightforwardness of the immune system. And it is all right that this conflict is there, it is natural to everyone, but it needs watching. In this conflict can be seen mind itself in its folly and awkward confusion. No blame. No judgment. Just something to see for what it is. The mind makes a terrible master, but it can make a wonderful servant. Play lightly with these conflicts. Don't let them, so to speak, eat you alive."

A week later Rena called to say that she was having more pain in her lower spine where the cancer had been the year before and had been radiated. "It could be a pulled muscle or it could be a tumor. Last time I had a tumor in the bone."

S: "Have you been working with sending any forgiveness and loving-kindness into that area?"
R: "No. I have thought about it but I am in such a bind. On the one hand, it doesn't feel right to attack it, and on the other, I just can't seem to accept it, to offer it any love."
S: "And there is the conflict again. But in the resolution of this conflict may lie your healing. The heart is the place of the coincidence of opposites. After working with so many people who have been seriously ill and seeing so many techniques used in so many different ways, we have come to the conclusion that all healing originates from the heart. That it is the heart strength, the attitude, that empowers the technique, whatever it may be, and propels the healing.

"And I don't even mean to say that the healing of your body is the only object of our work together. It is the healing of the heart. If you should save your body but remain in such conflict that you are 'brokenhearted,' what is furthered? So I am suggesting that you investigate yet more deeply that friction, that heat produced by these oppositions in the mind. If you can see this conflict for what it is, you might get a glimpse of the mind as just old confusions in their age-old holy war. But you don't have to make your body the battlefield.

"In an odd way it feels as though it is not death that you are fighting but life itself. If this were another's body, you would have no trouble, I suspect, sending love to the area of another's stress. But because it is your body, all the ways you have never allowed yourself to love yourself, to just be, are now manifesting themselves. Clearly, this is nothing new, but it has never been so obvious as it is now. This is a time for much kindness and self-forgiveness. This is a time to treat yourself like your only child. To allow yourself to simply be, in love and self-care."
R: "Well, in some ways I feel pretty optimistic because I have

seen so many conflicts resolved, though I hear what you are saying and I know that it is true."

When I asked Rena what she was optimistic for, was it that her body would remain or that the inner changes would take her beyond identification with the body, she said, "Both. Either/or. Even though things seem to be getting worse, I give a certain amount of credence to the thought 'Things can get better.' I don't want to die yet. I still haven't finished my work. I really would like to get my book done, at least before I go. I really want to leave something like that behind."

S: "This desire to be remembered is quite natural. But much that is natural nonetheless blocks us from seeing beyond to our real nature. But since we have a contract 'to push beyond,' let's explore this one, as frightening as it may be. What does it mean when you say 'you' want to leave something behind? Is that another way of not letting go? Of maintaining some control even after you have died? Isn't that looking for a kind of immortality which the body simply doesn't possess? To be immortal you must have been born, but who you really are was never born and can never die. So I guess immortality is out of the question, because you are already so much more than any form, no matter how subtle, and who you are is beyond time. It has always been and always will be, so why bother with piddling ideas of 'eternity,' which is still just more time, or 'immortality,' which is just more space. In a way, you are shortchanging yourself by not looking deeper, by not letting go past the mind and body into the direct experience of who you really are. And you know this from various glimpses into the mystery which you have related to me. Now your work is to trust what you have seen without holding onto it. To allow yourself to die into the moment, into just this much, which goes beyond immortality or eternity and comes into the edgeless nature which is beyond definition and beyond 'knowing.' You can only be it."
R: "Oh, this mind! I know what you are saying is so. I have even seen it at times for myself. It is trust, or should I say distrust, that keeps me from letting go into it. Maybe I feel that finishing up this book is completing the cycle of this life, a coming to closure. Sometimes when I talk to you I feel afterward as though I have

shown you the least of me. But I guess that is why we're talking. A few days ago when I was feeling really bad, though, I just settled into it. In that moment it was really OK if I didn't finish my book. Sometimes it is OK if my time is coming up now. I have been trying to work in the house on ordering my priorities. That is the hard part for me now. Though I would love to finish this book before I die."

S: "That is quite understandable, but let's for a moment just investigate that place where you want people to say, 'Oh, how wonderful Rena was; oh, how well she did!' It is the same old looking for approval that has kept life so narrow. It causes such suffering. Maybe it is time for you to let go of your suffering. Which doesn't mean not to write the book, but to do it lightly and with love and self-acceptance rather than some tense furrowing of the brow that only gives you a headache afterward."

R: "You are hitting a real painful one for me now. Keep talking."

S: "I know it is a painful one. I saw it in the part of the book that you sent to me. In it you seem to be so 'heroic'—you only showed your ups and never your real pain, your fear or confusion. This kind of trying to appear as 'something for someone' only creates more self-denial, less room in your heart for you. You wrote as though you were the person you have always wished you were instead of the beautiful person you are. But you and I know better. The pain you feel, even the confusion, is OK too. You are not any less beautiful for being human. Maybe the person you always wanted to be is just an ideal, a model that has always gotten in your way and has so often limited your trust in just being yourself. I think the writing of your experiences is a good thing and could even be healing for you and others to the degree that your honesty allows you refuge in your heart. But the attachment to appearing so 'together' is toxic and leaves you with a feeling of isolation and 'undoneness.' "

R: "This is a real confusing one for me. It is even painful to have to look at these thoughts. Should I stop writing the book?"

S: "Not necessarily. I think the writing could be very therapeutic to the degree you will just let yourself be. But my sense now is that it is just causing you more suffering, because it is more wishful thinking and more self-rejection of those parts you wish were not there. You know, in Zen they say, 'The greater the impediment, the greater the enlightenment.' If you could write a book of the deep investigation of that which makes you feel partial, you might well come into your wholeness. The exploration of that which you are denying—your fears, your confusion, even your cancer—may be the path through for you. But the denial of these things, the covering over of them to make yourself appear more whole than you really feel you are only leaves you with a feeling of being more fragmented.

"Your whole life you have been told to 'be someone,' that you must get somewhere in your career, that you must posture in the world to gain its acceptance, and now death approaches and you think, 'This is my last chance to be someone, to get somewhere,' and the pain of life only becomes more evident. To be 'someone' is to fear death."

R: "My cancer and my book in a way feel like the same thing except going in opposite directions. Maybe somewhere inside of me I feel that one can cancel out the other. That the book will somehow neutralize the effects of the cancer. I don't know."

S: "Well, in that I hear two things. First, I hear that if the book will cancel out the effects of the cancer, that somehow you feel that since cancer represents the possibility of death to you that the book may represent 'never dying.' Perhaps once again you are looking in the wrong place for who you already are, which is so much more than you imagine. Also I sense that they are not going in opposite directions but maybe moving on the same track. Maybe your not loving yourself enough to allow it to 'all hang out' in the book is the same momentum that keeps you from sending love into your cancer. Both are a kind of loveless rejection of some part of yourself."

R: "Well, you are a writer. How do you deal with wanting to appear to be 'someone' in the eyes of those who read your writing? It is such a painful attachment."

S: "It sure is, and one I am not unfamiliar with. But there is nothing to judge in the attachment. It's just something to notice. It's just the mind's play. I am all too familiar with that situation of sitting there with my pen in my hand, where I am still someone doing something, and feel so separate from the beings I am talking to about oneness. I mean the absurdity of that. And we all have it. But writing, like healing, comes through all by itself when there is 'no one' to block it.

"I can see how writing is a beautiful mirror to see where we are, to discover deep feelings, even to resolve certain conflicts, at least for a while, in the mind. I think that kind of separation, that self-interest and desire to be someone, much less to be 'better than we are,' is completely natural, but it is so painful, and it seems to separate us so from life, much less death. When I see it in myself, all I can do is be compassionate and recognize how strong our conditioning is. I greet that insecurity with more friendship and warmth as time goes on. It doesn't so much frighten me or cause me to get lost in the subtle judging and self-doubt as it once did. It's the same old stuff. No big surprise that it is there. It has been there so many times in the past that it has its own momentum. But we can greet it with loving-kindness instead of self-judgment.

"When we meet these states with awareness, they melt. The power of clear attention cannot be overrated. It is the closest thing to magic that I know of."

R: "Well, this has been a good conversation for me. Lots for me to think about. I think I will go sit for a while and then reread the book so far. I'll be talkin' to ya."

A week later Rena called, a bit more breathless than the last time we had spoken: "Well, it seems like this thing has really gotten into my lungs. I am having quite a bit of difficulty breathing and almost no energy at all. Maybe this is it. But what I wanted to talk to you about is that recently I have this incredible desire to pull back, you know, be by myself, sit alone, and just sit. But I feel like I am letting my kids down if I do that, and part of me feels like I have the time and could be doing more with it."

S: "Well, my friend, it does sound like you are moving into the end game, and your desire to be quiet and alone is a natural part of that process too. Don't judge it, just hang out with it. Let your intuition guide you on this one from moment to moment. Your acceptance of that one too takes you to perhaps a deeper healing than you imagined when you were fighting with the body. If you can accept the natural changes in this process as the body weakens, as you can't be who you always wanted to be, you may find that your heart opens to you and allows a certain gentle ease that you have seldom known.

"Part of your opening to this process now includes recognizing how tricky such thoughts as 'I haven't done enough for my children' can be, because I know you to be a very good mother and a real giver to your children; yet nonetheless, the old confused mind still causes that thought to arise. In the *Bhagavad Gita* it says something to the effect that one does what one does and then must surrender the fruits of their labors. We live our life, and at the end of it we must let go completely without holding on or looking back. These thoughts about our children are so seductive and really stick to our 'not enoughness.' But who needs to die with that sort of self-denial in their minds? With their heart closed to themselves? Look at this one now as it is: just another bubble passing through the vastness of who you really are. It is time to let go of your case of mistaken identity, mistaking yourself for each thought rather than focusing on the spaciousness out of which they arise and into which they disappear. This practice of letting go, of coming to the edge and gently going beyond, is the practice of mercy. It is the very opposite of the cruelty and attachment the mind has accumulated through tens of thousand of moments of self-rejection and judgment."

R: "I think that brings the most pain, that 'not enoughness.' "

S: "But if you really see that state of mind as just the bubble it is, floating in the spaciousness of your deathless nature, you will experience your wholeness, your enoughness."

R: "Well, the other day when I was writing, for the first time I came into a place of 'things are OK just the way they are.' It was OK that I am not healing and I could forgive that one too. And it was OK that I am dying. But then after I napped for a while, as soon as I opened my eyes, I could feel how caught up I was in all of it again."

S: "Obviously, our clarity comes and goes and our attachment to that one is as good a thing to watch as any. Just noticing the process of our opening and closing can breed such deep compassion for ourselves. A lot of this fear and good old insecurity comes from a lack of trust in the process. What is happening now is not random. It is all unfolding perfectly. If you watch how thoughts end, how one thought dissolves into the next, you will see the process of thought itself and won't get so lost in any single thought being who you are. You don't have to understand what happens after death or even how to die any more than you need to know how the stars come out or how the earth was formed to see the perfection of this process. In just 'this much' which is given, the whole truth can be received and the perfection of the process can be experienced. Just as one thought leads perfectly into another, into the next, into the next, so one day does, and one year does, and one lifetime does. We are creation constantly in the act of becoming. We are evolution itself unfolding from moment to moment. This process which includes love and loss, life and death, is our perfect evolution. It is not other than who you really are.

"You said before that your 'oversoul had enough wisdom to take on this curriculum,' and here we all are and the teaching of our dying is just a deeper teaching in life. We are a process constantly evolving beyond itself. Within itself. And in a very real sense we don't even know what is good for us or for others. We are constantly attempting to protect ourselves and others from pain, yet it seems to be the opening to this pain that makes life so much more livable and death so much less frightening.

"All of us have periods of change in our lives where we go from one octave to the next. And dying is in many ways no different than any of these other transitions we have made. As one friend used to say, 'Death is just a change in life-styles.' With each of our changes, of our 'movings on,' we have always had to let go of the last stage before we could fully enter the next. It is like swinging on a set of children's monkey bars where you really can't go on to the next rung until you have let go of the last one. Sometimes when I am with my kids in the park, I will see how they trust the process of their momentum so much that they seem almost to fly across those bars without holding to any of them. But then I will see some of us old adults, so conditioned to distrust our natural momentum, and when they go across the bars, they refuse to let go of one until they have securely grasped the next. They hang there like herniated chimps grasping onto one but not letting go of the last. When the children go across, you see that there are moments when they have completely let go of the last rung and their hand hasn't quite reached the next, but it is the trust in their momentum that keeps them from falling. When we have that kind of trust, we just move from bar to bar, or level to level, in a continuing movement that maintains itself effortlessly. In all growth we must let go of the last stage before the next can fully develop. In a sense, we are constantly having to die in order to be reborn. And here we all are, learning to let go and to move into the next unknown moment."

Although I felt that her heart's surrender would allow a new freedom, I sensed that this was not what she was going to do— that a lifetime of resistance and control might cause her to die "full-minded" instead of "openhearted," and that too was OK, had its own dignity, and that all I could do was to send her love and try to deepen her confidence and trust in what was to come. If I had to give a simple definition of what conscious dying might be, it is to let go of the last moment and open to the next. No life, no death, just moment-to-moment change floating in pure awareness.

R: "It is true. My mind keeps grasping at straws. Sometimes I get caught up in understanding what it is all about. It is like I was reading the other day and became very stimulated by all the exciting ideas that tied things to physics and consciousness and spirit and all that sort of thing. It is such fun to play mind games, but it is like getting a really big rush from this input and then realizing that all of it is real interesting but 'so what?' "
S: "Right, the mind sees how everything connects, but the mind doesn't feel particularly connected."
R: "Some of what you have said about 'understanding being the ultimate seduction of the mind' hit me when I put down the book. I saw how I was so busy understanding that I didn't feel particularly connected to myself or to anything at all."
S: "It is time to let the mind sink into the heart. It is like a friend of ours said a day or two before he died: 'It is time to let go of my someoneness and explore some oneness.' "

Two weeks later Rena's husband Spence, whom we had spoken to many times before, called to say that Rena seemed to be "getting near death." When I asked him how she was doing, he said with a bit of frustration, "Well, we are talking through a few things we haven't touched on much before. For a long time there has only been so much that Rena wanted to hear. In the last week or so she and I have been talking out some stuff, but still she seems a little 'wary,' if I can use that word."

When I asked him how it was for him, he said, "In some ways it is so beautiful for both of us. We have both grown so much in these last years. There are moments we share that are so precious, but still she seems to be holding."

S: "What is she holding to?"

Sp: "Everything being in order. She is concerned about the funeral and the arrangements after the funeral and all that. All those things have to be set up. It has to be ordered and controlled and organized. There is a lot of planning. I know you have been talking to her about letting go of control, and a while ago when she was doing those meditations on letting go, we did some of them together and it felt like everything was opening up quite a bit, but then I think she just got scared and withdrew. She started to talk about her book a lot and would almost quote it like 'holy scripture' at me. Now she is even trying to control what will happen after her death."

S: "And that is OK too. All of that is just her form of preparation. Our conditioning has such extraordinary momentum. Don't let it frighten you or get you stuck in feeling that she is putting you out of her heart. She is just dying her death as she has lived her life. It may be very difficult at moments for both of you. But if you are to be there for her in whatever way she needs in that moment, you will have to keep your heart open to things as they are with no need to change her death or make her die any other way than what feels right to her."

Sp: "Sometimes we meditate together and it is so quiet. But a moment after we have opened our eyes, all this planning is coming out of her and she is talking the silence away. Sometimes I just want to cry with her, but because she is so together, or what seems like together, and everything seems just fine, I don't know what to do with these feelings when I am around her."

S: "All you can do is love her and let her be. Her fear has to be allowed if you are to touch the love that is just beneath the surface. She has done a lot of work on herself over these last years, and even though it may not be evident to you right now, the momentum of this work will go on long after she has left the body and has seen that that too was not who she really was. Just watch any place within yourself that you would like her to be different and see how that blocks you from letting her completely into your heart at this most precious time. And for you, my friend, all I can say is just cry when you cry and laugh when you laugh."

Sp: "I know. I just wanted to hear myself say it, I guess. We have shared so much over the last twelve years and I guess some of my anger is not so much at her as it is at my losing this."

Spence called a few days later to say that Rena had "died mid-sentence." "It was just like her. And what was strange was what happened just after she died when I was trying to get things together just as she had requested. She had made me promise that before anyone saw her I would close her eyes and put her makeup on and set her body straight and put a smile on her face. But when I tried, I couldn't close her mouth! So there she lay, all made up in the long purple dress she liked so much, with her mouth wide open. I guess it is true that we die the way we live."

We see Spence occasionally in our travels across country and he says that everything is going well. He has since remarried and says that thinking back to the day of Rena's death, though he still feels sadness, it also makes him smile. "It was such a serious time in those last few days and I was scared that I might be left with a sense of not having finished things up, but when I couldn't close her mouth, I laughed so hard that the cosmic humor of it brought it all into perspective. And every once in a while, I think back to that old saying in the Haight-Ashbury days, 'May the baby Jesus shut my mouth and open my eyes.' And I try to look out into the world wider than ever before."

When We Let Go
of Everything,
Only Love Remains

MARTINE

Martine's husband, Frank, called us at their counselor's suggestion. Martine had come to the last stages of her cancer and was now experiencing considerable disorientation from a brain tumor. After Frank and I talked for a few moments, he put on Martine. She spoke very simply with long pauses between phrases, her tone a bit like that of a lost child. As we spoke, it was immediately evident that she couldn't comprehend very much having to do with abstractions or concepts. Because of the tumor her circuitry had become blocked, her ability to reason diminished by insufficient current to that part of her brain. Not being allowed "to figure it all out" in the way she had in the past, all one could feel was the love that remained. As Frank put it, "I wouldn't say she has lost her mind, I would say she has found something better." We told Frank we would be glad to get together with him and Martine but that after speaking to her we did not feel there was anything we needed to "teach" her. That her work was in her heart and that all the two of them really needed was to "just hang out together." We suggested that perhaps they might like to attend an upcoming workshop in their area and just be there in whatever way felt right to them.

Two weeks later Martine and Frank came to a Conscious Living/Conscious Dying workshop.

Frank spoke first. "Sometimes I get real brave and I really feel

OK at times. I talk to a lot of people who are giving me a lot of courage about this, but often I don't know what to do and it can end so quickly."

He went on to tell the story of how Martine had found a lump in her breast some years earlier and had gone through all the medical strategies available to her until at last a secondary tumor from the breast cancer had "lodged in her brain" and the doctors had said, "There is very little we can do at this point."

F: "I don't know where to start. There have been so many friends there for us. And it seemed like we were working with this disease in her body, but then when the brain became involved, we would be sitting with friends and if there was the least distraction to what was being said, Martine just sort of sat there blank-faced, and I knew that she didn't understand what was being said. Sometimes she would say something that had nothing to do with what was going on and I would just bite my tongue. It was very confusing to occasionally lose our communication, which had been such a benefit to us both when times got tough. There had been times in the past when she had been so out of it on drugs from her operations and the doctoring she had to go through that she couldn't understand what I was saying and couldn't speak very well, but this was different. At some times she would be clear and at other times she didn't understand what was happening. And it frightened us both at first. Martine was having a really hard time. Her mind was not responding as one would expect it to. She was starting to lose control of speech and she couldn't remember anything. And the more this happened the more upset and emotionally uptight we became. It was a kind of Catch-22 thing—we went around in circles. When she was clear, we worried about the 'confusion,' and when she was confused, we felt like two small circles of light that somehow couldn't merge. I felt very alone and I think she did too.

"Then one night in the middle of our trying to understand this all, Martine just stopped and cocked her head as if she were looking at the ceiling, and she became real quiet. It was sort of like she thought of God or something. And she went out into the kitchen and came back about ten minutes later, and she was just clear as a bell. She had worked through something. That is what she called her 'first reincarnation' and mine too. And since that time she seems to have accepted death, which is something I had not thought about before. Our accepting of this confusion was our first step in really accepting death, and it was a complete turnaround, a whole new way of looking at it for me.

"Since then, except for a few times, she has been really clear, even about being confused. Only occasionally will she say, 'Well, I'm not thinking clearly.' And then she will sit there sort of musing, not being able to figure even what thinking clearly might be, or something like that. And then she will turn to me and say, 'I am going to die and I love you so much.' And in that moment, even in this confusion, there is a different kind of clarity."

As Frank shared the story of their past two years, the hundred or so people in the group, almost en masse, responded with a wave of kind sadness. As the story went on, one could feel the group slowly getting drawn into feeling sorry for her. This went on for a few minutes until, recognizing that nearly everyone had gotten lost in thinking that Martine was a victim of circumstances, I asked Martine if she would like to share.

M: "It's a weird position to be in. I've always been so healthy. Never had the flu or even a cold hardly. About a year ago I was having some emotional problems, and in five seconds or so they would just go away. I was taking fifty vitamins a day and I was so convinced that I was going to cure myself, but it seems that I didn't and now I am dying. And now sometimes, it is like I have been in this workshop for the last few hours and I didn't know what was going on. Sometimes I would understand but often the words just went over my head.

"But there is something I would like to say to you all. I would like you all to pay attention, please . . . more than anything else, be nice to everybody, because it can end so quickly. It is so important to love each other and to help each other. That is what it is all about. And you know what? There is something wonderful happening now . . . I can tell everyone now that I love them, and it's so wonderful because I felt that for thirty-two years. I felt like I wanted to tell everyone that I loved them, and I was afraid to. There were very few people I could tell that to. And it doesn't matter now, I can tell you all."

Turning to the group, I asked, "Now do you feel sorry for her? She has a perspective that a lot of people would give their eyeteeth for. She is in an extraordinary state. She cannot rely on her mind. She cannot always walk a straight line, but her heart is wide open. All the ways the mind is used to holding, to protecting, to posturing, are no longer allowed. In a manner of speaking she is free, because she no longer has to rely on understanding the world. All she has to do is be in it. What is happening is that she can't understand from the conceptual realm, and that is usually our defense in the world. The mind filters everything. But her filter doesn't work anymore. She is directly experiencing life. She is not experiencing life as most do, as an afterthought, as an idea about what is happening. She is just the happening itself. She is not existing in a realm where everything has a name and a place and a category by which we never directly experience it. In a sense, she is a reflection of her true nature, which is the openness of her heart. Which is not to say there is not still a place in her which wants to be clear and sometimes says, 'Oh, how wonderful, I'm clear now.' But these are only in the times when 'the mind is working again,' because as she says, 'When it goes out, I go with it.'

"Ironically, it is only when she has a little 'clarity' about herself as a separate being that she feels bad about not being clear at other times. Our clarity is greatly overrated. That old conditioning we all carry to be clear, to be understood, is still functioning, but it seems to be diminishing. To the degree that this old conditioning is functioning, it is causing her pain. And when that goes, she couldn't care less whether she can understand you or you can understand her or not, and those are the times when she is free. In a sense, she has broken through the 'bondage of concepts,' for it is our constant conceptualizing, of turning the world into ideas, that keeps us from living in the world and directly experiencing it—of directly touching, smelling, hearing, seeing, tasting life. It is our concepts that keep us thinking life instead of living it. That keep us always just out of reach of the moment."

The group formed an oval, joining hands across the open space, forming a "human cradle" into which Martine was gently placed. Circles and circles growing out from the center of that mandala of caring and love, slowly the group rocked her back and forth singing the Hallelujah Chorus. For fifteen minutes the group was joined in a single supportive openness. And when Martine was placed gently back on the floor, after lying there a few minutes, her eyes opened and she said, "Ooooh. Wonderful. And now I want to do it for each one of you, but I can't figure out how."

At the end of the retreat it seemed like all one hundred people came up to hug Martine and Frank. They had become the center of the personification of feelings of love for the group. They had become the perfect mirror for each being's original nature. Although most had come to the retreat "to gain some deeper wisdom and understanding," at the end of the retreat it was the purity of Martine's love that they were most drawn to. It was "the wisdom of love" that they had heard so clearly and shared in those five days. Martine had become a perfect teaching in "unconditional love." Because her mind was not so involved in conditions, the love that came out of her was a kind of universal love that knew no bounds or limitations. "I just love everyone. I can't help it." Her willingness to experience the present as it was happening was one of the great teachings of the workshop for everyone involved. About two weeks after the workshop we received a card from Martine on which was written, "Ahhh. . . ."

In the mid-1970s, while working with Ram Dass (*Grist for the Mill,* 1976) and teaching meditation in the California prison system, STEPHEN LEVINE met Elisabeth Kübler-Ross. For the next few years he led workshops with her and learned from the terminally ill the need for deeper levels of healing and profound joy of service (*A Gradual Awakening,* 1979). In 1980 he began teaching workshops with his wife, Ondrea, as they continued to serve the terminally ill and those deeply affected by loss as Co-Directors of the Hanuman Foundation Dying Project. (*Who Dies?,* 1982). For three years Ondrea and Stephen maintained a free-consultation telephone line for those confronting serious illness or the possible death of a loved one (*Meetings at the Edge,* 1984). As the Levines continued to gain insight from those who overcame illness and surpassed death, their explorations deepened while further meditative techniques were developed to "let the healing in". Their guided meditations for the healing of illness, grief holdings, heavy emotional states, and sexual abuse and subtler forms of life/death preparation brought them international recognition (*Healing into Life and Death,* 1987 and *Guided Meditations, Explorations and Healings,* 1992), having aided thousands of people worldwide. Presently Stephen and Ondrea Levine are living in the high mountains of the Southwest, "attempting to practise what we preach" in the silence of the deep woods. They are seeking the "healing we took birth for", working on a long-awaited new book, *Relationships as a Path to Awakening,* feeding the animals and the trees, and "examining the weatherbeaten out-croppings and the sun-dappled forests of the mind, sipping at the clear wellsprings of the heart".